DISNEYANA:

Walt Disney
Collectibles

DISNEYANA:
Walt Disney Collectibles

- Cecil Munsey -

HAWTHORN BOOKS, INC.

Publishers / NEW YORK

The views expressed by the author are not necessarily those of Walt Disney Productions.

DISNEYANA: WALT DISNEY COLLECTIBLES

Copyright © 1974 by Walt Disney Productions. Copyright under International and Pan-American Copyright Conventions. All rights reserved, including the right to reproduce this book or portions thereof in any form, except for the inclusion of brief quotations in a review. All inquiries should be addressed to Hawthorn Books, Inc., 260 Madison Avenue, New York, New York 10016. This book was manufactured in the United States of America and published simultaneously in Canada by Prentice-Hall of Canada, Limited, 1870 Birchmount Road, Scarborough, Ontario.

Library of Congress Catalog Card Number: 73-19381

ISBN: 0-8015-2138-6

1 2 3 4 5 6 7 8 9 10

There are countless people throughout the world, who, like me . . .

my wife Dolores . . .

and my son Cecil III . . .

have experienced the joys of owning Walt Disney character merchandise as youngsters and of collecting Disney memorabilia as adults. It is to these people that this book is dedicated.

Contents

List of Tables

Acknowledgments

An ancient Egyptian, whose name has long ago been lost to recorded history, once declared: "A man hath perished and his corpse became dirt. All his kindred have crumbled to dust. But his writings cause him to be remembered in the mouth of the reciter." To this I would add that for every person who has written there are countless people who have throughout his development, in numerous ways, made his writing possible.

I am lastingly grateful to my wife Dolores and my son Cecil III for their continued love and support. Their inspiration, advice, and help during the three months I spent in research at the Walt Disney Studio in Burbank, California, and the period spent writing my manuscript was truly invaluable. I am also indebted to my mother Alma (Northup) Munsey, who introduced me to Mickey Mouse in 1936 and encouraged my fascination with Disneyana for over thirty years.

I owe a special debt to Vincent H. Jefferds, who is in charge of character merchandising for Walt Disney Productions, for his foresight and assistance in making this work a reality. I am also grateful to Don MacLaughlin of the Character Merchandising Division for his interest and help during the initial stages of research.

To David R. Smith, director of the Walt Disney Archives, I am especially indebted. With patience, understanding, enthusiasm, and kindness, he shared his office with me for three months, facilitated my search for historical material, and helped me obtain most of the photographs presented. In addition, much of the reference material presented in the appendixes is the result of an earlier effort by Dave in 1967.

I acknowledge with gratitude the help provided by Les V. Perkins and Carol Svendsen of the Walt Disney Archives. Les, with the enthusiasm of a fellow collector, facilitated my research in numerous ways. Carol, with dedication, guaranteed the prompt reply to my many letters seeking information.

To Dave Spencer and the entire crew of the Still Camera Department at Walt Disney Productions, I owe appreciation. They provided me with faultless and prompt service.

I am grateful to Professor William D. Wilkins and his wife, Rosemary, of Bonita, California, for special encouragement that enabled me to survive completing a doctoral dissertation and starting this work in the same month. I am also grateful to them for introducing me to their daughter, Mary Elizabeth Wilkins, curator of the Mother Colony History Room of the Anaheim (California) Public Library. Mary Elizabeth deserves special thanks for providing me with research assistance whenever needed.

I am also very grateful to Bob Clampett of Hollywood, California, for taking time away from his famous cartoon characters Beany and Cecil in order to provide me with information and photographs about his part in the creation of the first stuffed Mickey Mouse dolls. Without his help the complete story could not have been presented.

I gratefully acknowledge, also, the help that Harry "Bud" Barber of Poway, California, provided. With patience and a good memory, he enabled me to complete the history of the role Courvoisier Galleries of San Francisco played in making original Disney art a collector's item.

A number of collectors of Disneyana participated in the preparation of this work by allowing me access to their collections and sharing their knowledge with me. I am grateful to Lois S. Beyrer of San Diego, California; Mel Birnkrant of Beacon, New York; Jeff Cain of San Francisco, California; John Fawcett of Warrenville, Connecticut; Ward Kimball of San Gabriel, California; Robert Lesser of New York City; Richard Lucy of El Centro, California; Roger Nelson of New Orleans, Louisiana; and Ernest Trova of St. Louis, Missouri.

Special thanks go also to James R. Kucera of San Diego, California, and Edward Roenker, Jr. of Santee, California, for their photographic assistance.

I am also indebted to Ruth White of San Diego, California, for typing the manuscript; to Judy O'Brien of Poway, California, for typing the appendixes; and to Louis Fournier of San Diego, California, for reading and criticizing the original handwritten manuscript.

Introduction

From humble beginnings in the 1920s, Walt Disney and his brother Roy built an entertainment business second to none in the world. It is impossible to completely assess the influence the characters invented or developed by the Disneys have had on the citizens of the twentieth century, although few would deny that this influence has been both positive and great. *in the media*

The creative activities of what is known today as Walt Disney Productions are providing entertainment for thousands of collectors. Beginning in the 1930s with a few collectors, growing in the 1940s to a fraternity of hundreds, and by the 1970s having enlisted thousands, the collecting of Disneyana is currently a major hobby activity. Unlike most collectors, Disneyana buffs range from people with a few items to those with thousands. In the case of the former, perhaps the term "collector" is not even an accurate descriptive word. There are thousands who have acquired examples of Disneyana as children, keep them for sentimental reasons, and add new items only occasionally during trips to Disneyland, Walt Disney World, and wherever such things are sold. In addition, there exist collectors who devote great amounts of time, energy, and money to their extensive collections. It is for all students of Disneyana that this book was written.

This book is extensive in its coverage of the history and collectibles of Walt Disney Productions, but it is not definitive in either case. There are too many aspects of this giant entertainment industry, and a number of books already exist that deal with the films, art, characters, and people that make up the world of Disney. Here a history of the two brothers and the business they built is provided as background, against which are set the collectibles that have been produced through the years. The coverage of the collectibles is representatively comprehensive but not exhaustive. Walt Disney Productions has been too prolific in its character merchandising (which makes up the bulk of what is collected) for one book to discuss and picture it all. Every effort has been made, however, to present illustrations and discussions of all of the categories that interest collectors of Disney artifacts. Many of the photographs presented are from advertisements and catalogues of character merchandise and, as such, they have the distinct advantage of illustrating the "direct" collectibles (the basic items) as well as the "indirect" collectibles (secondary items, such as packages).

Of the thirty chapters offered, twenty-two develop the history of character merchandising chronologically. In addition, eight chapters called "photo-chronologies" are interspersed throughout the book and present a chronological coverage of the items featured. The reader should note that most of the items illustrated are presented in groups according to the time periods in which they were manufactured, in order to facilitate using this book as a reference tool. Along the same lines, an annotated table of contents is presented so that the reader can quickly and easily determine where specific items of interest are illustrated; generic names for the categories are used in most cases.

Dating memorabilia is almost always of major importance to collectors and just as frequently a major problem to authors. Every effort has been made to date the items illustrated, although some circa dating has been used, and in a few cases it has not been possible to offer a date. One of the major problems in dating artifacts stems from Walt Disney Productions' program of reissuing certain of its classic films periodically. Along with each reissue there are generally numerous pieces of character merchandise produced. This, then, precludes dating merchandise by characters and original release dates in most cases. *Snow White and the Seven Dwarfs*, for example, was reissued in 1944, 1952, 1958, and 1967; *Pinocchio* was reissued in 1945, 1954, 1962, and 1971; and *Fantasia* in 1946, 1956, 1963, and 1969.

To aid in dating, seven appendixes have been assembled, which allow the student of Disneyana access to numerous facts not included in the body of the text. In addition, there is a comprehensive index. It is hoped that all collectors will discover that for the first time they have the literature necessary for them to more adeptly pursue their interest in Disneyana.

1. Before Mickey Mouse

Contrary to what most collectors of Disneyana believe, the history of Walt Disney character merchandise does not begin with items featuring Walt's most famous cartoon character, Mickey Mouse. In August of 1927, after having produced a series of fifty-six silent cartoons featuring a live-action figure called Alice, Walt introduced a new silent cartoon series named *Oswald the Lucky Rabbit*. Twenty-six Oswald cartoons were made. Oswald has the distinction of having been the first Disney character featured on character merchandise.

The Oswald series was distributed by Universal Pictures Corporation. The first Oswald merchandise item was announced on page 32 of the August 20, 1927, issue of the *Universal Weekly*, the house organ for Universal Pictures Corporation. Since the first item was a chocolate-coated marshmallow candy bar called Milk Chocolate Frappe, it is doubtful if collectors will ever have the opportunity to include such a perishable article in their collections. There is a chance, however, that a small number of the waxed paper wrappers is still extant. Printed on the wrapper is a likeness of Oswald tossing six-lettered balls that spell his name. Below the figure is "The Welsh Rabbit, a Rare Bit," and on one end the buyer is told to "Watch for OSWALD in Universal Pictures." Printed on the left side is "Milk Chocolate Frappe," and on the right side, "Vogan Candy Corporation, Portland, Oregon." There is an even better chance that collectors may find examples of the two-column newspaper advertisements that were used to promote the new candy bar or the three-panel counter cards or the window stickers that were also used to advertise the chocolate bar.

In August of 1927 a pin-back celluloid-covered button featuring the likeness of Oswald was announced in *Universal Weekly*. This desirable collectors' item was manufactured by the Philadelphia Badge Company. A third piece of Oswald merchandise was announced in the April 21, 1928, issue of *Universal Weekly*; it was an "Oswald Stencil Set," which was produced by the Universal Tag and Novelty Company.

It is rather ironic that except for providing the art work for the Oswald merchandise (the art was actually drawn by Ub Iwerks and other artists working for Walt; he had abandoned drawing himself by then in favor of coordinating the creative efforts of his staff from a production standpoint), Walt had nothing to do with and made no profit from these first Disney character merchandising items. It is probable that Walt was satisfied with the publicity generated by the Oswald merchandise. Even if he had been concerned and had wanted to exploit his cartoon character to his own financial advantage as he did in later years with other characters, he would have learned that under the contract that he had signed with Charles Mintz, who distributed his cartoons through Universal Pictures, he did not own the Oswald character—Mintz did!

The first merchandising item authorized by

Walt Disney himself featured Mickey Mouse, but before discussing that more specifically it would perhaps be better to learn more about the man who created that world famous cartoon character.

Walter Elias Disney was born in Chicago on December 5, 1901, and was the next to the youngest in a family of four boys and one girl. His father, Elias Disney, was a Canadian of Anglo-Irish descent and his mother, Flora (Call) Disney, an American of German descent. At the time of Walt's birth Elias was a struggling building contractor, who operated out of the Disney home at 1249 Tripp Avenue. Before Walt was born the Disneys had lived in Florida, where they had owned and operated a citrus grove. In fact it was in Florida that Elias met and married Flora Call, who was at the time a school teacher. While Flora was not a native of Florida, having been born in Ohio in 1868, she had lived there since she was sixteen years old.

Five years after Walt was born, the Disney family moved from Chicago to Marceline, Missouri, to operate a forty-eight acre farm they had purchased. They farmed for four years, until 1910. Shortly after moving to the farm, Walt's two oldest brothers left home and moved back to Chicago. Herbert, the oldest, became a mailman, and Raymond, next to the oldest, eventually became an insurance salesman. While life on the farm was a hard one for Walt, he loved country living and was influenced by it throughout his life, as a careful examination of his many accomplishments will evidence. It was during the four years on the farm that Walt first expressed an interest in drawing—an interest, incidentally, of which his father did not approve. Elias could see no future in art and encouraged Walt to take up more practical pursuits.

Walt did not heed his father's advice and in 1914, four years after the family had moved to Kansas City, Missouri, he persuaded his father to allow him to enroll in Saturday morning classes at the Kansas City Art Institute. Walt was thirteen at the time. Life in Kansas City for Walt was even harder than it had been on the farm. Elias had taken six thousand dollars of the money he received from the sale of the farm to purchase a newspaper route. While Ruth, Walt's younger sister, stayed at home and helped with house-

work, Walt and his older brother, Roy, joined their father in delivering two thousand newspapers twice daily. The three Disneys began their deliveries at 3:30 A.M. every morning and suffered the ravages of Kansas City weather year round.

In 1917 Elias decided to sell the newspaper route, which had grown to include three thousand customers, and move back to Chicago. He took the money from the sale of the route and invested it in a share of a small jelly factory. Roy had left home in 1914 and was working as a teller in the First National Bank of Kansas City. Walt did not make the move with the family right away. He was allowed to stay in Kansas City to finish his school term and to work with the man who had purchased the newspaper route. When school recessed, Walt took a summer job as a "news butcher" (candy, fruit, soft drink, and newspaper salesman) on the Santa Fe Railroad. From this experience Walt gained a lifelong love of trains. (In later years he built and enjoyed a miniature railroad at his Hollywood home.) After two months as a news butcher, Walt joined his mother, father, and little sister in Chicago.

In Chicago, Walt was enrolled at McKinley High School. Still interested in drawing, Walt frequently contributed to the school newspaper. In addition, he attended the Chicago Academy of Fine Arts three nights a week. He studied cartooning under Leroy Gosset, a cartoonist for the *Chicago Record*. In addition to his studies, he worked with his father at the jelly factory and held several part-time jobs at various times.

On June 22, 1917, Roy joined the navy. Walt was only fifteen at the time, but a few months later he tried to follow in his older brother's footsteps. The navy refused to let Walt enlist because he was only sixteen. That turned out to be only a minor setback—Walt learned that to join a civilian Red Cross ambulance unit he had only to be seventeen and have parental consent. He somehow managed to provide the necessary papers, and was accepted and sent to Sound Beach, Connecticut, for training.

While Walt was at Sound Beach, the Armistice was signed. It looked for a while as if Walt would not get to Europe after all, but, since there were sick and wounded still in France, he was one of a group of fifty sent to replace ambulance drivers who were returning. He eventually wound up in Neufchâteau, assigned to a canteen unit. Once settled, his interest in art surfaced, and he began painting posters; drawing cartoons that, when sent to *Life* and *Judge* magazines, were rejected; painting the Croix de Guerre on his buddies' jackets; camouflaging footlockers; and painting camouflage on German helmets, which were then sold by a buddy to soldiers who had just arrived in France and were eager for "genuine" German sniper helmets. He was paid small sums for his art work and that money, plus some he won in a dice game, enabled him to send home approximately five hundred dollars, which was later to come in handy to help finance one of his early cartooning attempts.

Walt returned home to Chicago in 1919. He stayed there only a few days. His father had a job for him at the jelly factory for twenty-five dollars a week, but Walt decided to return to Kansas City and become an artist. Once back in Kansas City, with brother Roy's help (Roy had returned from the navy to his job as a bank teller), Walt secured employment with Pesmen and Rubin, a commercial art firm. He worked for the art firm for two months (October and November) at fifty dollars a month. Since he was only helping out during the Christmas rush, he was let go.

However, while working at the agency, Walt met another young artist, Ubbe Iwerks. "Ub," as he was called, and Walt, who were laid off at the same time, discussed their mutual problem, and decided to form a partnership and go into business for themselves. They convinced a man named Carder, who published a newspaper called the *Restaurant News,* to give them space (enough for two desks) in his office and $10 a week to draw for his paper. Walt sent for the money he had saved in France and bought two desks, two drawing boards, an air brush, and a tank of compressed air. Soon Walt and Ub were hard at work. They solicited business from a number of sources and made $135 plus their $10 weekly salary their first month in business. Since Iwerks was pronounced "eye works," they named their newly formed firm Iwerks-Disney Commercial Artists instead of Disney-Iwerks, which, Walt reasoned, sounded too much like an optical firm.

In February 1920, Walt left or became a silent partner and took a job more to his liking with the Kansas City Film Ad Company. Walt earned forty dollars a week with this firm, where his drawings were made into crude animated films that were shown as commercials in the local theaters. Two months later Ub gave up the business he and Walt had started and joined Walt at the Kansas City Film Ad Company. Both men were fascinated with animation and worked very hard to learn everything they could about the art. The work being done at Kansas City Film Ad was rather crude and consisted mainly of stop-action photography of jointed figures. Such a technique really prevented any serious attempt to achieve naturalism. Walt learned all that he could, then borrowed a camera from his boss and began to experiment in the evenings in a garage. The results of his experimenting were a series of short topical cartoons and commercials that he sold to a man named Newman, who owned a chain of theaters. The "Newman Laugh-O-Grams," as he called them, were successful but not profitable, because Walt sold them to Newman at cost so that he could continue his experiments.

Walt continued his work with Kansas City Film Ad and was soon earning sixty dollars a week. With the extra money he purchased a new camera and returned the borrowed one and soon quit his job to go into business on his own. His next step was to bring other artists in to help produce the Newman Laugh-O-Grams. Most of the artists at first worked for no pay just to gain the experience; one of the artists was Walt's friend and co-worker at Kansas City Film Ad, Ub Iwerks. With the added help Walt began work on a series of up-dated fairy tales, including *Cinderella, The Four Musicians of Bremen, Goldie Locks and the Three Bears, Jack and the Beanstalk, Little Red Riding Hood,* and *Puss in Boots.* The fairy tales were called "Laugh-O-Grams" and belonged to a corporation that Walt formed called Laugh-O-Gram Films, Inc. The firm was initially capitalized at fifteen thousand dollars. The fairy tales did not do well, and the one film distributor in New York City who was interested went bankrupt before Walt could make any real money. Since there was no money to pay the artists, Walt let them go.

Walt did not give up, as many probably would have. Instead he went to work on a cartoon called *Alice's Wonderland,* which featured a live-action figure named Alice. By combining a film of Alice shot against a white background with a film on which the animation was shot, he achieved the effect of blending the real Alice with the cartoon characters. The film was good, but Walt had exhausted all of his credit producing it. As a result Laugh-O-Gram Films, Inc., went bankrupt. Walt stayed in Kansas City and did free-lance photography on special assignment for Selznick News, Pathe Newsreel, and Universal News Reels. He made little money and was forced to sleep in the studio of the defunct Laugh-O-Gram Films, Inc., where the rent had been paid in advance.

In July of 1923 Walt, who was then twenty-one years old, decided that his future in Kansas City was not promising and that he would move to Hollywood and seek work. He took with him one copy of the film *Alice's Wonderland*. After being in Hollywood for several months without finding work, Walt finally interested Margaret J. Winkler, a New York film distributor, in his Alice film. After some negotiations, he signed a one-year contract to produce a series of Alice Comedies—one a month at fifteen hundred dollars each. That was October 16, 1923.

Walt went to his brother Roy, who had moved west in 1920 for his health, and convinced him to join the cartoon business. Walt and Roy had $290 between them plus another $500 that they had borrowed from their uncle, Robert Disney (who had been providing Walt with room and board for $5 a week since he arrived in Hollywood). With their $790, Walt and Roy rented space in the rear of a building at 4651 Kingswell, which was also occupied by the Hollywood-Vermont Realty Company. Later, they moved next door to 4649 Kingswell. It was at this time they hung out their first sign, which read: DISNEY BROS. STUDIO.

Virginia Davis, who had starred in Walt's original *Alice's Wonderland*, was brought out from Kansas City to continue with the series. Eventually she was replaced by Dawn O'Day for one picture; the series ended with Margie Gay as Alice. The first Alice Comedy made in Hollywood cost $750, which left Walt and Roy with a $750 profit from the $1,500 that they received for the film. It was called *Alice's Day at Sea* and released on March 1, 1924. The New York film distributor wasn't especially pleased with the early films, because only approximately three hundred of the

nine hundred feet of each film was animated, while the other six hundred feet featured Alice and other children in live action. The problem stemmed from the fact that Walt could not draw enough of the animation all by himself. Hence the brothers employed several assistant artists and convinced Ub Iwerks to leave his job in Kansas City and join them in California. The films improved and became modestly popular.

As the business grew, employees were added. One of the new employees was a Lewiston, Idaho, girl named Lillian Bounds. She and Walt fell in love and were married in July of 1925. Roy, however, was the first of the team to marry; he married his Kansas City sweetheart, Edna Francis, on April 11, 1925.

On July 6, 1925, it was determined that the business was successful enough to have its own building. Walt and Roy took four hundred dollars of their profits from the Alice Comedies (which were selling then for eighteen hundred dollars each) and bought a lot at 2719 Hyperion Avenue in Hollywood. By January of 1926, they had erected and moved into a single-story building with enough space to contain their blossoming cartoon business. Walt and Roy produced successful Alice Comedies until 1927. By then their popularity had fallen off to the point where Walt decided to begin instead another series of totally animated cartoons, and Oswald the Lucky Rabbit was chosen to be the star.

Margaret Winkler, who had been the distributor of Walt's early Alice films, married Charles Mintz in 1924. So it was with Mintz that Walt signed a one-year contract for the distribution of his new Oswald series. Mintz was at the time associated with Universal Pictures Corporation, and Oswald was distributed through this firm. Oswald films became quite popular during that first year, earning the Disney brothers $2,250 a reel.

As indicated earlier, there was a flaw in Walt's contract with Charles Mintz. Technically Mintz owned the character Oswald. Thus when it came time to negotiate a new contract, Walt went to New York City. There Mintz offered Walt a contract that, instead of increasing the price of each film by $250 as Walt had requested, reduced the amount to be paid for each film. When Walt refused, Mintz broke the news that his wife's brother (George Winkler) had persuaded several of Walt's best animators to join Mintz in producing Oswald cartoons without Walt. By not accepting less money for his cartoons, which were increasing in popularity and earning more money, Walt had no alternative but to return to Hollywood and develop a new character. Oswald did survive as a cartoon character and eventually became the property of the famous animator Walter Lantz.

Page 32 of the August 20, 1927, issue of *Universal Weekly* shows Vogan Candy Company trucks advertising "Oswald Milk Chocolate Frappe Bars," a two-column newspaper ad, a window sticker, and a three-panel counter card advertising the Oswald candy bar. Such items are considered to be among the first examples of Walt Disney character merchandise.

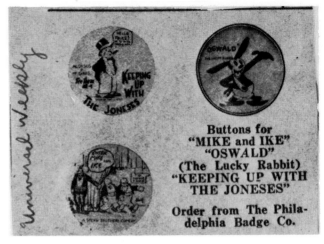

Three pin-back, celluloid-covered buttons made in 1927 by the Philadelphia Badge Company. The one shown in the upper right portion of the advertisement clipped from an August 1927 issue of *Universal Weekly* features Walt Disney's character Oswald the Lucky Rabbit.

A waxed paper wrapper for the Oswald chocolate candy bar. Because most wrappers were destroyed when used, the few examples still in existence are rare collector's items.

Part of a two-page advertisement from the August 20, 1927, issue of *Universal Weekly*. Walt Disney's character Oswald the Lucky Rabbit was used to advertise films distributed by Universal Pictures.

OSWALD STENCIL SET AN EXPLOITATION WOW

Universal's Lucky Rabbit Gets Biggest Tie-up In Short Subject Film History

NEVER before in the history of short subject exploitation has there been such a tremendous tie-up as that recently effected in connection with Oswald the Lucky Rabbit. Universal's comedy rabbit, created by Walt Disney and produced by the Winkler Productions, has been made the subject of a novelty stencil set for children. The set will be distributed through five and ten cent stores and other chain stores all over the country, which means reaching millions of purchasers and movie-goers.

The set consists of stencils cut in bright, firm paper, crayons and drawing paper. The parts that are cut have to be pushed out by the young owner of the set before the stencil can be traced with a pencil on a sheet of drawing paper. The real fun begins when the child comes to coloring the outline drawing with gay crayons. The

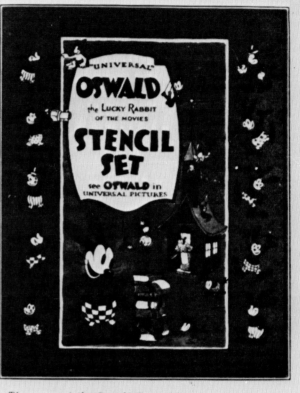

The cover of the Oswald Stencil Set is gaily colored in red, yellow and black, making it an eye-catching toy for five-and-ten cent store distribution.

instruction sheet, shown on the lower left hand corner of this page, shows the completed pictures of Oswald as an aid to coloring them. The little cartoons are familiar to all movie fans as one of the most amusing comedy subjects on the screen today. Youngsters will go wild over the set as surely as they laugh with delight at the films of Oswald.

The cover of the box has been designed with a view to catching the passing eye. The background is in bright red and yellow, while the cartoons of Oswald are silhouetted sharply in black.

These Oswald Stencil Sets can be effectively used as prizes at Oswald matinees, or tied-up with newspaper contests for little folk. The set will make sure-fire window displays in local stores together with announcements of playdate and theatre. The sets may be bought from the Universal Toy and Novelty Company, 2329 Third Avenue, New York City, for nine cents each. Make the favorite comedy character even more famous by tying him up with this newest drawing novelty.

The distribution of the stencil set will be as wide as Oswald's fame and appeal directly and instantly to the very youngsters who are Oswald fans all over the country.

OSWALD Playing Bandit

OSWALD The Sheik

Instructions

Push out parts that are cut, then place each stencil on a sheet of paper and follow the outlines with a pencil, then color with crayons.

OSWALD Marathon Runner

OSWALD The Jazz Singer

A box of bright crayons is attached in this space to the instruction card.

OSWALD Painting the Town

OSWALD The Athlete

Page 22 of the April 21, 1928, issue of *Universal Weekly,* featuring an "Oswald Stencil Set." These sets were manufactured by the Universal Toy and Novelty Company of New York City, and their original wholesale cost was 9¢ each.

Articles about Oswald the Lucky Rabbit from (*above*) the September 2, 1927, issue of *Motion Picture News* and (*right*) the June 14, 1928, issue of *Universal Weekly*.

Oswald The Lucky Rabbit

There is something about the character of Oswald that makes people laugh. Only less than a year old, this clever little cartoon rascal has won his way into the hearts of movie goers. He is acknowledged the peer of all comedy characters today. He isn't just funny, he has got personality, he is unusual, he does unusual things and does them in a mighty interesting way.

1928 is going to be Oswald's biggest year. He will be two years old and he will know a lot of people. Oswald fits it on any program. He is like cream in your coffee or salt in your soup or like sugar in your breakfast food. His presence makes the thing a complete success. He gives it that added touch that makes picture shows exceptional, that send people away talking, creating great word of mouth advertising.

Title frame from the first Oswald film produced by the Disneys. While the film was copyrighted in 1927, it is most likely that it was not distributed until 1928.

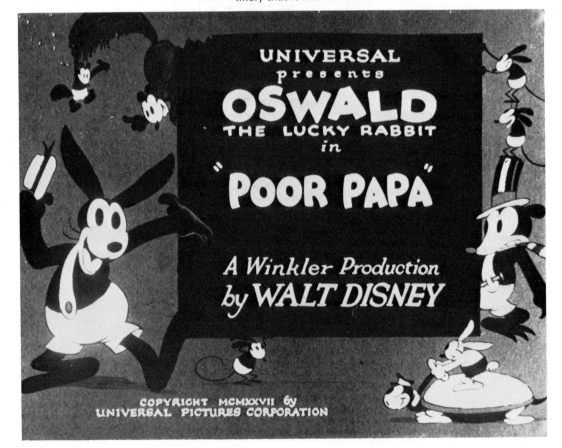

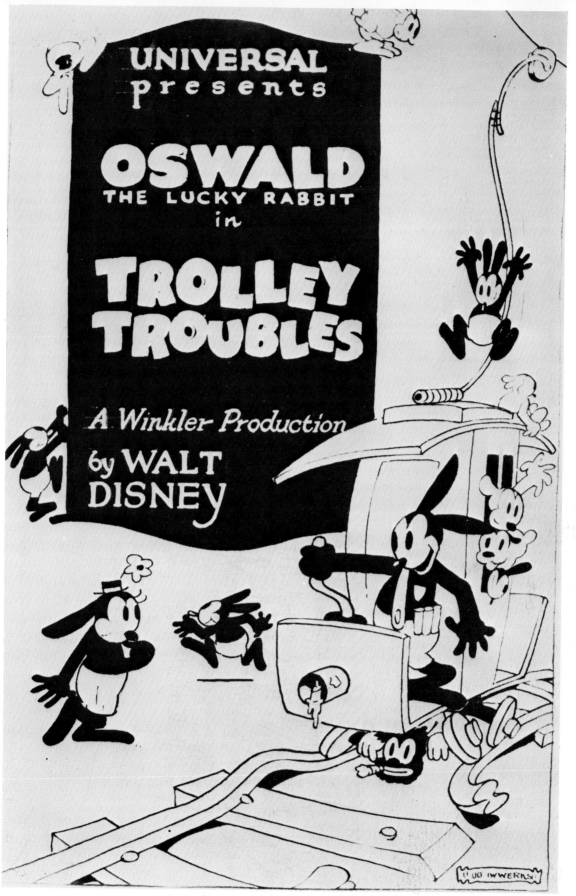

Poster from one of the first Oswald cartoons released by the Disneys (1927).

A poster used in late 1922 or early 1923 to advertise *Little Red Riding Hood,* a cartoon produced by Walt Disney's first company—Laugh-o-Gram Films, Inc. No examples of this poster are known to exist—this photograph is a blow-up of one portion of the wall of Walt's office in 1923.

A poster used in 1924 to advertise the Alice comedy *Alice Gets in Dutch*.

A 1925 poster, drawn by "UB Iwwerks" [sic], advertising the twenty-fifth Alice Comedy, *Alice in the Jungle*. It is interesting to note that the mouse sitting on the giraffe's head resembles Oswald the Lucky Rabbit more than his yet-to-be-invented relative Mickey Mouse.

The thirty-sixth Alice Comedy, *Alice Helps the Romance*, was released in 1926. The individual film distributor, Joseph P. Kennedy, listed in the upper left corner was the father of President John F. Kennedy.

Walt Disney and his associates standing in front of the Disney Bros. Studio at 4649 Kingswell in Hollywood in 1924. Ub Iwerks is on the extreme left; Walt is in the center; and Roy Disney is on the extreme right.

2. Mickey Mouse, Star of Films and Comic Strips

The loss of his cartoon character Oswald the Lucky Rabbit had only a slight slowing effect on Walt's career. Walt, Roy, and Ub Iwerks, who had recently become a partner in the Disney Brothers Studio, immediately got to work developing a new animated star to replace Oswald. A mouse character was selected. When first drawn, the new character resembled Oswald a bit, but because of its more simplistic design the mouse was easier to draw. The new mouse was tentatively called Mortimer. The name was changed to Mickey when Walt's wife suggested that Mortimer was perhaps a bit pompous for an animated mouse.

The first Mickey Mouse cartoon was started in April of 1928. It was called *Plane Crazy* and was animated entirely by Ub Iwerks. The cartoon was a "silent," filmed in black and white, as were all films in those days. Mickey, during his early period, was more functional (from an animator's standpoint) than other characters. Basically he consisted of two large circles—one for the body and one for the head—with two smaller circles for ears. His legs and arms looked like pipe cleaners, and to them were attached large feet and hands. He wore short pants and large shoes; later, he wore gloves as well. He did not have the unique personality a bit of aging and a voice would soon give him, but he was consistent with Walt's philosophy on such matters. Mickey was not altogether animal nor altogether human, but he did think for himself.

When *Plane Crazy* was finished in mid-1928, a second film, *Gallopin' Gaucho,* was begun. Be-

cause of Warner Brothers' talking picture *The Jazz Singer,* starring Al Jolson, which had been released approximately nine months earlier in October of 1927, silent films were not selling. *Plane Crazy* and *Gallopin' Gaucho* were no exceptions, and Walt was unable to find any distributor to take these films on. Walt quickly decided that Mickey Mouse had to have a voice if he was to become a star in the new era of sound films. Thus, early in the summer of 1928, Walt began to produce his third Mickey Mouse film—his first with sound—called *Steamboat Willie.* This first Disney sound cartoon was not to be a "talkie" but rather a film in which Mickey's action would be coordinated with a strong rhythmical music track. The technicalities of such a project presented many difficulties to Walt and his staff, but by September 1928 the film was finished and an accompanying musical score had been written. Walt took the film and the music to New York to have it recorded. This attempt to make the recording cost Walt approximately twelve hundred dollars—and the recording was not even synchronized with the film! After Walt had wired Roy for more money, a second recording was made; this time it came out right.

Walt then took the finished product around New York trying to interest distributors. Eventually he convinced Harry Reichenbach, the manager of the Colony Theater in Manhattan, to show *Steamboat Willie* for two weeks at his theater for five hundred dollars a week. Thus, on November 18, 1928, Mickey Mouse made his debut. *Steam-*

boat *Willie* was an immediate success and, as a result, the film was next booked at the prestigious Roxy Theater. During the film's run at the Roxy, Walt signed an agreement with a distributor named Pat Powers. It was a one-year agreement that called for Walt to receive a percentage of the rental fees.

Walt quickly sent for a Kansas City theater musician, Carl Stalling, to help him put musical sound tracks to *Plane Crazy* and *Gallopin' Gaucho,* which were still unsold. Stalling was an old friend of Walt's and had, in fact, once loaned him $250 to continue his early efforts in animation. At any rate, Stalling went to New York and helped Walt add sound to his first two Mickey Mouse cartoons and to one recently completed called *The Barn Dance.* When Walt returned to California he had left with Pat Powers four Mickey Mouse cartoons with sound. Carl Stalling returned to Hollywood with Walt and took over the musical part of the business.

During this early period the Disneys were putting most of their profits back into the business. Walt took home only fifty dollars a week and Roy thirty-five dollars; when expenses exceeded income, they did not draw their salaries. The cost of each cartoon, at this time, was approximately five thousand dollars. Their cartoons were, however, selling—and, in fact, Mickey Mouse was more often than not receiving marquee billing right along with feature-length films.

With the help of Carl Stalling, the sound half of the business soon became as sophisticated as Ub Iwerks's and the other animators' half. In fact, one of the innovations was to actually write the musical score from the story before the animation was done. After the musical score was recorded, the animators drew the cartoon to fit it.

Early in 1929, even though Mickey cartoons were taking the film industry by storm, Walt decided to diversify. He started a new series of cartoons called Silly Symphonies. In the spring of 1929 Walt sent the first of his new series, *The Skeleton Dance,* to Powers in New York. Powers returned it and told Walt to stick to Mickey Mouse. Walt, being the confident innovator that he was, immediately arranged to have *The Skeleton Dance* previewed at the Roxy in New York. It was a success. Walt then clipped the local press notices and returned the film with the notices to Powers. That convinced Powers, and he arranged to distribute the film. It was released in July of 1929. The only concession Walt made to Powers was to agree to have the film released with the introduction "Mickey Mouse Presents a Walt Disney Silly Symphony."

As was previously stated, the first merchandising item authorized by Walt Disney himself featured Mickey Mouse. In the fall of 1929 Walt made a trip to see Powers. In his own words, "I made the first commercial [merchandising] deal. . . . I was in New York and a fellow kept hanging around my hotel waving $300 at me and saying that he wanted to put the Mouse on the paper tablets children use in school. As usual, Roy and I needed money, so I took the $300." Since no record of this transaction can be found in the very complete files of Walt Disney Productions and none of the tablets have ever been located, some collectors have speculated that Walt's story was just that—a story. However, just before his death in 1971, Roy verified the story; but, like Walt, he could only remember the time, amount of money, and the item. Until further facts emerge, such as the name of the man who paid the $300, the name of the firm that produced the tablets, or examples of the actual tablets, the story told by Walt will have to remain an incomplete one and collectors will have to begin their collections with items produced in 1930.

Speaking further of the school tablet incident Walt recalled:

> That suggested other ways to exploit characters like the Mouse. The most obvious was a comic strip. So I started work on a comic strip hoping I could sell it to one of the syndicates. As I was producing the first one, a letter came to me from King Features wanting to know if I would be interested in doing a comic strip featuring Mickey Mouse. Naturally I accepted their offer.

Accepting the offer was one thing, but producing the strip was another. In a letter dated October 19, 1929, Walt wrote to King Features:

> Due to the fact that we have increased our production schedule from twelve to thirty-one pictures for the coming year, we have been unable to devote much time to the making up of the

specimens of the MICKEY MOUSE COMIC STRIP that you requested. The comic strip is an entirely new angle for us and we have been somewhat puzzled as to the best policy to carry out in this strip. The artist that we have had working on this angle [Ub Iwerks] has made up quite a few specimens but we have not as yet been able to satisfy ourselves with the results.

On November 19, 1929, Walt wrote to King Features:

> I mailed you yesterday the first specimens of the MICKEY MOUSE Comic Strip. . . . The popularity of MICKEY has been increasing by leaps and bounds and the pictures are now being distributed in every country in the world. Several of the big theatre circuits in this country have already re-booked the first series . . . to play return engagements in their theatres. We are also starting a national campaign on what is known as the MICKEY MOUSE CLUB.

Several days later Walt received a letter from King Features dated November 21, 1929, which reads:

> I just received the six strips of "Mickey Mouse" and everyone here thinks they are great. We believe Mickey has the makings of a top-notch strip judging from these samples . . . we would like to have another six strips right away. One reason for this is that Mr. Hearst will be here next week and we want to show "Mickey Mouse" to him.

On December 18, 1929, Walt sent the second batch of six strips—one for each day of the week except Sunday.

As 1929 drew to a close, negotiations between Walt and King Features reached the telegram stage. On December 30, 1929, King Features sent the following telegram:

> NEW YORK MIRROR WISHES TO BEGIN PUBLICITY ON MICKEY MOUSE NEXT WEEK AND START STRIP WEEK THEREAFTER STOP IN ABSENCE OF FORMAL CONTRACT MAY WE HAVE YOUR PERMISSION TO TELL MIRROR TO GO AHEAD STOP WHEN WILL THIRD SET RELEASES REACH US STOP PLEASE WIRE COLLECT ANSWERS BOTH THESE QUESTIONS STOP PROSPECTS EXCELLENT THAT MICKEY WILL BE BIG COMIC HIT OF NINETEEN THIRTY.

On the same day Walt replied:

> PERMISSION REQUESTED YOUR TELEGRAM GRANTED . . . THIRD SET RELEASES MAILED LAST WEEK FOURTH SET TO FOLLOW THIS WEEK.

While the actual contract was not signed until January 24, 1930, the first *Mickey Mouse* comic strip appeared on January 13, 1930. From January 13 through February 8, 1930 (a period of five weeks), strips by Ub Iwerks were used. Some of these first strips were actually published with a credit to Iwerks. Ub, however, severed his association with the Disneys shortly after the comic strip first appeared. Collectors, as a result, consider the *Mickey Mouse* strips by Iwerks quite rare and valuable.

One other Disney collectible by Iwerks was marketed early in 1930, before he left the Disney fold. This rare item is a circular cardboard disk measuring eight inches in diameter. Around the edge of the disk almost-two-inch vertical slits are cut. Just below the slits are eight drawings of Mickey. By sticking a pin through the center of the disk, holding the disk before a mirror, looking through the slits, and then spinning the disk Mickey appears to move. The disks were developed to promote Mickey Mouse cartoons. They were marked: "Mickey Mouse Movies/ Walt Disney's Famous Cartoon Character/ Drawn by 'Ub' Iwerks." While the disks are identified as having been copyrighted in 1929, they were not produced and distributed until early in 1930.

From February 10 through May 3, 1930, Win Smith, who had inked the strips for Iwerks, drew and inked the *Mickey Mouse* daily comic strip. From May 5, 1930, until the present, Floyd Gottfredson has drawn the *Mickey Mouse* strip. It is interesting that Gottfredson was assigned the task of drawing the *Mickey Mouse* strip in 1930 only on a temporary basis. With tongue in cheek he says, "Walt just never got around to replacing me." The truth is that he did such a good job there was no need to seek a replacement.

Through January and February of 1930, the content of the strip consisted of unconnected gags, but beginning in March it began to have a continuing story. In the first story Mickey was a castaway on a desert island loaded with cannibals.

By March 19, 1930, Mickey was back on the farm, his usual environment. On April 1, he was introduced to a villain named Sylvester Shyster, who was described as "a crooked lawyer—the kind of guy who'd stick a knife in your back, then have you arrested for carrying concealed weapons." Clarabelle Cow was first used in the comic strip on April 2, 1930, and Horace Horsecollar joined the group on April 3.

By April 7, 1930, each strip was given an individual title. On April 14 Pegleg Pete, described as "old Shyster's henchman, fiendish but dumb," first appeared in the strip. He was not called Pegleg Pete, however, until April 24. Eventually Pete was drawn without his peg leg; the generally accepted explanation for the elimination of the peg leg is that Gottfredson had difficulty remembering which leg it was that had the wooden appendage.

In 1931 Walt offered, in the comic strip, an autographed picture of Mickey free to interested readers. Within two weeks, eight to ten sacks of mail were being received each day. The sacks contained thousands of letters requesting the autographed picture. Today, of course, those autographed pictures of Mickey Mouse are extremely rare collectors' items. As with many of the less durable Disney artifacts, most of the thousands of pictures that were given away have been destroyed over the years.

Among collectors of comic strips, the Disney strips have long been favorites. As a result many were saved and are available today. People often save newspapers for years, and such accumulations are an excellent source of comic strips. Other sources are public libraries, which frequently will give away newspapers after they have been microfilmed.

The daily black and white *Mickey Mouse* strip, which began on January 13, 1930, is still being published. The Sunday *Mickey Mouse* comic page in color began on January 10, 1932, and is also still running. Another Disney color comic page, called *Silly Symphonies,* began on Sunday, January 10, 1932, and ran through July 12, 1942. On December 12, 1937, another Sunday color page was started. This one was centered around the animated characters of full-length feature films, beginning with *Snow White and the Seven Dwarfs.* This series ran through December 16, 1951. In 1952 it was retitled *Treasury of Classic Tales,* and it is still being published under that title. *Donald Duck* began as a daily strip in black and white on February 7, 1938, and is still running. The first Sunday color *Donald Duck* page began on December 10, 1939, and is also still being produced. *Uncle Remus,* a Sunday page in color, began on October 14, 1945, and ran through December 31, 1972.

There were a number of other Disney comic strips and pages produced and published over the years. A complete listing of all the Disney strips and pages, their dates, the artists, the writers, and the inkers is offered in this book as Appendix A to guide interested collectors.

The following table, based on 1966 statistics, will give an indication of the extent to which the Disney comic strips and pages have grown since 1930.

Table 1

Growth of Disney Newspaper Comic Strips, 1930–1966

FIVE DAILY BLACK AND WHITE FEATURES

	START	TERM	PAPERS		WEEKLY CIRCULATION (U.S. Only)
Mickey Mouse strip	Jan. 1930	36 years	*Total:*	113	5,000,000
			U.S.	67	
			Foreign	46	
Donald Duck strip	Feb. 1938	28 years	*Total:*	322	13,000,000
			U.S.	225	
			Foreign	97	
True Life Adventures panel	Mar. 1955	11 years	*Total:*	163	8,000,000
			U.S.	71	
			Foreign	92	
Scamp strip	Oct. 1955	11 years	*Total:*	166	9,000,000
			U.S.	81	
			Foreign	85	
Christmas annual strip	Nov. 1960	6 years	*Total:*	276	8,000,000
			U.S.	77	
			Foreign	199	

FIVE SUNDAY COLOR FEATURES

Mickey Mouse page	Jan. 1933	33 years	*Total:*	120	15,000,000
			U.S.	78	
			Foreign	42	
Donald Duck page	Dec. 1939	27 years	*Total:*	155	15,000,000
			U.S.	104	
			Foreign	51	
Uncle Remus page	Oct. 1945	21 years	*Total:*	95	10,000,000
			U.S.	63	
			Foreign	32	
Treasury of Classic Tales page	July 1952	14 years	*Total:*	85	10,000,000
			U.S.	50	
			Foreign	35	
Scamp page	Jan. 1956	10 years	*Total:*	76	10,000,000
			U.S.	43	
			Foreign	33	

Approximate Combined Weekly Circulation: 100,000,000

Ub Iwerks, Walt's chief artist and animator, in 1929, just before he severed his association with the Disneys.

These early black and white *Mickey Mouse* daily newspaper strips were written by Walt Disney, penciled by Ub Iwerks, and inked by Win Smith. *Top:* January 15, 1930. *Center:* February 3, 1930. *Bottom:* February 10, 1930.

A circular cardboard disk created by Ub Iwerks in 1929 and marketed early in 1930 by the Disneys to promote Mickey Mouse films. The disk is eight inches in diameter. By sticking a pin through the center, holding the disk before a mirror, looking through the slits, and then spinning the disk, Mickey appears to move.

This *Mickey Mouse* daily newspaper comic strip was published May 5, 1930. It was written by Walt Disney and penciled and inked by Floyd Gottfredson.

The first two *Mickey Mouse* newspaper comic strips in which it was announced that readers could obtain a free autographed picture ot Mickey. *Top:* May 18, 1931. *Bottom:* May 19, 1931.

Black and white *Mickey Mouse* newspaper comic strips for May 20, 1931 (*top*), and May 21, 1931 (*bottom*), in which free autographed pictures of Mickey Mouse are offered.

Mickey Mouse newspaper comic strips for May 22, 1931
(*top*), and May 23, 1931 (*bottom*).

The black and white *Mickey Mouse* newspaper comic strip
of May 25, 1931 (*top*), in which the free photograph of
Mickey Mouse is illustrated for the first time. In comic strip
of May 26, 1931 (*bottom*), Disney continues to offer a free
picture of Mickey Mouse.

In the *Mickey Mouse* newspaper comic strips of May 27, 1931 (*top*), and May 28, 1931 (*bottom*), the offer for a free picture of Mickey Mouse is continued. Reference is also made to the abundance of mail being received.

Mickey Mouse newspaper comic strips of May 29, 1931 (*top*), and May 30, 1931 (*bottom*). The May 30 strip mentions that the first of the requested pictures are being mailed.

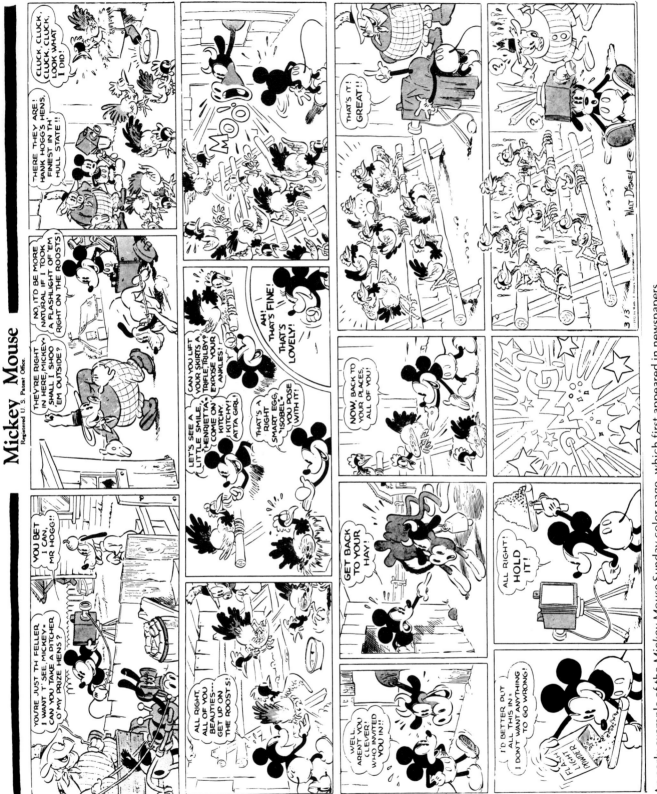

An early example of the *Mickey Mouse* Sunday color page, which first appeared in newspapers on January 10, 1932. This particular example was published on March 13, 1932. It was written and penciled by Floyd Gottfredson and inked by Al Taliaferro and Ted Thwaites.

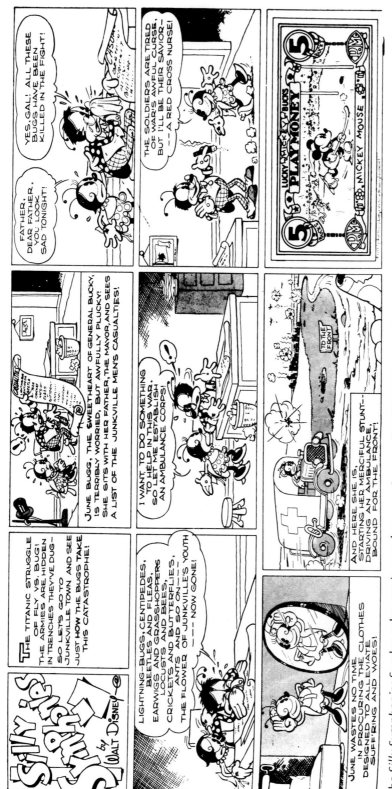

The *Silly Symphonies* Sunday color comic page began on January 10, 1932. This example was published on January 1, 1933, and featured Bucky Bug. The page was written, penciled, and inked by Earl Duvall.

On December 12, 1937, newspaper began to carry a new series called Early Sunday Color Comics. The subject of the first series was *Snow White and the Seven Dwarfs*. This example is the first one of the series. It was written by Merrill de Maris and penciled and inked by Hank Porter.

This is the first black and white daily *Donald Duck* newspaper comic strip. It was written by Bob Karp and penciled and inked by Al Taliaferro. This strip began on February 7, 1938.

This is an example of the first *Donald Duck* Sunday color page, which began on December 10, 1939. Bob Karp wrote it, and Al Taliaferro penciled and inked it.

This is the first of the *Uncle Remus* Sunday color pages. It was published on October 14, 1945. The series ran until December 31, 1972. The first one was written by Bill Walsh, penciled by Paul Murry, and inked by Dick Moores.

3. The Decision to Merchandise Mickey Mouse

The trip to New York late in 1929, which netted Walt three hundred dollars for the use of Mickey Mouse on character merchandise in the form of school tablets, came at about the time (December 16, 1929) Walt Disney Productions, a partnership, was formed into three corporations: (1) Walt Disney Productions, Ltd., and its subsidiary, the Disney Film Recording Company, Ltd., which carried on the production of pictures; (2) Walt Disney Enterprises, which engaged in ancillary activities—eventually the licensing of the use of names and characters on merchandise; and (3) Liled Realty & Investment Company, which owned or held real estate used or occupied by the other two corporations. The trip to New York, however, was not for the purpose of selling character merchandise, but to meet with Pat Powers, who was distributing Walt's films, and to obtain a long overdue accounting of their business relationship and discuss another contract.

Reminiscent of that fateful visit to New York in 1928 when Walt lost his cartoon character Oswald the Lucky Rabbit, Walt found himself in a similar situation with Powers. When Walt hesitated to sign another contract that would allow Powers to continue distributing the money-making Disney cartoons, Powers produced a contract he had signed with Walt's leading animator, Ub Iwerks; he suggested that if Walt renewed their contract, he would tear up Iwerks's contract. As much as Walt disliked losing his best animator, he refused. The result was that Iwerks sold his share of the business to Walt and Roy and went

to work for Powers drawing a cartoon character called Flip the Frog. (Flip the Frog was moderately successful for several years and was featured on character merchandise that today is considered quite collectible. Approximately ten years after leaving, Iwerks returned to work for the Disneys as a special effects innovator.)

To compound Walt's problems during this period, his musical director, Carl Stalling, who probably feared that the business would not survive after Iwerks quit, left the employ of the Disneys. Stalling eventually became a musical director for Warner Brothers.

Once again Walt was able to overcome the disaster of losing talented employees. He did not attempt to find just one man to replace Iwerks, who could produce as many as seven hundred quality drawings a day; instead Walt hired a number of apprentice and experienced animators. Stalling was similarly replaced.

In January of 1930, Bob Clampett, an artist, was asked by an enterprising lady named Charlotte Clark to design a Mickey Mouse stuffed doll, which she thought she could successfully market. Until then Charlotte had been making her living selling cookies and novelties to large markets. The fourteen-year-old Clampett could not locate a drawing of Mickey, so he took his sketch pad to the Fox Alexander Theater in Glendale and made some sketches from a Mickey Mouse cartoon that was being shown. From the sketches he and Charlotte made the first Mickey Mouse stuffed doll. When Clampett's father learned of the plan to manufacture the dolls, he advised his son and Mrs. Clark to obtain Walt's permission, because Mickey was a copyrighted character. Clampett's father went even further and drove Clampett to the Disney studio with the first doll.

Both Walt and Roy were delighted with the doll. They were so pleased with it, in fact, that they rented a house near the studio (eventually nicknamed the "Doll House") and set Charlotte Clark up in the business of making Mickey Mouse dolls. Bob Clampett, his father, and six young women joined Charlotte Clark at the Doll House and helped make and sell Mickey Mouse dolls. Bob's function was to help stuff the dolls and to brush all the excess kapok off the completed dolls. He earned approximately thirty cents per doll. His father became the head salesman, and the six young women sewed and helped stuff the dolls.

Bob Clampett eventually became famous for drawing the first *Merrie Melodies* sound cartoon for Warner Brothers' cartoon studio; for drawing the first *Bugs Bunny* cartoon and giving Bugs his first carrot; for creating Tweety and the Puddy Cat; and later for winning three T.V. Emmy Awards for his "Time for Beany" show.

Walt was slowly beginning to realize that his cartoon characters were natural subjects for character merchandise. It was not a difficult conclusion to make, because many earlier cartoon characters had been featured on various types of merchandise. He recalled his casual experience with Oswald the Lucky Rabbit items and the easy three hundred dollars he had made by letting Mickey appear on school tablets.

At first his thoughts ran along the lines that such merchandise would provide valuable publicity for his characters and therefore make his films very popular. He discussed the idea carefully with Roy. (They both had received a number of letters asking for permission to use Mickey Mouse on merchandise.) Together they reasoned that not only would character merchandise increase the popularity of their films but it would bring additional revenue to the firm which, in turn, would allow them to make better films.

It was at this point that Walt turned the idea over to Roy for implementation. This was consistent with the relationship the two brothers had long maintained; Walt handled the creative and production end of the business, and Roy handled the financial matters. Roy once remarked, "My job is to help Walt do the things he wants to do."

Over the years countless words have been written about Walt Disney, his characters, his art, his parks, and the like. Comparatively little, however, has been published about his brother Roy. This was by design. From the very beginning of their long business relationship in 1923, Roy insisted that it be Walt who would be the public figure. An historian examining the corporate history of the business, however, cannot overlook Roy's contributions. This is especially true about the merchandising aspects of the business.

Roy Oliver Disney was born in Chicago on June 24, 1893. He attended grammar school in Chicago and high school in Marceline, Missouri. Both Roy and Walt helped run their father's forty-eight acre farm, and later when the family moved to Kansas City, Roy helped with the newspaper route.

In 1914, at the age of twenty-one, Roy left home and went to work as a teller for the First National Bank of Kansas City. He held that job until he joined the navy in 1917. For over a year he served as a petty officer on the U.S.S. *Adonis*, a cargo ship which worked the New York to France route. Later he served on the cruiser *Houston*.

After Roy was discharged in 1919, he returned for a short time to his position as bank teller in Kansas City. However, he came down with tuberculosis, which the navy ruled the result of exposure while in the service. In 1920, after a brief stay at a Kansas City hospital, the navy sent him to New Mexico to recuperate. From New Mexico he was sent to a hospital in Arizona and then finally to Sawtelle Veterans' Hospital in Los Angeles.

When Walt ran into financial difficulties with his Laugh-O-Gram Corporation in 1922, Roy sent him approximately thirty dollars a month of his eighty-five dollars a month pension. Roy continued to periodically help Walt out financially after he moved to Hollywood in 1923.

After Walt had signed the contract with Margaret Winkler in October of 1923 to produce the Alice Comedies, Roy left the veterans' hospital to help Walt get the business started. They became partners in the Disney Brothers Studio. Until Roy had completely recovered from his bout with tuberculosis, he worked only half days at the business; his afternoons he devoted to a nap, at Walt's insistence. Roy's recovery paralleled the growth of the business, and his responsibilities as the financial leader soon became a full-time job.

So in 1930, when it became Roy's responsibility to exploit the Disney names and characters on merchandising, he tackled the project with enthusiasm. On February 3, 1930, the first contract was signed.

A page from the October 1930 issue of *The Toy Trader*, an English toy magazine, introducing Ub Iwerks's Flip the Frog as a promoter of merchandise.

FLIP THE FROG

WE are the inventors of
"FLIP THE FROG" SOFT TOYS

which are our Registered Designs, Nos. 754778 and 757013, and are produced by us in collaboration with **UB IWERKS**, who designed the Film Cartoons, and **CELEBRITY PRODUCTIONS, INC.,** who produced them.

WE are the only persons who have been duly authorised by these parties to make
"FLIP THE FROG" SOFT TOYS.

OUR Trade Friends who handle and sell
"FLIP THE FROG" TOYS

made by us under our Design Registrations quoted above, can safely ignore vague threats of proceedings issued over the name of any other toy manufacturer, or any other person or firm.

TRADE   MARK

MADE IN ENGLAND
by
DEAN'S RAG BOOK CO. LTD.
ELEPHANT AND CASTLE, LONDON, S.E.1.

Showroom Address :
29 KING STREET, COVENT GARDEN, W.C.2.

Say you saw the advertisement in " THE TOY TRADER."

Page 1 of the October 1930 issue of *The Toy Trader,* featuring an advertisement by Dean's Rag Book Co., Ltd. The ad is for Flip the Frog soft toys. This firm also made and sold a great deal of Disney character merchandise, including one famous version of the Charlotte Clark stuffed Mickey Mouse doll.

Page 9 of *The Toy Trader* for October 1930, featuring an advertisement for Flip the Frog character merchandise and other items.

WHYTE, RIDSDALE & CO. LTD.

Telephone No.: Avenue 6740 (3 lines)   Telegrams: "Whytsdale, Ald, London"

72, 73, 74, 75, 76 HOUNDSDITCH, LONDON, E.C. 3

WHY NOT PAY US A VISIT?

We pay carriage on all orders to the invoice value of £10

DIP TOYS and BAZAAR GOODS in great variety

THE MOST COMPREHENSIVE COLLECTION OF
FANCY GOODS, TOYS AND NOVELTIES
IN LONDON.
DELIVERY FROM STOCK.

7/F8012. CHIMPEE TEA PARTY.

A Zoological Novelty three miniature monkeys at tea in charge of their keeper. All metal, enamelled in colour and neatly boxed, exact as sketch.

PRICE .. .. 8/- dozen sets.

LEAGUE FOOTBALL.

The best indoor football game yet produced; all the thrills of a real match, with Penalties, Free-kicks, Corners, etc., all embodied in this exciting game. Two sizes.

7/M3033. Size of box, 11 x 8in.   8/- dozen.
7/M3034.   ,,   ,, 15 x 12in. 20/- dozen.

"FLIP" the FROG.

The children's latest film star enters TOYLAND. A characteristic soft toy in rich quality Green and Gold mohair plush, made in the following sizes—

7/R4241.	Height, 5 ins.	15/-	doz.
7/R4242.	,, 6½ ,,	22/6	,,
7/R4243.	,, 8 ,,	35/-	,,
7/R4244.	,, 9¾ ,,	46/6	,,
7/R4245.	,, 11½ ,,	63/-	,,
7/R4246.	,, 14½ ,,	87/-	,,
7/R4247.	,, 16 ,,	120/-	,,

7/M3047. BIJOU GOLF.

A table game of skill. Complete 9 hole course with many novel bunkers, etc., fixed ready for play. Packed in box complete with specially designed flippers and galalith counters. With Golf rules. Cloth measures 35 x 17 ins.

PRICE .. 28/- dozen

7/T5191. CRAZY GOLF PUZZLE.

This popular pastime is now made as a Glass Top Puzz'e fitted with steel ball and assorted in four different courses.   Length 6ins.

PRICE .. .. .. 4/3 dozen

7/F8898. "AQUADUCK."

The latest swimming toy. Strong clockwork nodding head, all-metal, gaily coloured, and packed each in decorated box. Length, 5in.

PRICE .. .. .. 8/- dozen

Write for our Illustrated Christmas Novelty Circular.

Walt Disney posing with the first large shipment of Charlotte Clark stuffed Mickey Mouse dolls. This photograph was taken early in 1930.

In 1931, when Walt offered in the daily newspaper comic strip to send a free autographed picture of Mickey Mouse to those requesting it, the studio was flooded with mail. This is a picture of Walt posing with ten sacks of mail received in one day. A large stuffed Mickey Mouse doll, made by Charlotte Clark, is standing on top of the stack of letters.

A formal portrait of Roy O. Disney, taken in 1971.

4. Produce the Doll!

February 3, 1930: Confirming your recent conversation with our Mr. Carl Sollmann regarding the manufacture and sale by us of Figures and Toys of various materials, embodying your design of comic Mice known as MINNIE & MICKEY MOUSE, appearing in copyrighted moving pictures, we submit the following: It is agreed that in consideration of your granting us the sole right in the United States and their possessions . . .

This was how the first contract began. The first firm to manufacture and sell Disney character merchandise was Geo. Borgfeldt & Co. of New York. While Walt, as president of the corporation, actually signed this and numerous other contracts, it was Roy who negotiated it. Roy's preliminary investigations showed that the Borgfeldt group had a long history of dealing with novelties. Borgfeldt had offices in a number of countries at that time, and through those they planned to license foreign as well as domestic manufacturers to produce specified novelties that they in turn would import and distribute.

On March 27, 1930, Borgfeldt issued its first license (through Waldburger & Huber of New York) to Waldburger, Tanner & Co. of St. Gall, Switzerland, to manufacture Mickey and Minnie Mouse handkerchiefs. The handkerchiefs were extensively sold and are very desirable collectors' items today. The Waldburger and Tanner handkerchiefs were marked: "MICKEY & MINNIE MOUSE, Copr. 1928, 1930 by Walt E. Disney." Over the years handkerchiefs featuring Disney

characters have proved a popular item and have been manufactured by a number of different companies.

While the lack of a well-developed line of domestic merchandise was a continuing concern of the Disneys during the duration of their first contract with Borgfeldt, it was the production of a quality Mickey Mouse stuffed doll that gave Walt and Roy some of their most frustrating times.

It will be recalled that Charlotte Clark began early in 1930 to manufacture, on a limited basis, a stuffed Mickey Mouse doll that pleased Walt and Roy a great deal. Initially the dolls were purchased from Mrs. Clark for casual distribution by the Disneys to friends, business acquaintances, and certain visitors to the studio. But after Walt was photographed with one of the dolls and the photograph was published in a magazine, *Screen Play Secrets*, and a number of newspapers, the demand for the dolls increased. Thus, both Walt and Roy were determined to have the Clark dolls manufactured and distributed on a national basis.

Mrs. Clark, being only a casual manufacturer of the dolls, was not equipped to fill the sudden demand. The plan, then, was to have Borgfeldt produce and market the dolls.

In September of 1930, the May Company and Bullock's, two large department stores in the Los Angeles area, expressed an interest in selling the dolls but refused to pay the $57.00 a dozen that Borgfeldt estimated they would cost. Roy, not wanting to lose the opportunity to have the dolls sold by the two large stores, went to Charlotte Clark, who quoted a price of $2.50 each or $30.00 a dozen. At Mrs. Clark's price the stores could sell the dolls for $5.00 each and make a nice profit.

By November of 1930, Mrs. Clark was producing three to four hundred dolls a week in her small "factory"—a house near the studio. To do this she had to employ six women to help her. While several hundred dolls a week may sound like a significant number, in comparison to the demand it was not. Roy continued to insist that Borgfeldt locate a manufacturer who could produce the dolls in keeping with the demand. Borgfeldt agreed to continue the search for such a manufacturer but meanwhile placed orders for dolls with the overworked Mrs. Clark.

In October of 1930, Dean's Rag Book Company in England was also producing the doll, under an agreement with Walt's representative in England, but the quality was such that the Disneys eventually refused to let them be imported. The Dean's doll is easy to identify because it featured a toothy sneer instead of the appealing one-line smile found on the Clark dolls.

Again Roy wrote to Borgfeldt, on October 29, 1930:

> We have no desire to go into the business of manufacturing or distributing toys and novelties, but we do very greatly desire to take advantage of the wonderful opportunity that exists today to see these dolls out on the market.

He warned:

> Before you folks go into any manufacturing arrangements on Mickey Mouse character dolls, we want to be sure that the doll put out is a good one, and a good likeness of our character. The one point that seems to take with everybody is that the doll we are having manufactured [by Mrs. Clark] is, as many buyers have stated, the truest character doll of its kind that they have ever seen.

The reply from Borgfeldt this time was, in part, a postponing:

> In the East we will turn out our own Mickey Mouse Doll and carry out your design exactly and if you could obtain for us from your manufacturer [Mrs. Clark] the name of the concern from whom they buy the material here in New York, we could go to the same people and obtain quotations from them.

Roy replied on February 4, 1931:

> We are serious when we say that we think there is a big possibility in marketing these Dolls, and that we want you to either seriously consider handling the article in an aggressive way or relinquish it entirely to our use . . . we are very reluctant to let this young lady [Mrs. Clark] go until we are satisfied that you can get someone else to manufacture an article equally as good.

Return mail brought Roy a letter from Borgfeldt dated February 7, 1931, which stated:

> As to the manufacture of a velvet Mickey Mouse Doll, we can have these made much cheaper here in New York by one of our factories. We are preparing two smaller sizes than the one you have made on the Coast, as we did not want to conflict with yours. . . .

Borgfeldt's answer, on February 25, 1931, was a confusing:

> It was our intention to try to have the three Dolls made in New York, but for the present we will continue to send orders to you on the Coast for the large Doll.

From Roy's desk came a salty:

> Walt and I are both very much put out regarding your continued delay in getting into proper production and distribution of these dolls. You have been talking a great deal and doing nothing. . . . You must realize that this means far more to us than the mere royalties involved in the sale of the dolls. It seems to be one article that has wide appeal for both children and grownups. In view of your delay, we ask that you withdraw that article from our contract arrangements, and allow us to have unhampered freedom and the right to properly exploit our character. I am making arrangements with Mrs. Clark to re-open her shop for the manufacture and sale of these dolls.

Eight days later Borgfeldt sent the following telegram to Roy: "SENDING FIRST SAMPLE VELVET DOLL MANUFACTURED IN OUR FACTORY TODAY."

The sample of the Borgfeldt doll arrived on

March 25, 1931, and, after showing it to Walt, Roy wrote:

> In the first place, I believe the doll is stuffed too soft to hold its shape. It came to us rather battered and was a very dilapidated, mis-shaped thing. Your doll weighs eleven ounces. Our doll weighs six and one half ounces, yet our doll is more sturdy; it is packed much tighter. . . . Mrs. Clark used Kapok. The legs of your doll are entirely too thick. The feet are too small— that is, they are too thin, not built up enough. The gloves are larger than those on our doll. The face and head are the poorest part of your doll, it being too thick and thereby losing some of its pleasing appearance. The ears are not cut with the round edge, but rather with a scalloped edge. The mouth is crooked and not as we like it. The oblong line of the eyes should be parallel with the line of the body.

On April 1, 1931, samples of the two small sizes of stuffed Mickey Mouse dolls arrived from Borgfeldt. Roy's comments were similar to the above:

> We are very disappointed . . . [they] look even worse than the large one and I want you to know that we do not like them and do not want you to manufacture and put on the market these dolls if they are going to look like these samples.

With little hope that Borgfeldt's doll manufacturer could produce dolls of the quality desired, Roy continued:

> I still believe that Mrs. Clark can do you and us more good in manufacturing these dolls . . . than you can do with an outsider, and again I ask you to make her a definite proposition whereby she can set herself up in proper shape, with an output she can count on.

In the reply, dated April 27, 1931, Borgfeldt ignored Roy's suggestion regarding Mrs. Clark.

> We are sending you new samples of the Velvet Doll in all four sizes to give you an idea of what progress we are making in the perfection of these Dolls. When you receive them will you please advise if you have any comments to make?

In the same letter a list of Borgfeldt's Mickey Mouse merchandise is listed. As of April, 1931, they had the following on the market: drum; metal drummer; sparkler; crickets; wooden squeak toy; wooden dancer; walking toy on board; express wagon; wooden jointed Mickey Mouse; tumbling circus toy; ring nose puzzle; rubber sport ball; four velvet dolls; wooden bobbing-head figure; shooting game; quoits game; and two stencil sets. They also indicated that they were working on a Mickey Mouse kite; marble game; celluloid rattle; speed boat; bubble pipe; inflated rubber doll; and a magic lantern with Mickey Mouse slides.

During the early part of 1931, Walt asked Charlotte Clark to make a Minnie Mouse doll. The doll was made and sent to Borgfeldt for inclusion in their line. On May 1, 1931, Borgfeldt indicated, "We are going to work on the Minnie Mouse Doll, in four sizes, and are doing a nice business on same."

On October 30, 1931, Roy wrote:

> I was in Bullock's Los Angeles store, recently, in the Toy Department, and had an opportunity to see, for the first time, a complete display of the various models of stuffed Mickey Mouse Dolls which Borgfeldt is now handling. I must confess that I am very disappointed. I think the workmanship and general appearance of all the Dolls . . . is nothing short of terrible. . . . The buyer at Bullock's has called the studio on at least two occasions, attempting to purchase Dolls from us direct because of the inferiority of Borgfeldt's Dolls. Walt had the opportunity of seeing the display of all Borgfeldt Mickey Mouse toys and novelties in the Biltmore Hotel. Walt was not disappointed, he was positively disgusted with the majority of the merchandise. . . . Evidently in your opinion this is good merchandise at the price and competition demands that you keep that price down. However, we have built our business on the theory of trying to make a better product than the other fellow, and we still believe we are right. Please take this letter seriously, and in the spirit in which it is intended, and try to improve the quality of your Mickey Mouse merchandise, particularly the Mickey Mouse stuffed dolls.

The situation did not change to Walt's and Roy's satisfaction, so they began to think along other lines. Roy reasoned that since they could not get Borgfeldt to produce the Mickey and Minnie Mouse dolls of the quality desired, and since Charlotte Clark's output was limited, they would have to get someone else to manufacture the dolls.

The "someone else," however, could not be a regular manufacturer because of the agreement with Borgfeldt.

The two brothers finally decided that the best solution would be to release the Charlotte Clark pattern to the public and let individuals make their own dolls. Since, as has already been stressed, it was not the profit from selling the dolls that was important to Walt and Roy but satisfying the demand for dolls, the solution was a good one. Roy, thus, arranged for the McCall Company of New York City to produce the pattern. The resulting pattern, McCall Printed Pattern No. 91, was released early in 1932. The pattern was printed in English, French, and Spanish. The envelope contained "twenty-seven pieces, one transfer and one tissue sheet of directions." From the McCall pattern, which cost thirty-five cents, three sizes of Mickey and/or Minnie Mouse dolls could be made: (1) eight and one-half inches, (2) thirteen and one-half inches, and (3) eighteen inches in height. The pattern suggested that for the heads and bodies flannel, sateen, cotton broadcloth, percale, or taffeta material was best, and that the clothes could be made from scraps of material.

The patterns sold well and even though the package carried the warning, "This pattern sold for individual use only and not to be used for manufacturing purposes," many fine seamstresses throughout the country made dolls in quantity and accepted "donations" from those who wanted dolls. During the Depression such activities were, of course, not uncommon.

Today, collectors prize well-made dolls from the McCall pattern as highly as those made by Charlotte Clark. Dolls made by Dean's Rag Book Company in England and Margarete Steiff & Company, Inc., in Germany (both imported for a time by George Borgfeldt & Company) are valued, too, by collectors, but more for their age than their beauty.

By 1934, Mickey and Minnie Mouse stuffed dolls were being manufactured by the Knickerbocker Toy Company of New York City. Knickerbocker made dolls of the quality the Disneys desired, and was able to satisfy the demand. This firm made the dolls until World War II. After the war, Gund Manufacturing Company of New York City made stuffed Disney character dolls until the 1970s.

McCall doll patterns were sold from 1932 through 1939. Charlotte Clark continued to make dolls on a limited scale for a number of years, but more importantly she designed dolls for the Knickerbocker Toy Company during the period that they manufactured Disney merchandise. She continued with the Gund Manufacturing Company when they took over and designed their Disney dolls until 1958. Charlotte Clark, it should be noted, designed a number of dolls for those companies—Donald Duck, Pluto, and others. Many of the Clark-inspired dolls bear a label that reads, "A Charlotte Clark Creation." Mrs. Clark died on December 31, 1960, at the age of 76, having been directly and indirectly associated with the Disneys for thirty years, and making a significant contribution to the field of Disney character merchandising.

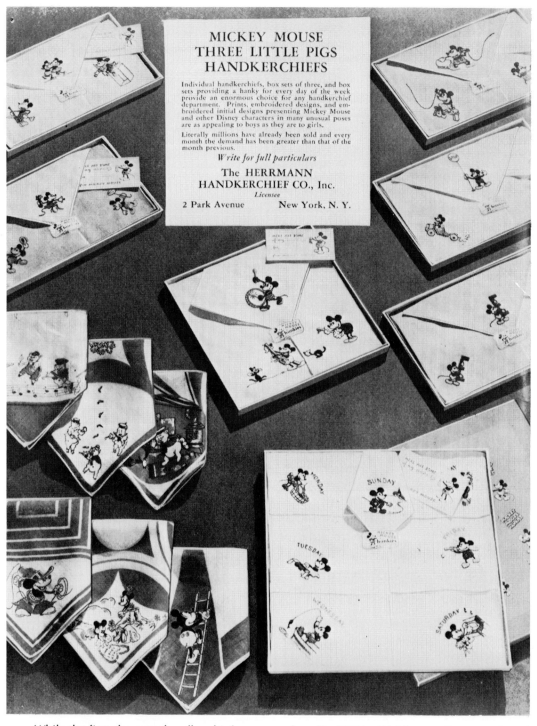

While the first character handkerchiefs were produced in 1930 by Waldburger, Tanner & Co. of St. Gall, Switzerland, and distributed through Waldburger & Huber of New York under a license granted by Geo. Borgfeldt & Co. of New York, in 1932, the Herrmann Handkerchief Co., Inc., of New York became the major manufacturer of character handkerchiefs featuring Disney characters. This photograph shows some of the Herrmann handkerchiefs for 1934.

Mickey Mouse character handkerchiefs made by the Herrmann Handkerchief Co., Inc., in 1936 to celebrate the firm's fourth year as a Disney character merchandise licensee.

Disney character handkerchiefs made in 1936 by the Herrmann Handkerchief Co., Inc. Note the "Silly Symphony Hankies" in the lower left.

Handkerchiefs, featuring Disney characters, that were
made in 1938 by the Bernhard Wolf Company of New York.

Handkerchiefs made in 1940 by the Herrmann Handkerchief Co., Inc., of New York. This selection features both embroidered and printed designs.

Handkerchiefs, featuring the characters from the film *Pinocchio,* made by the Herrmann Handkerchief Co., Inc., in 1940.

The original sketch by early Disney artist Burton "Bert" Gillett for the first toy made by Geo. Borgfeldt & Co. of New York, a wooden Mickey Mouse with jointed hands, arms, legs, and a wire tail. This toy was made in 1930 in two sizes: 7¼" and 9¼".

Toys and dolls featuring Mickey Mouse and sold by Geo.
Borgfeldt & Co. in 1931.

A 1932 advertisement of Geo. Borgfeldt & Co. of New York, showing some of the character merchandise available that year.

A 1930 photograph of a display of stuffed Mickey Mouse dolls made by Charlotte Clark. This display was in the window of Bullock's department store in Los Angeles.

A 1932 picture of Walt Disney posing with Mickey Mouse character merchandise.

Mickey and Minnie Mouse stuffed dolls produced by the Knickerbocker Toy Co. of New York. Of the dolls produced in great quantities, these were the first that Walt liked.

In addition to the standard Mickey Mouse stuffed doll, the Knickerbocker Toy Co. was producing dolls with costumes in 1935.

These mean your biggest year in dolls

In 1936 the Knickerbocker Toy Co. was producing these dolls. Note the addition of a stuffed Donald Duck doll.

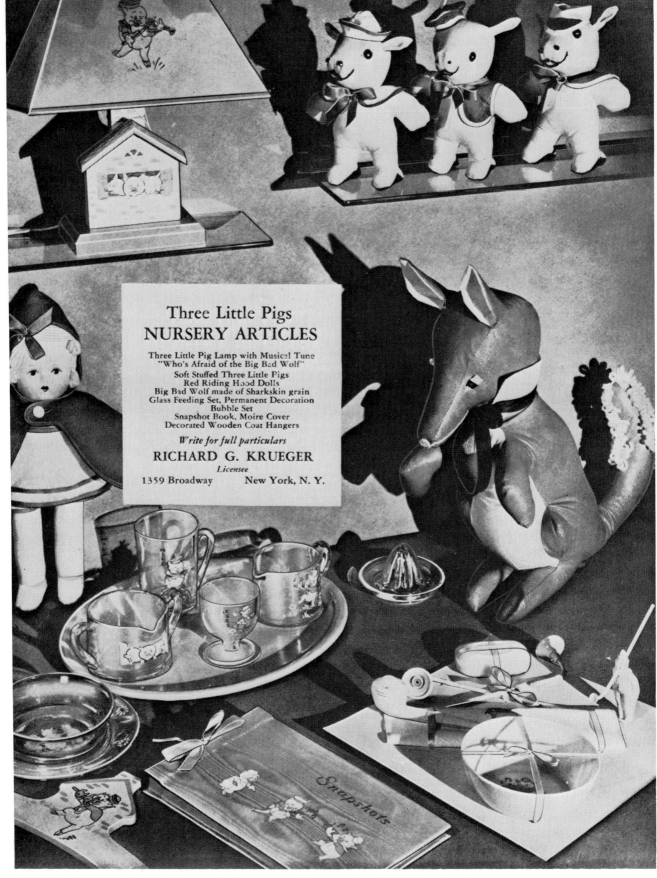

Three Little Pigs
NURSERY ARTICLES

Three Little Pig Lamp with Musical Tune
"Who's Afraid of the Big Bad Wolf"
Soft Stuffed Three Little Pigs
Red Riding Hood Dolls
Big Bad Wolf made of Sharkskin grain
Glass Feeding Set, Permanent Decoration
Bubble Set
Snapshot Book, Moire Cover
Decorated Wooden Coat Hangers

Write for full particulars

RICHARD G. KRUEGER
Licensee

1359 Broadway   New York, N. Y.

While the Knickerbocker Toy Co. was the largest manufacturer of stuffed dolls, other firms produced some dolls. The items pictured here, including the small stuffed dolls, were made by the Richard G. Krueger Company of New York in 1934.

A 1934 advertisement featuring items produced by the Geo. Borgfeldt Corp.

PLUTO THE PUP

DONALD DUCK

BIG BAD WOLF

ROBBER KITTEN

ELMER ELEPHANT

ORPHAN KITTENS

MISS COTTONTAIL

TOBY TORTOISE

Stuffed dolls made in 1936 by Richard G. Krueger of New York. This firm's line included Disney characters from Silly Symphonies as well as Walt's more famous Pluto, Donald Duck, Big Bad Wolf, etc. All of the dolls shown sold for $15 a dozen except Robber Kitten, which sold for $22.50 per dozen.

In 1938 the Ideal Novelty & Toy Company produced these dolls in a variety of sizes. The Disney characters represented in this line are Snow White and the Seven Dwarfs. The Dwarfs retailed for $2.00 each.

Stuffed and wood-composition dolls produced in 1938 by the Knickerbocker Toy Company, Inc., of New York. These dolls sold in 1938 for $1.00 and up.

A display house and complete set of *Snow White and the Seven Dwarfs* (top), *Snow White and Seven Dwarfs* dolls and traveling case (*middle*), musical Dwarfs dolls (*bottom*). All were produced in 1938 by the Knickerbocker Toy Company, Inc.

Disney character dolls manufactured in 1938 by Richard G. Krueger, Inc., of New York. By the dozen the prices were: Snow White, organdy dress—$22.50; Snow White, velvet, silk-lined cape—$36.00; Dwarfs, washable sharkskin grain material—$14.40; Dwarfs, velvet—$18.00; fawn—$15.00; birds—$7.20; chipmunk—$10.50; bunny—$10.50; Donald Duck—$14.40; Elmer Elephant, plush—$18.00; Pluto, velvet—$14.40; Orphan Kittens—$15.00; Robber Kitten—$27.00. Dolls with music were $15.00 additional per dozen.

Dolls and stuffed animals made by Richard G. Krueger of New York in 1940. The Pinocchio dolls (approximately 15" tall) were made with jointed legs and arms or with stuffed bodies; both had "life-like wool hair." Ferdinand the Bull, Donald Duck, and the Dwarf were made in a glazed fabric that looks like leather. Elmer Elephant is made in "plush" material. All dolls retailed between $1.50 and $5.00 each.

Walt Disney's Pinocchio dolls and animals manufactured in 1940 by the Knickerbocker Toy Co., Inc., of New York. The items came in a variety of sizes.

These dolls and animals made in the likeness of Disney characters were made in 1940 by the Knickerbocker Toy Co., Inc. They came in various sizes.

Bongo (*right*) and Lulubelle (*left*), stuffed dolls produced by the Gund Manufacturing Company of New York. These dolls, based on characters from the Disney film *Fun and Fancy Free,* were made in 1947.

In 1947, after World War II, the Gund Manufacturing Company of New York became the prime manufacturer of stuffed Disney character dolls. These dolls were made of "softest velvet and pile fabrics."

Mickey and Minnie Mouse stuffed dolls produced by the Gund Manufacturing Company in the 1950s. The dolls both have black plush heads and vinyl faces, hands, and shoes. They stand 20" high and were sold for $9.00 each. Minnie is wearing a blue printed taffeta dress and matching pantaloons; Mickey is wearing black and white checked taffeta trousers, a red felt cutaway jacket with organdy cuffs, a yellow felt vest, and an embroidered dickey.

In the 1950s and 1960s the Gund Manufacturing Company began to modernize their line of stuffed dolls.

64

Contemporary Mickey Mouse (*left*) and Minnie Mouse (*right*) dolls produced by the Gund Manufacturing Company.

Disney character stuffed dolls made by the Knickerbocker Toy Co. of New York in 1934.

5.
Photo-
Chronology One

In addition to the Three Little Pigs, already shown, there are two versions of the Big Bad Wolf and one Mickey Mouse hard rubber doll. These, too, were manufactured by the Seiberling Latex Products Company.

A different grouping of the hard rubber dolls made by the Seiberling Latex Products Company in 1934. These dolls sold originally for 39¢ each. The Three Little Pigs are 6" tall, the Big Bad Wolf is 10" tall, and the Mickey Mouse is 6¼" tall. All have movable heads.

Hard rubber dolls of the Three Little Pigs by the Seiberling Latex Products Company of Akron, Ohio, 1934. This firm made a number of rubber character items over the years.

These are rubber dolls and balls made by the Seiberling Latex Products Company in 1940. Pinocchio, Figaro the Cat, and Jiminy Cricket are approximately 6" tall. All of the dolls have whistles except Cleo the Goldfish, who squirts water through her mouth. The dolls retailed for 25¢ each and the balls 5¢ to 50¢ each.

ber dolls and balls made in 1938 by the Seiberling Latex ucts Company. These dolls and balls, featuring Snow te and the Seven Dwarfs, were sold individually or in

Left to right: (1) Donald Duck, with his blue sailor suit and hat and red tie painted on his body; (2) Mickey Mouse dressed in a red striped cotton sunsuit; (3) Minnie Mouse with white shoes and gloves and red dotted dress. These dolls are made of soft vinyl, measure 11″ in height, and when squeezed make noises. The dolls, made by the Sun Rubber Company of Barberton, Ohio, sold originally for $1.98 each.

This is a soft rubber Cleo the Fish from Walt Disney's feature-length animated film *Pinocchio*.

Inflated dolls and balls produced in 1936 by the Seiberling Latex Products Company of Akron, Ohio.

These rubber toys, Pluto (*left*), Donald Duck (*center*), and Thumper (*right*) from the film *Bambi,* were made in 1949 by the Sun Rubber Company. They came in pastel colors and were equipped with a noise maker.

Plastic inflatable dolls and balls made in 1949 by the Vanguard Corporation of Chicopee, Massachusetts. These toys are made of 12-gauge Vinylite with silk-screened 3-color artwork. The figural toys were sold for 98¢ each and the balls, according to size, sold from 98¢ to $2.98 each.

Two dolls made in 1940 by the Ideal Novelty & Toy Company of New York. The subject is Pinocchio. The doll on the left is 10″ tall and has a wood composition body with movable head and jointed legs and arms; it sold originally for $1.50. The doll on the right is 12″ tall and features woven wire legs and arms and a movable head; it sold originally for $1.00.

"Paper Slotties," featuring Disney characters, by the Container Corporation of America in Chicago, Illinois. These dolls, retailed in 1947 at 50¢ for a box of 6, came in flat sheets. The figures were die-cut and had to be punched out and fitted together. The dolls were used as premiums and were sold as a set.

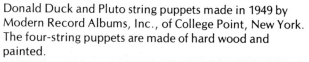

Donald Duck and Pluto string puppets made in 1949 by Modern Record Albums, Inc., of College Point, New York. The four-string puppets are made of hard wood and painted.

A Donald Duck string marionette by Peter Puppet Playthings, Inc., of Brooklyn, New York. The puppet has a vinyl head, painted composition body, sponge rubber feet, and is 7″ tall.

Hand puppets made by the Gund Manufacturing Company of New York in 1949. With vinylite heads, the puppets sold for $1.19; without, they sold for 89¢ each.

Donald Duck, Mickey Mouse, Minnie Mouse, Pluto, and characters from the Disney film *Snow White and the Seven Dwarfs*. These marionettes were manufactured in 1938 by the Alexander Doll Company of New York.

Bisque figurines distributed by the Geo. Borgfeldt Corporation of New York in 1934.

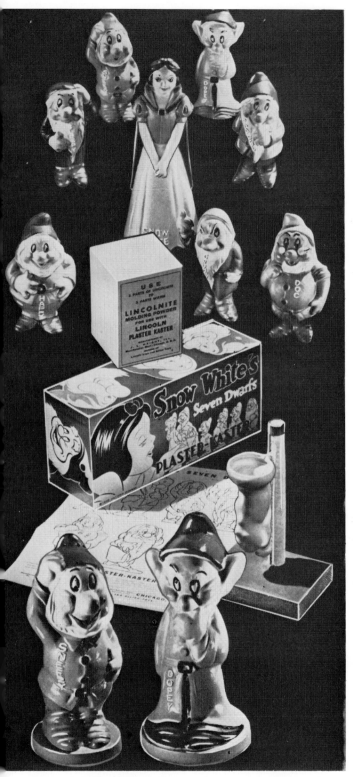

Molded wood fiber figures and plaques made in 1940 by Multi Products of Chicago, Illinois. Pinocchio (*lower right*) is 7″ tall; the sizes of the other items can be judged relatively.

Molded wood fiber novelties made in 1940 by Multi Products. The pictured fountain pen sets, bookends, and brush sets sold originally for $1.00 each.

Figures, salt and pepper shakers, and cast sets made in 1938 by J. L. Wright, Inc., of Chicago, Illinois. Snow White and the Seven Dwarfs are figures made in metal. The cast set allowed the creation of 4″ figures of the Seven Dwarfs. The Dopey and Sneezy metal salt and pepper set (*bottom*) are highly favored collectibles today and command a good price on the collector market.

Dolls, banks, and statuettes of Pinocchio made by the
Crown Manufacturing Company, Inc., of New York in
1940. The large doll (*right*) is 12" tall and has movable
arms, legs, and head. The banks are made of wood pulp
composition and have a lock and key.

Mechanical dolls and figurines distributed by the Geo.
Borgfeldt Corporation of New York in 1940. The large,
key-wound mechanical Pinocchio doll is 10½" tall. The
small Pinocchio doll on the shelf (*center*) is of wood. All
other figures are made of bisque.

The National Porcelain Company, Inc., of Trenton, New Jersey, produced these china figures in 1940. They came in white (pictured), tinted shades, and in full color. The smaller 2½" figures in white or tinted colors retailed for 10¢ each and the larger 3¼" figures in full color sold for 50¢ each.

In 1940 Brayton's Laguna Pottery of Laguna Beach, California, produced these pottery figures based on characters from the Disney film *Pinocchio*.

Disney characters made in 1940 by Brayton's Laguna Pottery.

Figurines based on characters from the first feature-length animated Disney film, *Snow White and the Seven Dwarfs*. These were all made in 1946 by the Evan K. Shaw Company.

Figurines made in 1946 by the Evan K. Shaw Company and based on characters from the feature-length Disney animated film *Pinocchio*.

Ceramic figurines based on Disney characters from the 1942 film *Bambi*. These were made by the Evan K. Shaw Company in 1946.

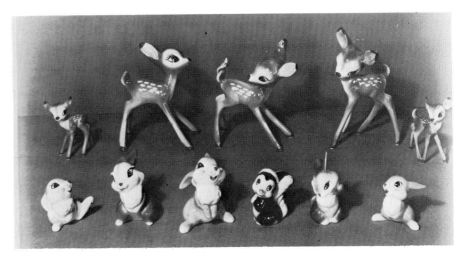

Disney character figurines made in 1946 by the Evan K. Shaw Company.

Ceramic figurines of Donald Duck (*left*), Panchito (*center*), and Joe Carioca (*right*) made in 1946 by the Evan K. Shaw Company. All of these Disney characters starred in the 1945 film *The Three Caballeros*.

Ceramic figurines produced in 1947 by the American Pottery Company.

Ceramic figurines made by the American Pottery Company of Los Angeles, California, in 1947.

Ceramic planters, cookie jars, banks, pitcher, plates, and salt and pepper shakers featuring Disney characters. They were made in 1947 by the Leeds China Company of Chicago, Illinois.

Planters, cookie jars, salt and pepper shakers, and figurines made by the Leeds China Company in 1949.

Ceramic figurines and Bambi dinnerware set made in 1949 by the American Pottery Company of Los Angeles, California.

Soap figurines made by the Lightfoot Schultz Company of New York in 1935.

Modeled soap made in 1938 by the Lightfoot Schultz Company. Such perishable items are rare today, for obvious reasons, and command a good price on the collector's market when made available.

In 1940 the Lightfoot Schultz Company produced these modeled soap figurines.

Molded figural soap made in 1947 by Kerk Guild, Inc., of Whitesboro, New York.

Character soap bars made in 1947 by the Monogram Soap Company of Hollywood, California. The complete line featured 48 different bars with Disney characters.

Molded wax candles featuring characters from the Disney film *Pinocchio*. These wax figurines were made by the Manhattan Wax Candle Company, Inc., of New York in 1940. Because most of the candles sold were used, few examples of these figural candles exist today.

6. Walt's Representative in London

In June 1930, William Banks Levy, already in England managing Powers Cinephone (which had recorded "Steamboat Willie" in New York), was tapped by Walt to be his representative. This was at the time when Mickey Mouse cartoons were beginning to become very popular not only in this country but in others. To Walt, England seemed to be the logical country in which to have a representative protect the Disney interests.

Levy had been in England representing the Disneys only a few weeks when he began receiving inquiries about the possibilities of using Mickey Mouse on character merchandise. The interest in England closely followed Walt's and Roy's recognition of character merchandising as a possible adjunct to their film business in the United States.

On June 17, 1930, Levy received a power of attorney from Walt that authorized Levy to license manufacturers to produce merchandise featuring Mickey and Minnie Mouse. Levy's official merchandising, then, began five months after that of George Borgfeldt & Co.

Unlike Borgfeldt, however, Levy was ready to quickly launch into the character merchandising business. He had accumulated all the paperwork associated with the many inquiries that had come in, and he quickly met and made deals with many of the firms represented. By September 14, 1930, he had twenty-eight licensees signed. Among the items being produced were:

Chocolate cartons; celluloid figures and rattles; novelty flower holders; jewelry and fountain pen clips; handkerchiefs, children's dress fabrics and cushion covers; design and motifs for embroideries; wallpapers and cretonnes; crepe paper serviettes and tablecloths; china containers and eggcups; children's slippers and babies' shoes; engraved subjects on pottery; children's attache cases and girls' pouchettes; silver charms; rubber Mickey Mouse; cycle and club pennants; plush mascots and hat ornaments; soap models; electro-plated and gold-plated articles; toilet sets; enamel powder compacts; rubber air balloons; decorative frieze; printed transfers; toys and books; child's chair; postcards and calendars; masks; perfumery bottles; tooth brushes; and Mickey Mouse candles.

Needless to say, both Walt and Roy were pleased with William Levy's achievements.

Levy's first contract was with Fred Butcher of a projection apparatus firm called Johnsons of Hendon, Ltd. Butcher suggested that, from selected illustrations already in existence, a series of Walt Disney stories could be printed on cellophane strips and sold with toy lanterns. The resulting product consisted of a battery-operated lantern projector with pictures mounted in groups of four between glass. This successful novelty has become a collector's item today. After World War II, the Johnson Disney Toy Projection Lantern was modified to carry filmstrips of twenty-four pictures instead of slides.

Another English pioneer in Disney character merchandise was Lewis Knight of Lewis Knight, Ltd. Knight furthered Mickey and Minnie Mouse's career by imprinting their likenesses on balloons.

What started off as a booming business for Levy in 1930 did not turn out to be one by mid-1931. In late July of 1931, Walt sent the following letter to a long list of English manufacturers (and a few others):

> We have been watching with interest the merchandise you manufacture which carries reproductions of our characters. We feel that these reproductions could be improved upon, insofar as they do not exactly conform with the way we know our characters to be. We would suggest, therefore, that you file these new designs we are sending you, until you are ready to consult them before making new merchandise. We feel that if you make your merchandise as nearly as possible like the ones enclosed, the result will be more satisfactory to both of us.

In a letter dated October 30, 1931, to Levy, Roy speculated:

> Mickey Mouse toy and novelty business in England and on the Continent has fallen off to a negligible amount, excepting on books. We have three books [published by Dean's Rag Book Company, Ltd.] over there which are going exceptionally well. [The first British Disney book was published in 1931; it was called *The Adventures of Mickey Mouse*.]

It will be recalled that the Disneys had similar problems in the United States. It took a number of years and a completely new world-wide merchandising plan before Roy could convince both manufacturers and distributors that Disney success in films was based on quality, and success in merchandising character toys and novelties must be based on the same premise.

The slump in England lasted for over a year. A similar slump in the United States was not noted, because Borgfeldt did not quickly develop as extensive a line of Disney merchandise as did Levy. Because of Levy's energetic approach to the business during that first year, collectors will find that many of their earliest items were either manufactured or distributed from the English base.

Levy and Borgfeldt, in some cases, had small problems over territory and merchandise. They occasionally ordered merchandise from the same Japanese, German, Swiss, Canadian, English, American, French, and other firms. For example, Dean's Rag Book Co., Ltd., of England produced a doll based on the Charlotte Clark design; for a while Borgfeldt imported the doll and sold it along with the Charlotte Clark originals. Hence, collectors will find some differences between the Disney character merchandise sold on the Continent and the United States during those early years, although much of it will be the same. In later years, the character merchandise produced here and abroad becomes more dissimilar because of more restrictive agreements with licensees.

Because of radical changes in the Disneys' approach to character merchandising in 1932, both Levy's and Borgfeldt's roles changed. Levy's merchandising contract was canceled on June 9, 1933. In a letter to Roy dated May 22, 1933, Levy reported that their deal of a 55/45 percent split of profits had earned the Disneys $19,343.18 and Levy $15,619.52, which were large amounts in those days. Levy stayed in England as a Disney licensee, and in February 1936 launched "Mickey Mouse Weekly" in partnership with the powerful Odhams Press, Ltd. Later Levy returned to the United States, to assist Roy Disney in launching the first public issue of Disney stock, and eventually to become "Worldwide Sales Supervisor" of the Disney films.

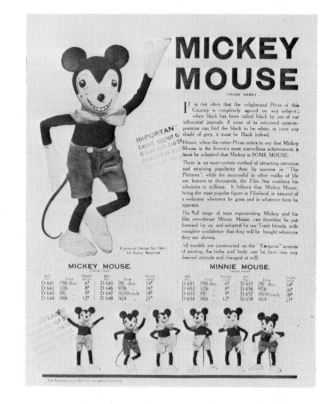

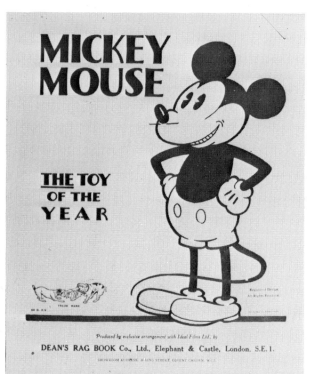

Pages 1 and 2 of a brochure from Dean's Rag Book Company, Ltd., of London, England. This piece of 1930s advertising (page 2) shows that this English firm produced and sold 8 sizes of Mickey Mouse dolls and 8 sizes of dolls in the character of Minnie Mouse. Unlike most American versions of Mickey and Minnie Mouse dolls, the dolls advertised here were jointed so that "the limbs and body can be bent into any desired attitude and changed at will."

Pages 3 and 4 of a brochure from Dean's Rag Book Company, Ltd. Advertised on page 3 are two pull toys, a hand puppet, and a "Jazzer," which is a doll that attaches to a record player and dances as records are played. On page 4 are the "Mickey Mouse Dancers"—dolls that move in unison; a "Mickey Mouse Skater"—a doll on wheels that is pulled; and the "Li-Vo Mickey"—a puppet that is manipulated through a hole in its back.

Volume 1, number 1, of William B. Levy's English version of a Mickey Mouse magazine—*Mickey Mouse Weekly*. This was a very successful publication; the first issue (Feb. 8, 1936) consisted of a sell-out printing of 375,000 and an additional printing of 25,000. Future issues were published in 450,000 lots. The magazine measures 11″ x 15″.

A view of the inside of the Ensign, Ltd., "Mickey Mouse Toy Lantern Outfit" box. Note the rather sophisticated pistol-shaped and battery-operated projector.

Photography equipment made in England. Mickey Mouse Camera (*top*) was the most popular of the line. The printing outfits (*bottom*) came complete with instructions and materials to allow printing of pictures and enlarging them. These items were produced in the 1930s by Ensign, Ltd.

85

7.
Photo-
Chronology Two

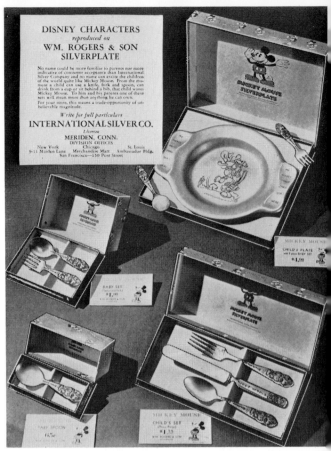

Four silver items made by the International Silver Company in 1934 are pictured. A child's plate (*top*) with a fork and spoon are offered for $4.00; a baby set of a fork and spoon (*middle*) for $1.00; a baby spoon (*bottom left*) for 65¢; and a child's set of a fork, knife, and spoon are offered for $1.75.

Six silver cups made by the International Silver Company in 1934.

Page 30 of the 1934 Kay Kamen character merchandise catalogue, advertising a silver baby plate (*top*), a porringer (*bottom left*), and a cereal bowl (*bottom right*). These Mickey Mouse items were made by the International Silver Co. of Meriden, Connecticut. The boxes in which they came are also of great interest to collectors.

Page 33 of the character merchandise catalogue of 1934 shows an advertisement for silverware and napkin rings by the International Silver Company. The silverware features reproductions of characters from the Disney film *Three Little Pigs*. The napkin rings feature reproductions of Mickey Mouse.

This is a 1938 advertisement by the International Silver Company for Snow White and the Seven Dwarfs fork and spoon.

Pinocchio fork, knife, and spoon by the International Silver Company. This set of Disney character silverware was produced in 1940.

This 1947 advertisement for children's silverware shows cups, forks, and spoons that were manufactured by Silvercraft of California (Los Angeles). The items pictured came in both sterling silver and silverplate, and featured Mickey and Minnie Mouse. The four-piece set (*upper right*) sold for $4.50 in silverplate and $16.00 in sterling; the fork and spoon set (*lower right*) sold for $1.95 in silverplate and $5.00 in sterling; and the cup and spoon set (*upper left*) sold for $3.00 in silverplate and $12.00 in sterling.

A 1934 advertisement for toothbrushes made by the Henry L. Hughes Company, Inc., of New York.

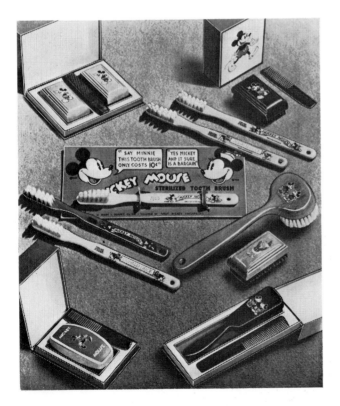

Mickey Mouse and Donald Duck brush and comb sets by Henry L. Hughes Company, Inc. The brushes came in satin or ebony finish or red and black enamel, and were manufactured in 1936. They sold generally from 59¢ to $2.00, depending on how they were grouped in sets. The toothbrushes sold for 10¢, and the bath brush retailed for 59¢.

A 1935 advertisement for Mickey Mouse hard rubber combs and cases by the American Hard Rubber Company of New York.

A 1935 advertisement for combs and brushes from the Henry L. Hughes Company, Inc., of New York.

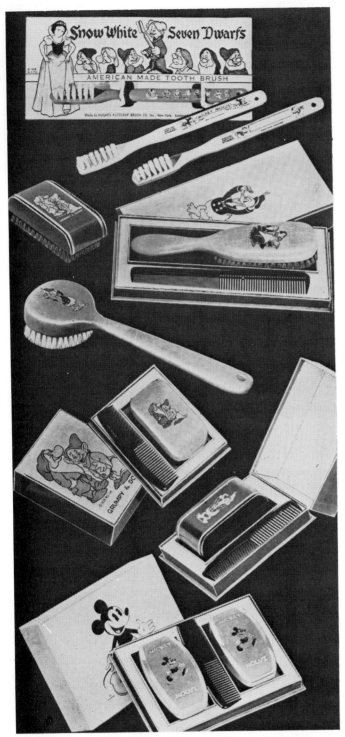

Brushes and brush sets made in 1938 by Hughes-Autograf Brush Company, Inc., of New York.

Hair ornaments, combs, fork and spoon sets made by Lapin-Kurley Kew, Inc., of New York in 1939.

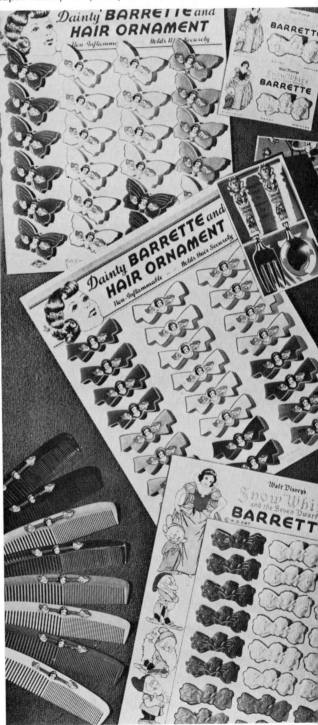

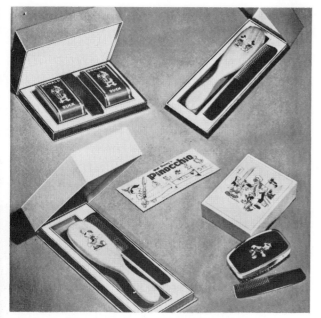

Combs and brushes advertised in 1940 by the Hughes-Autograf Brush Company, Inc., of New York.

A three-piece Snow White dresser set advertised in 1947. The set is made of translucent pastel plastic. The manufacturer was the Herbert George Company of Chicago, Illinois.

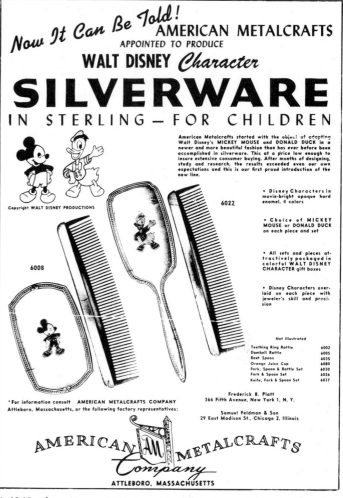

A 1948 advertisement (*National Jewelers Magazine* and *Jewelers Circular Keystone*) for sterling siverware brush, comb, and mirror.

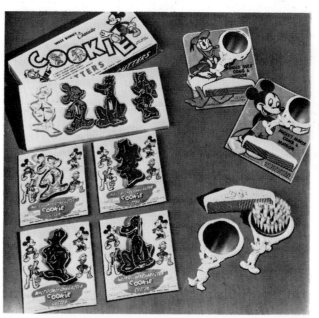

Cookie cutters, comb, brush, and mirror made in 1949 by Loma Plastics, Inc., of Fort Worth, Texas.

A 1932 advertisement for Mickey Mouse china by Schumann of New York.

A 1934 advertisement for chinaware and figural mugs by the Salem China Co. of Salem, Ohio.

Mickey Mouse chinaware made in 1936 by the Salem China Company of Salem, Ohio. This firm made an extensive line of such items featuring Mickey Mouse. Because of the high quality and beauty of this line, collectors eagerly seek examples for their collections.

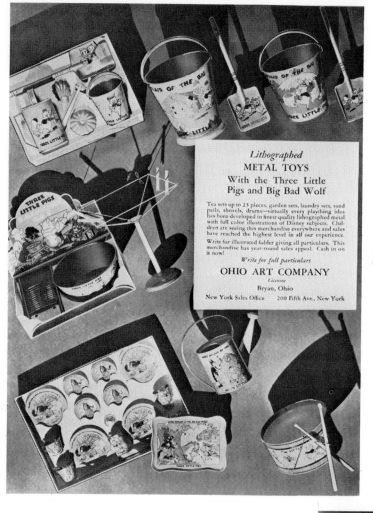

A 1934 advertisement for lithographed metal toys of the Ohio Art Company of Bryan, Ohio.

A 1934 advertisement for lithographed metal toys of the Ohio Art Company.

A 1935 advertisement for an aluminum tea set, coffee maker set, and baking set featuring Mickey Mouse. These items were made by the Aluminum Specialty Company of Manitowoc, Wisconsin.

More items featuring Mickey Mouse that were advertised in 1935 by the Aluminum Specialty Company. Pictured are a percolator set, a baking set, and cookie and biscuit cutters.

A 1935 advertisement for a "Mickey Mouse Lunch Kit" from the Geuder, Paeschke & Frey Company of Milwaukee, Wisconsin. This firm made a complete line of Disney character items in lithographed metal.

Toys and chinaware marketed in 1936 by the George Borgfeldt Corporation of New York.

Metal waste baskets and lunch kit of 1936. These were produced by Geuder, Paeschke & Frey Company of Milwaukee, Wisconsin.

Lithographed metal toys advertised in 1938 by the Ohio Art Company of Bryan, Ohio.

A portion of the line of metal toys offered in 1938 by the Ohio Art Company.

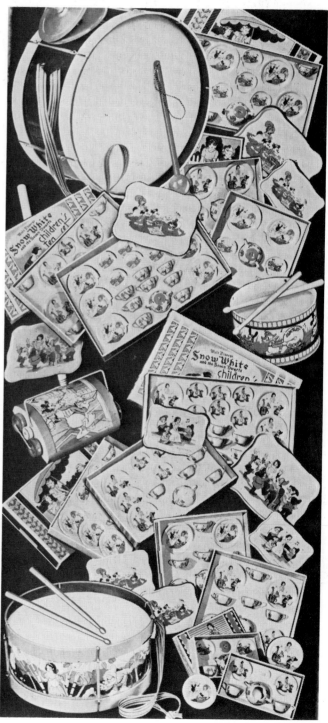

Toys and novelties marketed in 1938 by the George Borgfeldt Corporation of New York.

Glass and metal containers produced in 1938 by the Libbey Glass Company and the Owens-Illinois Glass Company, both of Toledo, Ohio. The milk bottles are especially hard to find.

Glass and metal containers advertised in 1940 by the Libbey Glass Company and Owens-Illinois Glass Company. To obtain the entire set of 12 Pinocchio glasses would be the goal of many collectors.

"Beetleware" dishes advertised in 1940 by the Bryant Electric Company of Bridgeport, Connecticut.

Dinnerware featuring Bambi. This line was produced by the Evan K. Shaw Company in 1946.

8. The First Mickey Mouse Club

In September 1929, Harry W. Woodin, manager of the Fox Dome Theater in Ocean Park, California, came to Walt with the idea of a theater-sponsored club that would be associated with Mickey Mouse. Walt liked Woodin's idea and asked him to work closely with Roy to develop it. Roy, too, thought that the club, like character merchandise, would help to promote the popularity of their cartoons.

Woodin went back to his theater in Ocean Park and, with the complete cooperation of the Disney studio, he organized the first Mickey Mouse Club. The club was so successful in its first months that Roy convinced Woodin to quit his job and come to work for the Disneys, organizing similar clubs throughout the country. Thus, late in 1929, Woodin joined the Disney organization as general manager of Mickey Mouse Clubs.

One of the first things he did as general manager was to write a monograph for theater managers outlining the Mickey Mouse Club concept. Because Woodin had to travel almost continually to help organize new clubs and maintain those already established, Roy made his own personal secretary, Lucille Allen Benedict, Woodin's assistant. Together she and Woodin developed a semimonthly newsletter called the *Official Bulletin of the Mickey Mouse Club*. This newsletter was published on the first and fifteenth of each month and was sent to the theater managers who had established clubs. The publication served primarily to advise clubs of new ideas and of the activities of other clubs. The first issue was published on April 15, 1930.

According to Woodin the two primary purposes of the club were: (1) to provide an easily arranged and inexpensive method of getting and holding the patronage of youngsters; and (2) through inspirational, patriotic, and character-building activities related to the club, to aid children in learning good citizenship, which in turn fosters goodwill among parents. There were also the unspoken purposes of making Mickey Mouse cartoons more popular and promoting character merchandise.

Mickey Mouse Club matinees were almost always held at noon on Saturdays. The theater manager usually had a working arrangement with a number of local merchants who were involved in selling products and services to children. Since the local clubs increased sales, it was not difficult to obtain the merchants' cooperation. Newspaper advertisements announcing programs and club activities were paid for by the cooperating merchants, who were listed as sponsors of the club.

Some of the businesses found most likely to participate in Mickey Mouse Clubs included: bakeries, which offered a free birthday cake each Saturday for children who had celebrated a birthday during the previous week; florists, which sent a small bouquet to sick club members and gave a big cheer as the recovered member was brought up on the stage and welcomed back; dairies, which offered prizes (ice cream) to club entertainers and contest winners; banks, which gave a free savings bank toy to club members on their birthday; department stores, which gave inexpensive toys to club members to encourage the purchase of more expensive toys from their toy department; stationery stores, which advertised their line of character merchandise by providing prizes; photographers, who took free pictures of the club officers (they were changed every eight weeks) and offered discounts on quantity purchases; and sporting goods stores, jewelry stores, candy stores, drugstores, shoe stores, music stores, and many others. Merchants were quick to grasp the opportunity to be associated with such a nationally accepted product as Mickey Mouse cartoons. In addition, of course, they received the benefits of having their firm's name flashed on the screen, posted in the theater lobby, printed in the newspaper, and their business identified by a poster as one of the sponsors.

The cost of a Mickey Mouse Club license, which included the *General Campaign Book* (the monograph previously described) and the bimonthly bulletin for a year, was twenty-five dollars. Membership cards and applications, store cards, posters, buttons, trailer (four hundred feet of film presenting the "Mickey Mouse Club Song"), birthday cards, and the like cost extra. It was estimated that it cost one hundred dollars, on the average, to get a club organized. This was generally no burden to the sponsoring theater, because the costs were most often shared by the participating merchants.

Among other things, the *Campaign Book* contained fourteen prewritten publicity stories, which were periodically placed in the local newspaper(s). If the newspaper selected to carry the stories was one in which the *Mickey Mouse* comic strip, handled by the King Features Syndicate, was published, the publisher almost always ran the club stories free to encourage more readership.

Local Parent-Teacher Associations and schools were often supporters of Mickey Mouse Clubs. Club members with high marks in school were given special membership cards, which gave them special privileges. Often the first slate of club officers was selected with the help of the school

on the basis of good grades and citizenship. Membership in the club was free, but the children paid to get into the theater.

In addition to showing Mickey Mouse cartoons, the theater booked a feature film especially selected for children, as well as a serial. The serial was important because it brought the children back week after week.

There was quite a ritual associated with each matinee meeting of Mickey Mouse Clubs. After beginning the meeting with a Mickey Mouse cartoon (to allow the children time to settle down and allow for late-comers), the officers of the club took their place in a semicircle on the stage. The officers consisted of a chief Mickey Mouse, a chief Minnie Mouse, a master of ceremonies, a cheerleader, a song leader, a color bearer, two sergeants-at-arms, and a courier. Next the chief Mickey Mouse read the creed of the Mickey Mouse Club:

> I will be a square shooter in my home, in school, on the playground, wherever I may be. I will be truthful and honorable and strive always to make myself a better and more useful citizen. I will respect my elders and help the aged, the helpless and children smaller than myself. In short, I will be a good American.

The audience then spoke the Mickey Mouse pledge in unison: "Mickey Mice do not SWEAR—SMOKE—CHEAT or LIE." Next the flag was brought on stage and saluted. Then one verse of "America" was sung. Various games were then played, acts presented, stunts shown, and contests held. Following that the group was led in the Mickey Mouse Club yell:

> HANDY! DANDY!
> SWEET AS CANDY!
> HAPPY KIDS ARE WE!
> EENIE! ICKIE!
> MINNIE! MICKEY!
> M-O-U-S-E

Finally, the "Mickey Mouse Club Song" was flashed on the screen, and everybody sang. The scheduled films were then shown.

Before 1930 drew to a close, there were hundreds of clubs all over the nation, and in other countries as well. Woodin did a great deal to build the popularity of Mickey Mouse cartoons and promote character merchandise—the latter was especially true in England.

The era of the first Mickey Mouse Club is an important one to collectors of Disneyana, who actively seek old Mickey Mouse Club membership application cards; the eleven-inch by eleven-inch black and orange store cards; club birthday cards; club buttons made of celluloid (one for members and one for each officer); club membership cards; club passes; student honor cards; and other items. The prices for these relatively rare items are surprisingly high.

At its height in 1932, the Mickey Mouse Club had over a million members in the United States—or, as a writer in the October 1, 1932, issue of *Motion Picture Herald* put it, the club's "membership approximates that of the Boy Scouts of America and the Girl Scouts, combined." At that time there were over eight hundred clubs in America, and they ranged in size from almost one thousand to almost five thousand members each. During the heyday years, regional conventions of Mickey Mouse Club members were held periodically.

By mid-1933, however, it was decided that the whole concept was too unwieldy to actively support. In a December 4, 1935, letter to a St. Louis theater manager who had requested information about establishing a Mickey Mouse Club, Lucille Allen Benedict explained:

> We found that granting exclusive rights to any theatre to call its junior matinee a Mickey Mouse Club in the long run caused us more trouble than it did good in the way of publicity. After all, all of the theatres are our potential customers, because if they don't buy one year they may the next. We ran into all kinds of difficulties and controversies over the Clubs and finally decided to do away with any connection with them. A great many theatres are still running such clubs, but they are doing so entirely on their own, and without any help or references from us. The success of each Club always depended upon the resourcefulness of the theatre manager, at any rate, and no matter how many suggestions we gave them from this end, the manager had to put it over in the long run. We also found that in the cases where the Club wasn't especially successful, the Managers felt "Mickey Mouse" was responsible and developed a resentment against the product in general.

Even though it was decided to let the clubs die a natural death, as Miss Benedict explained, many theater managers who had successful clubs were reluctant to disband them, and as a result there were Mickey Mouse Clubs around for years.

A conspicuous example of the above was the chain of Odeon theaters in England. In 1939 they reported, "The Clubs organized in this circuit are flourishing. . . . There are 160, attracting about 100,000 children every Saturday." The chairman of this large theater chain, Oscar Deutsch, even wrote and had published a small book about the Mickey Mouse Club. He titled it *Citizens of To-Morrow* ("A survey of a great Youth Movement —how it began and how it has steadily progressed —and a tribute to the part that entertainment has played in the development of good character and good habits"). Mr. Deutsch's introduction to the book is interesting:

> Ever since the day when the first of the Odeon Theatres was opened, I have always made it a point of my policy to take special interest in the welfare of children in relation to the cinema. Wherever possible, some part of Saturday has been devoted regularly to special performances for boys and girls; and from humble beginnings something has been evolved which is, I believe, of national importance. Children's Circles, as they were then called, sprang up in all parts of the country, and the year 1937 saw the birth of a unified Movement called Odeon Mickey Mouse Clubs [four years after the Disneys had withdrawn their support of the Club concept]. . . . The guiding principle throughout the whole Movement has been to promote in the minds of the youth of this country a sense of responsibility that will serve them well in the part they are to play in the civic life of Britain. In this book I have dealt with the aims, objects and the development of these Clubs as fully as space allows and I sincerely hope you will find it of interest.

One other man stands out in the history of the first Mickey Mouse Clubs; he was Sonny Shepherd, who managed the Biltmore Theater in Miami, Florida. Shepherd was so taken with the club concept that he operated a club at his theater well into the 1950s. One of Shepherd's notable ongoing projects was a Mickey Mouse Club orchestra, which was the pride of the community.

As originally conceived and put into practice,

the Mickey Mouse Club was unwieldy; but, as has been shown with the foregoing two examples, there were many desirable aspects to the concept.

With modification, and using television as its vehicle, Walt later revived the Mickey Mouse Club with great success.

THIS AGREEMENT, made and entered into this_____day of _____, 193____, by and between WALT DISNEY

PRODUCTIONS, LTD., a California Corporation, (hereinafter called Licensor), and_____
(Manager, Owner or Lessor)

of_____Theatre, (hereinafter called Licensee).

W I T N E S S E T H :

1. Licensor owns and/or controls a copyright upon a system or idea designated as "Mickey Mouse Club," together with other copyrights, trade marks and/or design patents in and upon certain motion pictures, designs and names designated and known as "Mickey Mouse."

2. Licensor hereby grants to Licensee and Licensee agrees to use an exclusive license to operate and maintain a Mickey Mouse Club at the theatre hereinabove set forth.

3. Licensee is hereby licensed to use and utilize for the term hereof, the Mickey Mouse Club idea and name.

4. This license is exclusive to Licensee as against competitive theatres located within the reasonable drawing territory of Licensee's theatre, and

more particularly described as_____
(Names of theatres, or specific limits of territory)

5. This license is non-assignable, and Licensee may not sell or assign, give away, transfer, encumber or otherwise dispose of the same or any supplies or anything appertaining thereto to any other theatre, person, corporation, or partnership, without the written consent of Licensor.

6. Licensee agrees in consideration hereof to pay Licensor the sum of Twenty-five Dollars ($25.00).

7. Licensor agrees to furnish Licensee one (1) General Campaign Book and Organization Chart and to mail to Licensee, monthly, a Bulletin heretofore known and designated as "Official Mickey Mouse Club Bulletin."

8. The term of this license and agreement shall be for the period of one (1) year. This license and the agreements contained herein shall be automatically extended at the option of Licensee from year to year, so long as Licensee shall contract for and play the full yearly series of Mickey Mouse Cartoons.

WALT DISNEY PRODUCTIONS, LTD.

Signed_____
Theatre

By_____By_____

A copy of the agreement theater owners and Walt Disney Productions, Ltd., entered into before establishing a new Mickey Mouse Club.

New York Office:
1705 Loews State Bldg.
1540 Broadway

ORDER SHEET

WALT DISNEY PRODUCTIONS, Ltd.
2719 Hyperion Avenue
Hollywood, Calif.

MICKEY MOUSE CLUB
L. A. BENEDICT, MANAGER

Mickey Mouse and Silly Symphony
Cartoons

REQUISITION NO._____ Date_____193____

Theatre_____ Manager_____ City_____

Starting Date_____ Time_____ State_____

Seating Capacity_____ Sound_____ Stage_____

SUPPLIES

Membership Applications M $1.25	Group Mats Set $1.50	Envelopes for Birthday Cards M $4.00
Membership Cards (2 colors) M $4.50	Full Page Mat ea. $1.50	Slides ea. 60c
500—$3.50	Announcement Folders M $4.50	Theme Song Trailer $16.50
Window Cards ea. 10c	(Imprinting) $2.00	Buttons M $15.00
(Imprinting) $2.00	Theme Song Folders M $4.50	Advance Trailer ea. $4.50
	(Imprinting) $2.00	
Passes M $1.25	Birthday Cards (2 colors) M $5.00	Officers Buttons (Set of 9) $1.25
Store Cards ea. 10c	500—$3.50	One Sheets (Not Imprinted) ea. 15c

ALL ORDERS FOR SUPPLIES SHIPPED C. O. D.

SPONSORS:_____

SPECIAL INSTRUCTIONS:_____

An order sheet from the *General Campaign Book* provided to owners and managers of theaters sponsoring a Mickey Mouse Club. The order sheet lists the items available from Walt Disney Productions, Ltd., to facilitate the operation of a club, and gives their prices.

An official application form for membership in a Mickey Mouse Club. Theater managers used this form to keep accurate membership records.

An official Mickey Mouse Club membership celluloid pin-back button that was given to each club member.

A replica of the official Mickey Mouse Club membership card. The cards were either dark or light blue and imprinted, in red, with the name of the sponsoring theater and consecutive numbers.

To_____

In recognition of your efforts and excellent work in attaining the

_____193____ Honor Roll of your school,

The Texan Theatre Mickey Mouse Club

extends to you, this invitation to be our guest at the Texan Theatre

at Lufkin, Texas on_____193____

Texan Theatre

By_____

A replica of the official Student Honor Card used by Mickey Mouse Clubs when working closely with schools and/or Parent-Teacher Associations. The cards were printed in two colors on vellum card and imprinted in green with a Mickey Mouse cut.

MICKEY MOUSE CLUB CREED

I will be a square shooter in my home, in school, on the playgrounds, where-ever I may be.

I will be truthful and honorable and strive always, to make myself a better and more useful little citizen.

I will respect my elders and help the aged, the helpless and children smaller than myself.

In short, I will be a good American!

A copy of the Mickey Mouse Club creed that was printed on the reverse of each official membership card.

An example of an official Mickey Mouse Club Officer Button. There were 9 buttons in the set, one for each of the club officers to wear.

To _____

Permit us to share the joys of this,

Your Birthday

by extending to you an invitation to attend the

Loew's Broad Theatre, Columbus, Ohio

This card will admit you and a companion, with our compliments

May each recurring birthday find you rich in
health and happiness

Loew's Broad Theatre

An example of the offical Mickey Mouse Club birthday
card. Birthday cards were printed in two colors and
featured a green imprint of Mickey Mouse.

MICKEY MOUSE CLUB

PASS (1) CHILD

To_____
NOT VALID UNLESS BEARING STAMP WITH THEATRE NAME AND CITY

Acct._____

Void After_____

NOT GOOD
SATURDAY, SUNDAY
OR HOLIDAY NIGHTS
_____
CHIEF MICKEY MOUSE

MUST BE PRESENTED AT BOX OFFICE WHEN ADMISSION IS DESIRED

A stock pass used on special occasions by theaters
sponsoring a Mickey Mouse Club.

UT MICKEY MOUSE **IN YOUR LOBBY**

nd *Children Business* in Your BOX-OFFICE!

vise showman knows that the backbone
gross is dependent on the volume of
n business he does. Children talk about
ure, drag their parents in, and are the
movie audience in the world. The
Y MOUSE sculptured figure shown on
ge, and illustrated as well in the lobby
section of this pressbook, is the official
Y MOUSE lobby fixture.

discount on each display

h a special arrangement with United
Pictures Corporation we are offering
are direct to the exhibitors at a saving
—our regular price is $4.00 per dis-
% discount bringing the net price
$3.00 each.

Y MOUSE relief statuette is a star-
attractive figure. The pants are red,
blue, shoes are orange, gloves a vivid
There is an easel on the back so that
stand it up in the lobby of your the-
if desired, you can remove the easel
nt it against the wall.

On the left is shown an
actual reproduction of
a dealer's window in
Norwich, New York,
showing how the Nor-
wich Knitting Com-
pany's products were
displayed in this
dealer's window. Fea-
tured in the center of
the display you can see
a MICKEY MOUSE
sculptured figure.

Laminite . . .

Exclusive Paper Mache

THIS MICKEY MOUSE figure
is made of Laminite (exclusive
paper maché), perfected by Old
King Cole, Inc. It will stand the
onslaughts of rough year and
hard usage. To even further preserve the life of this display it
can be varnished so that it can
be used in front of your theatre
or on the marquee.

**Perfect for Merchant Dis-
plays . and Dept. Store
Windows . . .**

Many of the MICKEY MOUSE
licencees as well as exhibitors
have taken advantage of the
smart appearance of this
MICKEY MOUSE display. They
know it attracts business and
dresses windows as well, and is
ideal for show rooms and department store window displays
as well as for the exhibitors
lobby.

Make good use of the coupon on
the left. As soon as your order
is received we will ship them
promptly to you.

dly send me F.O.B. Canton
___ Mickey Mouse Displays
3.00 each ($4.00 less 25%)

OLD KING COLE, Inc.
Canton . Ohio

An official Mickey Mouse Club store window card. These
11" cards were black and orange in color, and were used to
help stores sponsoring or carrying Mickey Mouse
merchandise to identify themselves.

Page 35 of the 1932 United Artists campaign catalogue,
featuring an advertisement by Old King Cole, Inc., of
Canton, Ohio. This firm offered theater owners and
managers a "Mickey Mouse relief statuette" for window
display. The statuette showed Mickey with red pants, blue
buttons, orange shoes, and yellow gloves.

Page 39 of the 1932 campaign catalogue published by United Artists. This page features an advertisement for Fisch & Company, Ltd., of Los Angeles, California, a firm that specialized in banners, caps, fezzes, vests, pennants, etc., for the first Mickey Mouse Club.

Page 34 of the United Artists Pictures Corporation campaign catalogue for 1932. The advertisement by Moviescope Corporation of New York is promoting a series of Motion Picture Books, nicknamed "Flickers," that were giveaway items at Mickey Mouse Club gatherings. Collectors eagerly seek such items in the hope of completing a set of 12.

The first meeting of Sonny Shepherd's Mickey Mouse Club at the Biltmore Theater in Miami, Florida. This club, which began in the 1930s, lasted well into the 1950s and became the oldest of the first Mickey Mouse Clubs. The first meeting (shown here) was attended by 300 children. Within three months the club had grown to 1,500 members.

9. The Man with the Keen "Sense-of-Sell"

By the end of 1931 it was costing Walt approximately thirteen thousand dollars to produce each of his cartoons. While some of the increased costs were attributed to economic conditions, most were caused by Walt's continual push for better quality. At thirteen thousand dollars, the studio was barely breaking even on each film.

The family of Disney characters was growing, and by 1930 it included not only Mickey and Minnie Mouse, but also Pegleg Pete, Horace Horsecollar, and Clarabelle Cow. Pluto, unnamed, was introduced in the 1930 film *The Chain Gang* and became "Rover" the same year in *The Picnic*. He became "Pluto" in 1931 in *The Moose Hunt*. Goofy first appeared in *Mickey's Revue* in 1932.

While Mickey was the most popular of all the Disney characters in 1932, Minnie was running a close second. The others were enjoying somewhat less popularity but enough so that they were being requested for character merchandise.

When, in 1929, Technicolor introduced a rather crude two-color film, Walt and most other film producers did not experiment with it. But in 1932, when Technicolor offered a greatly improved three-color process, Walt, suddenly seeing an opportunity to further improve his cartoons, decided to become involved in color. At that time he was producing a Silly Symphony called *Flowers and Trees*; in fact, the film was already over half completed in black and white. At great expense, Walt discarded what had already been made and started again, this time with the new Technicolor film. He proceeded, however, only after over-

coming Roy's objections to spending additional money on a cartoon that was part of a presold series. Walt argued that while there would be no additional income to cover the additional expense of color as the contract was drawn, there would be the needed additional income from increased bookings. In addition, Walt had convinced Technicolor to give him an exclusive two-year franchise on the three-color process in the cartoon field.

Flowers and Trees premiered at the famous Grauman's Chinese Theater in Hollywood on July 30, 1932. It was the success Walt had predicted it would be. As a matter of fact, in 1932 it won the Disney studio its first Academy Award, for the best cartoon short subject of 1931–32. That same year the Academy of Motion Picture Arts and Sciences also presented a special Academy Award to Walt for the creation of Mickey Mouse.

While Walt continued to produce his Mickey Mouse cartoons in black and white until 1935, all Silly Symphonies after *Flowers and Trees* were produced in color.

Early in 1932 Walt received a long distance telephone call from Herman "Kay" Kamen, a Kansas City advertising executive. Kamen was born in Baltimore in 1892 and began his successful career, as a hat salesman, in 1918. In 1926, with Streeter Blair, he formed the Kansas City advertising agency called Kamen-Blair. At the time he made the call to Walt, he was considered one of the country's leading promotion men.

Kamen explained to Walt that he was interested in working with Disney character merchandise.

After hearing a few of Kamen's innovative ideas, Walt invited Kamen to come to Hollywood for further discussions. Showing the enthusiasm and dedication to an idea for which he was famous, within a few hours Kamen was on a train to California. Upon arrival he immediately made his way to the Disney studio for a meeting with the surprised Walt Disney. After Walt located Roy, all three of the men sat down in Walt's office, and Kamen began to outline his merchandising ideas in detail. Both Walt and Roy liked Kay Kamen and found his ideas full of promotional potential.

It will be recalled that at this time George Borgfeldt & Co. of New York and William B. Levy in London were handling the character merchandising business for the Disneys. Borgfeldt was having difficulty in providing a complete enough line of quality merchandise. Levy was having similar problems with quality aspects, and business on the Continent was in a slump. The Disneys frankly discussed their merchandising concerns with Kamen during that first meeting, and made clear their desires regarding *quality*. Kamen's ideas and response to the needs as expressed by Walt and Roy must have greatly pleased the Disneys, because they sent Kamen away with the assignment to further develop his thoughts on exploiting Disney characters through character merchandise.

The result of the first and subsequent meetings with Walt and Roy netted Kay his first contract with the Disneys on July 1, 1932. Because both Borgfeldt and Levy had certain exclusive rights within their specified territories, Kamen's contract did little more than make him Walt's representative in matters of character merchandise. The letter sent to all licensees explained the agreement as follows:

> We have recently made an exclusive contract with Kamen-Blair of Kansas City, to represent us in all matters pertaining to contracts with authorized licensees of Disney products, and to assist you by presenting to you new ideas for the exploitation of Mickey Mouse merchandise.

While legally Walt had hired Kamen as his representative in character licensing matters, the implication was that as soon as the Borgfeldt and Levy agreements ran out Kamen would succeed as the sole representative for Disney character merchandise.

During the first year in which Kamen represented the Disneys, he completely familiarized himself with the merchandising business and began to license manufacturers for products not covered in the Borgfeldt agreements, which specified "Figures and Toys of wood, metal, rubber, celluloid, china, glass, papier-mâché, cardboard, textile fabrics, chocolate, candy and other food substances." Anticipatory of later merchandise catalogues Kamen was to produce, United Artists Pictures Corporation published a forty-eight page campaign catalogue that was mailed to fifteen thousand film exhibitors. The book outlined numerous exhibitor tie-ups with local stores for Mickey Mouse and Silly Symphonies showings. Character merchandise was conspicuous in the featured lobby decorations and Mickey Mouse Club awards. The book showed how the local exhibitor displayed advertisements for the local merchants in his theater and how the merchants in turn advertised the films in window displays, newspaper advertising, and in other media. The campaign book was also circulated in eighty-eight foreign centers in the languages of the countries involved. This 1932 campaign book and the six subsequent merchandise catalogues (1934; 1935; 1936–1937; 1938–1939; 1940–1941; 1947–1948; and 1949–1950) produced by Kamen are not only excellent reference sources for a study of Disney merchandising history but are highly desirable collectors' items. The Kamen catalogues are very scarce today, even though thousands were issued. The rarest is the first one, produced in 1934; it was circulated to 25,000 exhibitors, manufacturers, and merchants.

At the same time, Walt was working on his latest Silly Symphony, *Three Little Pigs*. This film, with its hit song "Who's Afraid of the Big Bad Wolf?" not only earned Walt his second Academy Award for the best cartoon short subject of 1932–1933, but it gave Kamen four more characters to license for Disney merchandise. Fiddler Pig, Fifer Pig, Practical Pig, and the Big Bad Wolf became very popular, and collectors today find a wide variety of toys, novelties, and the like featuring these characters. Fifi, Pluto's girlfriend, was also introduced in 1933 in the film *Puppy Love*. Fifi, however, was not popular enough to have been featured on more than a few pieces of character merchandise; therefore, collectors cannot expect many Fifi items.

Three Little Pigs was released on May 27, 1933, and just a little over a month later (July 1, 1933) Kamen signed his first big contract with Walt Disney Enterprises. The contract called for Kamen to receive "40% of all monies received from licensees and Disney 60%. This is the basis of the split up to $100,000. On any and all money received over $100,000 Kamen is to receive 50% and Disney 50%." The territory embraced under the terms of that contract covered the United States and its possessions and all the countries of the Western Hemisphere.

Being the Disneys' sole representative, Kamen set about examining all of the contracts Borgfeldt and Levy had granted. As quickly as possible, he canceled those with manufacturers who lacked prestige or aggressive merchandising ability. He also canceled contracts with the firms who had raised the price of their products as a result of their license to use Disney characters. Kamen insisted that the only time a licensee could raise his prices—excluding normal economic factors—was when he had improved his product. He also sent his nephew, George Kamen, to England to administer the business on the Continent.

Kamen was one of the most itinerant executives in America. He traveled extensively and continually on behalf of Disney merchandise. One of his unusual methods of approach was to send a firm he wished to visit a telegram reading: "Kay Kamen will visit you tomorrow morning at eight o'clock." Just as the wire was being delivered by messenger, Kamen would enter the office. This almost always got him the desired time with the executive.

His logic in selling Mickey Mouse to a firm was simple and honest. He would explain the risks and expenses involved in developing and making popular a trademark or name. Then he would point out how the name of Mickey Mouse had already been established, and that Mickey Mouse's name was continuing to be built every time a new film was released or a comic strip appeared. This approach worked as well with firms with established names and trademarks as with firms with new products.

Like many of the men who worked for the Disneys over the years, Kamen was very successful in his field. In 1933, after having been in charge of Disney character merchandising for only six months, he was able to report the sale of several million dollars' worth of merchandise. During the summer months, he had facilitated the sale of 10 million Mickey Mouse ice cream cones (a Disney item not likely to be collected today). Another 1933 highlight was the sale of 900,000 Ingersoll watches and clocks.

Character watches were among the most successful merchandise items. Between June 1933 and June 1935, 2.5 million were sold, according to an article in the July 1935 issue of *Printers' Ink*. By 1939, the Mickey Mouse watch was such a well-known product that one was sealed in the World's Fair time capsule buried in New York. In a letter dated April 11, 1940, from C. H. Granger, president of the Ingersoll-Waterbury Co., to Kay Kamen, some interesting figures are presented. "From 1933 to 1939 inclusive we sold a total of $4,771,490.96 of Disney production merchandise, which represents nearly a quarter million dollars paid in royalties." That figure is not hard to accept when one notes that early in the venture Macy's Department Store in New York City sold as many as eleven thousand watches in *one* day. After a slack period caused by material shortages during World War II, business picked up, and in 1948 Kay Kamen presented Walt with the five millionth Mickey Mouse watch. In 1957 Walt was presented with the twenty-five millionth Mickey Mouse watch.

By 1958 the fad of character watches seemed to have run its course, and they were discontinued. Ten years later, in 1968, the demand for Mickey Mouse watches brought them back. In that same year comedian Bill Dana gave his new Mickey Mouse wrist watch to Walter Schirra, who carried it with him on the Apollo spacecraft. In 1969 Gene Cernan wore his Mickey Mouse watch during the Apollo 10 mission into space. The watches were also popular back on earth. From the May 8, 1969, issue of *Women's Wear Daily* comes this paragraph: "Among the first to arrive: Teddy Kennedy (Joan is rehearsing for 'Peter and the Wolf' with the Boston Symphony) and trim and suntanned Ethel Kennedy, wearing her Mickey Mouse watch and a black wool-and-leather little mini nothing." Still another 1969 article reported, "Carol Burnett once refused an offer of $500 for her watch, a gift from Joe Hamilton. Sammy Davis, Jr., 'Ironside' T.V. star Don Galloway, and impersonator Rich Little are among the many celebrity mouse owners." While the watches made after 1968 are popular as collectibles, it is the watches of the 1930s that sell today for hundreds of dollars.

By February of 1934 Kamen had departmentalized his organization in order to improve his service to manufacturers and distributors. One department was concerned with the technicalities regarding the licensing of manufacturers. An advertising agency designed packages, products, and promotion. The other department was for retail store exploitation. During the Christmas season of 1933, the latter department helped approximately fifty of the nation's leading department stores use Mickey Mouse as the central theme.

The 1934 year ended with $35 million worth of Disney character merchandise having been sold, which was a great increase over the several million dollars worth reported for the previous year. One of the Disney books sold 2.4 million copies.

While Kamen was making impressive strides in the merchandising business, Walt was busy in Hollywood. Donald Duck made his first appearance on June 9, 1934, in the Silly Symphony *The Wise Little Hen*. The appearance of Donald is significant, because his popularity was soon to equal and even surpass that of Mickey Mouse. Kamen, of course, was quick to make Donald Duck available for character merchandise. By the end of 1935, Mickey and Minnie Mouse, the characters from *Three Little Pigs*, Pluto, and Donald Duck were to be found on the majority of the Disney merchandise. Collectors, as a result, can expect that most of what they accumulate in the way of Disneyana from the mid-1930s will feature these characters.

By mid-1935 it was reported internationally that the favorite toys of the famous Dionne quintuplets of Canada were Mickey Mouse rattles. That is rather interesting when it is remembered that the quintuplets themselves were featured on hundreds of pieces of merchandise.

The release of the first Mickey Mouse cartoon in color (*The Band Concert*) on February 23, 1935, further stimulated sales for Kamen and his licensees. In England one manufacturer reported a 500 percent increase in sales of a game after he put an illustration of Mickey Mouse on the box. Also in England, it was reported that the queen and the duchess of York had purchased six hundred Mickey Mouse mugs to give as gifts to children in London hospitals.

Kamen reported that as of October 1935, he had turned down over a thousand applications for licenses to use Disney characters. Walt and Roy had definite ideas about the types of products that were appropriate for endorsement by Mickey Mouse and his friends. Such things as cigars, cigarettes, alcohol, and patent medicines, it was felt, were not the types of items that Disney characters should recommend. Ashtrays, however, have been produced featuring Disney characters. Also, at least one patent medicine received Mickey's endorsement: In 1935 Mickey was allowed to promote a Scott & Bowne product called Scott's Emulsion. The emulsion was cod liver oil. Walt did not allow Mickey to promote it in the United States, but he did grant permission for Mickey to recommend it in South America because of the high incidence of rickets there. The free booklet in Spanish that accompanied Scott's Emulsion in South America has become a very popular collectible item. Although three million were printed during the first promotion, few exist today.

The year 1936 began with six million orders for Mickey Mouse cereal bowls from the Westinghouse Electric & Manufacturing Corporation. It was a Mickey Mouse world. As one 1935 writer put it:

> Shoppers carry Mickey satchels and briefcases bursting with Mickey Mouse soap, candy, playing cards, bridge favours, hair-brushes, chinaware, alarm clocks and hot-water bottles, wrapped in Mickey Mouse paper, tied with Mickey Mouse ribbon and paid for out of Mickey Mouse purses with savings hoarded in Mickey Mouse banks. At the lunch counter—Mickey Mouse table covers and napkins—they consume Mickey Mouse biscuits and dairy products while listening to Mickey Mouse music from Mickey Mouse phonographs and radios. Then, glancing at their Mickey Mouse wrist-watches, they dash away to buy Mickey Mouse toothbrushes—they wear Mickey Mouse caps, waists [shirts or blouses], socks, shoes, slippers, garters,

mittens, aprons, bibs and underthings, and beneath Mickey Mouse rain-capes and umbrellas they go to school where Mickey Mouse desk outfits turn lessons into pleasure. They play with Mickey Mouse velocipedes [tricycles], footballs, baseballs, bounce-balls, bats, catching gloves, doll houses, doll dishes, tops, blocks, drums, puzzles, games—paint sets, sewing sets, drawing sets, stamping sets, jack sets, bubble sets, pull toys, push toys, animated toys, tents, camp stools, sand pails, masks, blackboards, and balloons— until day is done, when they sup from Mickey Mouse cups, porringers [bowls] and baby plates and lie down to sleep in Mickey Mouse pajamas between Mickey Mouse crib sheets, to waken in the morn smiling at Mickey Mouse pictures on the nursery walls covered with Mickey Mouse wallpaper.

Walt Disney Studio, as it appeared in 1931.

A picture of Kay Kamen (*left*) taken with Walt Disney (*right*) in 1948 just after they had signed their last contract, and shortly before Kamen met a tragic and untimely death.

The cover of the 1932 campaign catalogue by United Artists Corporation. This booklet contains some character merchandise and other things of interest to collectors.

The covers of the 1934 (*left*) and 1935 (*below*) Kay Kamen character merchandise catalogues. Not only are such catalogues collector's items in themselves but they are excellent reference books for collectors; they contain a great deal of the merchandise sold for the years specified.

The cover of the 1936–37 *Mickey Mouse Merchandise* catalogue (*left*) and the cover of the 1938–39 *Walt Disney Character Merchandise* catalogue (*below*) produced by Kay Kamen, who was in charge of licensing manufacturers to use Disney characters on their merchandise.

The Kay Kamen character merchandise catalogues for 1940–41 (*top left*); 1947–48 (*top right*); and 1949–50 (*bottom left*). While all catalogues of Disney merchandise are collectible as such, they are perhaps more valuable as reference tools for collectors who wish to know and look at much of the merchandise being distributed for the period specified on the catalogue cover.

TIME INSTRUMENT

James R. Putnam, Waterbury, Conn., assignor to Waterbury Clock Company, Waterbury, Conn., a corporation.

Application May 22, 1933, Serial No. 672,195.

5 claims (Cl. 58--126)

1. A time instrument comprising: a dial having time indicia thereon; rotatable seconds, minute and hour members; a figure mounted on said rotatable seconds member and fixed thereto so as to rotate therewith and simulating the body of an animate being; and a time indicator mounted on and rotatable with each of said rotatable minute and hour members and simulating a part of said animate being.

The Ingersoll-Waterbury Clock Company of Waterbury, Connecticut, produced the first of the famous Mickey Mouse wrist watches in mid-1933. This is a copy of the drawing that accompanied the patent application, which was filed on May 22, 1933. The patent was granted on February 5, 1934.

This is a copy of the drawing that accompanied the Ingersoll-Waterbury Clock Company's patent application for the classic Three Little Pigs and Big Bad Wolf pocket watch.

Late in 1933 the Ingersoll-Waterbury Clock Company produced its first Three Little Pigs and Big Bad Wolf clock, featuring the characters as drawn by Disney artists. This is a copy of the drawing that accompanied the application for the patent—from it can be determined that the firm claimed to have been producing the clock since November 17, 1933; the application was filed on April 18, 1934; and the patent was granted on July 17, 1934.

NEW MICKEY MOUSE
Alarm Clock

On the dial is an animated Mickey Mouse head wagging, hands pointing the time. Choice of red or green case. Packed in a self-display carton which makes selling easy. $1.50 retail, $1.05 trade.

MICKEY MOUSE DISPLAY

—a sure attention-getter for your windows. Also valuable as a counter sales-card. Places on it for 3 pocket watches and 2 wrist watches. FREE DISPLAY.

INGERSOLL MICKEY MOUSE
POCKET WATCH AND FOB—

complete in a colorful gift box. Mickey's own hands point the time, getting into comical positions doing so. It's the watch sensation of the decade and a wonderful value at $1.50 retail. $1.05 trade.

INGERSOLL MICKEY MOUSE
WRIST WATCH—

with Mickey's hands telling the time. A million have already been sold—more millions will be. Leather band or metal Mickey Mouse strap. $3.75 retail. $2.50 trade.

Advertising for the famous Mickey Mouse wrist watch (and band), the Mickey Mouse pocket watch (and fob), and the Mickey Mouse alarm clock. After only eight weeks of production, which began in mid-1933, the demand for the wrist watch was so great that the Ingersoll-Waterbury Clock Company had to add 2,700 employees to its 300-employee payroll.

INGERSOLL
THREE LITTLE PIGS
ALARM CLOCK

The Big Bad Wolf's hungry jaws open and close in rhythm to the clock tick. It's a great clock and a sure-fire seller. The dial and case are bright red. The display carton in which the clock is packed has original Walt Disney drawings on it. You'll sell a lot of these clocks. $1.50 retail. $1.05 trade.

FREE display card for the 3 Little Pigs Watch. The pigs and wolf drawn by Walt Disney himself. A sure "stopper" for your window.

Ingersoll Three Little Pigs Watch and Fob

The wolf's evil eye is winking. The 3 Little Pigs are right there on the red dial. It's a great watch and you ought to sell a pile of 'em! The back makes the watch a good luck token because it has a personal message from Walt Disney: "May the big bad wolf never come to your door"... But loads of customers will come into your door if you display the watch in your window. $1.50 retail. $1.05 trade.

A 1934 advertisement for the Three Little Pigs and Big Bad Wolf alarm clock and pocket watch. While both of the items were big sellers, it was the Mickey Mouse wrist watch that was the company's big seller.

A 1935 advertisement for the famous Mickey Mouse wrist watch made by the Ingersoll-Waterbury Clock Company of Waterbury, Connecticut. By March of 1935, the firm was Disney's biggest licensee. On June 1, 1935, the firm announced that it had sold 2½ million Mickey Mouse wrist watches. Note that the price in 1935 was $2.95 retail; the retail price in 1934 was $3.75. This advertisement shows very clearly the watch band most collectors prefer—the watch also came with a leather band.

As this illustrated display shows Mickey—The Magician—pulling watches out of thin air, so Ingersoll-Mickey Mouse wrist and pocket watches maintain their miraculous sales volume, in season or out. Pocket watches with fob retailing at $1.50—Wrist watches with ornamental bracelet or strap at $2.95—Alarm clocks at $1.50—have taught and are teaching millions of youngsters the correct reading of time. Stock up and maintain your stocks!

Write for full particulars

INGERSOLL-WATERBURY COMPANY
Licensee
Waterbury, Connecticut

A 1935 advertisement for Mickey Mouse pocket watches and Mickey Mouse wrist watches with a leather band.

This photograph was taken on February 26, 1935, at the Marshall Field department store in Chicago. The display features a giant-size pocket watch held above the counter as a canopy. Four wooden cutouts of Mickey Mouse, standing in a characteristic pose on the show cases of the counter square, support the display. Revolving around the top of the watch canopy are all of the famous Walt Disney characters that Ingersoll had incorporated with their watches and clocks. The watch canopy was 6' in diameter, and the Mickey Mouse cutouts were 3' high.

This is a 1936 advertisement for Mickey Mouse watches. In the ad the pocket watch (*lower left*) is described as a "Mickey Mouse Lapel Watch," the watch is so named because it came with a cord and button.

A 1938 advertisement for Mickey Mouse watches made by the Ingersoll-Waterbury Company. Besides showing the new "deluxe" model of the Mickey Mouse wrist watch (*top*) the ad shows the new version of the Mickey Mouse pocket or lapel watch (*bottom*), which sold for $1.50.

An Ingersoll-Waterbury Company advertisement for 1938. The ad introduces a "new and smaller deluxe Mickey Mouse wrist watch" that is rectangular in shape. The new watch sold for $3.95 while the original round type (still a best seller) sold for $3.25. The new wrist watch came in a choice of three bracelets—the two pictured and the classic metal band.

This 1940 advertisement shows the line of Mickey Mouse and Donald Duck watches by the Ingersoll-Waterbury Company for that year. The Donald Duck and Mickey Mouse pocket watches sold for $1.00; the Mickey Mouse wrist watch with a chromium finish sold for $2.95; and the Mickey Mouse wrist watch with a goldplate finish sold for $3.95. Note that the company no longer offered the traditional round Mickey Mouse wrist watch by 1940.

In 1947 the price of a Mickey Mouse wrist watch was $6.95. It came with a red vinylite plastic strap with a leather back. While the advertisment indicates that the watch was produced by the United States Time Corporation, that means only that the original Ingersoll-Waterbury Clock Company was operating under a new name.

Ingersoll (U. S. Time) produced these timepieces featuring Mickey Mouse and Donald Duck in 1947. Note that the alarm clock came with luminous hands.

In 1948 Ingersoll was manufacturing 10 Disney character wrist watches. Each watch sold for $6.95. Pictured here are 5 of the watches.

Mickey Mouse

Daisy Duck

Pluto

Bambi

Joe Carioca

Five of the Disney character wrist watches being produced by Ingersoll in 1948.

Bongo

Donald Duck

Pinocchio

Dopey

Jiminy Cricket

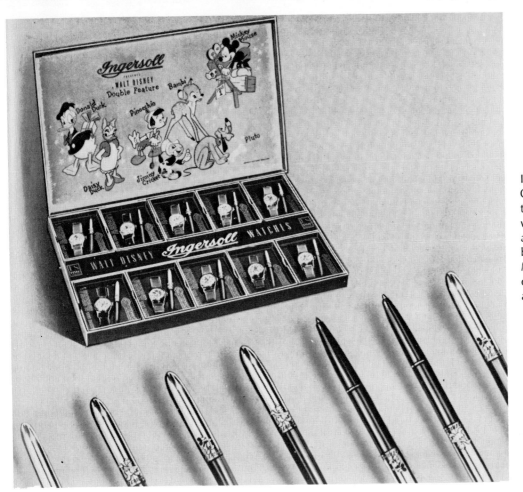

In 1949 the Ingersoll
Company (U.S. Time) offered
the same 10 Disney character
wrist watches for $6.95 but
also offered accompanying
ball-point pens, with Mickey
Mouse or Donald Duck
decals on them, for an
additional $1.00.

An Ingersoll Mickey Mouse
alarm clock for 1949 is
pictured here, along with
Mickey Mouse and Donald
Duck wrist watches. The
clock sold for $3.45; the
watches sold for $6.95 each.

10. Mickey's Merchandising Magic

By the mid-1930s Mickey Mouse, in the words of one journalist, was "the best-known and most popular international figure of the day." Mickey cartoons were being shown in eighty-eight foreign centers, in addition to being viewed in over ten thousand theaters in the United States. The audience in the United States alone was estimated to be an annual one of 600 million. Mickey's popularity through comic strips was such that he was reaching 20 million daily readers in approximately three hundred newspapers.

L. H. Robbins, a puzzled writer, asked the following question of his readers in the March 10, 1935, issue of the *New York Times*:

> Why is it that university presidents praise Mickey Mouse, the League of Nations recommends him, Britain's *Who's Who 1934* and the *Encyclopedia Britannica* give him paragraphs, learned academics hang medals on him, art galleries turn from Picasso and Epstein to hold exhibitions of his monkey-shines, and the King of England won't go to the movies unless Mickey is on the bill?

He could also have asked, why does the Goodyear Rubber Company stop making blimps to turn out a fifty-foot inflatable Mickey Mouse to lead the famous Macy's Christmas parade, why does General Foods spend $1.5 million to acquire the right to use Mickey's name on Post Toasties, why does the famous jewelry firm Cartier, Inc., sell Mickey Mouse charms and bracelets in gold and platinum set with diamonds for as much as $1,250, why do department stores spend as much

as $25,000 on a single Mickey Mouse window display, and why do over 200,000 retail stores sell Mickey Mouse merchandise?

As the journalist in the first paragraph wrote, Mickey Mouse was the best-known and most-popular figure of the day. In the area of character merchandising, whatever Mickey endorsed sold and, in most cases, sold very well.

Perhaps Mickey's most spectacular merchandising success was his association with the Lionel Corporation. On May 7, 1934, the Lionel Corporation went into a receivership with liquid assets of $62,000 and liabilities amounting to $296,000.

On July 19, 1934, Kay Kamen licensed Lionel to manufacture "a toy propelled by either mechanical or electrical movement with or without tracks." The toy turned out to be a tin wind-up handcar with Mickey and Minnie Mouse at the handles. The handcar came with a 27-inch circle of track and sold for one dollar a set. In four months 253,000 sets were sold.

Shortly after signing the contract with the Disneys, the receivers of the Lionel Corporation were permitted to borrow $350,000 from the banks on court orders to be paid on January 15, 1935. The loan was paid in full two months early, on November 30, 1934, and the $296,000 owing to creditors was paid in full on December 31, 1934. As of January 1, 1935, the firm reported $500,000 in cash and accounts receivable. An inventory showed approximately $400,000 in liquid assets and a total of $920,000 in current assets. Total assets, it was estimated, amounted to more than $2,000,000. On January 21, 1935, a U.S. District Court in Newark, New Jersey, on the basis of the foregoing record, turned the then financially healthy company back to its owners.

Simple arithmetic quickly reveals that the sale of Mickey and Minnie handcars could not account for all of the increased assets of the Lionel Corporation; in fact, the handcars accounted for only approximately 5 percent of Lionel's business during the period discussed. Still, Mickey won special mention by the judge who handled the receivership, because through Mickey's association with Lionel their other products suddenly became very popular.

Newspapers in many parts of the world ran the story of Mickey's successful association with Lionel. Because of the association, the firm captured 65 percent of the toy train business in 1934. The successful association between Mickey and Lionel lasted through 1938. During that period a number of mechanical toys were produced featuring Disney characters, such as a circus train with a tent that is hauled by a windup Commodore Vanderbilt and stoked by Mickey Mouse. This circus train was first made in 1935. Several mechanical freight trains and passenger trains were made with Mickey Mouse stoking the engines. In addition several handcars were produced. One featured Mickey and Minnie at the handlebars, while another showed Santa Claus at the handlebars with Mickey Mouse riding in his pack and a Christmas tree at the front.

While most of these toys were sold in the United States, thousands were shipped to Spain and Portugal, Italy, France, and Canada. It is in all of these countries, then, that collectors can expect to find one or more of the famous Lionel toys featuring Mickey Mouse or other Disney characters of the period.

Mickey's success did not stop with the Lionel Corporation. Early in 1933 the Ingersoll-Waterbury Company of Waterbury, Connecticut, applied for and was granted a license to produce watches featuring Mickey Mouse. While this firm, which had been producing Waterbury clocks since 1856 and Ingersoll watches since 1892, was not in receivership when the contract with the Disneys was signed, it was almost bankrupt and had been in receivership earlier. The great company was still financially shaky when it produced the first Mickey Mouse wrist watch in mid-1933. Kay Kamen helped get the watch featured at Macy's Department Store in New York City. The novel watch was an immediate success, and it was reported that as many as 11,000 were sold in a single day. At any rate, sales were such that after only eight weeks of production the Ingersoll-Waterbury Company had to add 2,700 employees to its 300-employee payroll to fill the demand for Mickey Mouse watches. By March of 1935 Ingersoll was the Disneys' largest licensee, and by June 1, 1935, the firm reported it had sold 2.5 million watches in the two years that it had been associated with Mickey Mouse.

In the small town of Norwich, New York, Mickey Mouse worked another of his merchandising miracles. In 1932, most of Norwich's employable citizens drew their salaries from the Norwich Knitting Company. Immediately following a shutdown of the textile mills, the Norwich Knitting Company signed a contract to put Mickey Mouse on sweatshirts. Like the Lionel handcar and the Ingersoll wrist watch, the Norwich sweatshirts became a big seller. By 1935 over one million sweatshirts a year were being sold, and one-third of Norwich's population was making enough money in overtime alone to support their families.

The Home Foundry Manufacturing Company of Chicago experienced similar success after being licensed to produce a Mickey Mouse Home Foundry. The firm was doing a good business selling casting sets for soldiers, cowboys, and Indians when it added Mickey Mouse to its line in 1935. Sales rapidly increased to the point where carload lots were being shipped to all parts of the country and sales of the Mickey Mouse casting sets equaled all of their other business. Because of Mickey Mouse, Home Foundry quickly became one of the country's leading manufacturers of casting sets.

Mickey's success was not restricted to the United States alone. An English firm introduced a new toffee in 1934 that featured Mickey Mouse. In the first week they sold 36 tons; six months later, they were selling 150 tons a week.

It is rather ironic that while the nation was suffering one of its greatest depressions, Mickey Mouse's popularity was such that his likeness on character merchandise made the economic difference for many floundering firms, and that indirectly he provided work for thousands of unemployed Americans. A 1934 survey of seventy manufacturers of Disney character merchandise revealed that approximately ten thousand jobs were created by Mickey Mouse.

When Walt decided in 1933 to produce color films, Mickey again was selected to introduce the new products. With the screened announcement that "Mickey Mouse Presents a Walt Disney Silly Symphony" for the showing of the *Three Little Pigs*, Technicolor was saved from possible bankruptcy. *Fortune* magazine put it this way:

Who's Afraid of the Big Bad Wolf? [the theme song of the *Three Little Pigs*] might also be considered the theme song in the drama of Technicolor's recovery, for it was Walt Disney's successful gamble with Silly Symphonies in color that drove the wolf from Technicolor's door.

Going a giant-step further, a writer in the November 28, 1935, issue of the *Dublin* (Ireland) *Evening Herald* wrote, "Walt Disney's bright idea of the 'Three Little Pigs' . . . appeared at the time of America's vast depression, and it was not too much to say that the quaint little characters saved the morale of America." He may have been right in his generous crediting, because for several generations after the Depression Americans followed the third little pig's advice of working and saving for that "rainy day."

A photograph of the original 50′ high rubber figural balloon of Mickey Mouse that was made by the Goodyear Rubber Company for the annual Macy's parade in New York City. Walt Disney is standing between the legs of the giant rubber model.

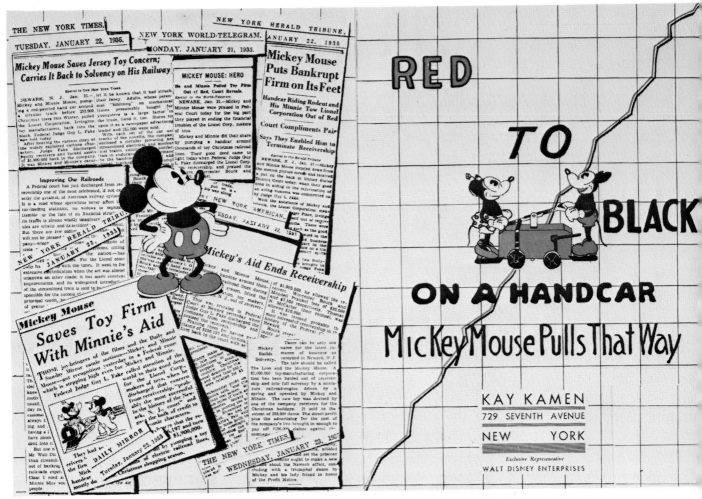

A magazine advertisement used by Kay Kamen in 1935 to publicize the fact that the Lionel Corporation was helped from possible bankruptcy when it obtained a license to use Mickey Mouse as the featured character on a toy train. Kamen not only obtained a good deal of publicity from the Mickey Mouse/Lionel relationship, but also signed up a number of new licensees.

MICKEY MOUSE HANDCAR
To Retail at $1.00
(No. 1100)

LIONEL'S famous Mickey Mouse handcar with Mickey and Minnie at the handle-bars. Loaded with fun and a thousand thrills, they circle the track ten or more times at a single winding, bending back and forth, pumping up and down. Handcar measures 7¾ inches long. Eight sections of curved track supplied with each outfit form a 27-inch circle.

SANTA CLAUS HANDCAR
To Retail at $1.00
(No. 1105)

SANTA'S taken to the handcar now. He's got a load that's packed with a Mickey Mouse who looks as if he is thrilled by the ride. The figure, the tree and the pack are moulded and hand-painted. Santa and his Christmas tree handcar measure 10½ inches in length, 6 inches to the crown of the head. Complete with eight sections of curved track forming a 27-inch circle.

Write for full particulars

THE LIONEL CORP.
Licensee
15-17-19 East 26th Street
New York, N. Y.
Chicago Office:
58 East Washington Street

An advertisement for the Mickey Mouse handcar that was produced by the Lionel Corporation of New York. The handcar was so successful that 253,000 were sold within the first four months. Also pictured (*bottom*) is a Santa Claus handcar produced by the same firm. The Mickey Mouse handcar was on the market in time for the 1934 Christmas season; the Santa Claus handcar was ready for the 1935 Christmas season.

No. 1532 Freight Outfit to retail at $1.25

No. 1534 Passenger Outfit to retail at $1.50

No. 1533 Freight Outfit to retail at $1.50

No. 1537 Passenger Outfit to retail at $4.50

MICKEY MOUSE, the movie star, is cast in a new role. He's stoking Lionel mechanical trains. Every time a tiny rod under the tender clicks against a tie, Mickey's body bends, his arms extend and the shovel sweeps forward. And just look at the locomotive he's working on. It's a New York Central Commodore Vanderbilt scaled down to size, equipped with the powerful Lionel clock-work motor, a ringing bell, hand brake and a headlight focused on the track.

Write for full particulars

THE LIONEL CORPORATION
Licensee
15-17-19 E. 26th Street, New York, N. Y.
Chicago Office: 58 East Washington Street

An advertisement for the various train sets featuring Mickey Mouse produced by the Lionel Corporation in 1935. These did not sell as well as the Mickey Mouse handcar, and as a result they are quite rare today.

In 1936 the Lionel Corporation introduced a Donald Duck rail car. The new addition to the handcar group sold for $1.25 and came complete with a 27-inch circle of track.

A 1932 advertisement for "Mickey Mouse Kiddie Jewelry" by Cohn & Rosenberger, Inc., of New York and Toronto, Canada.

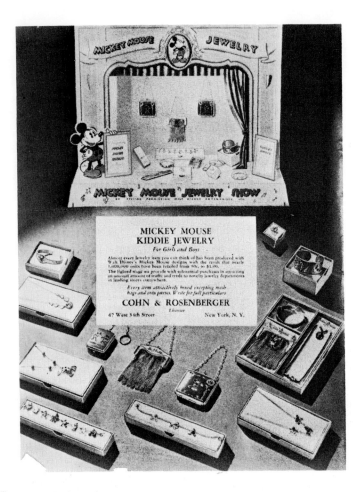

A 1934 advertisement by Cohn & Rosenberger, Inc., for Mickey Mouse jewelry.

Jewelry by Cohn & Rosenberger, Inc. The pieces pictured feature the characters from the Disney short *Three Little Pigs*.

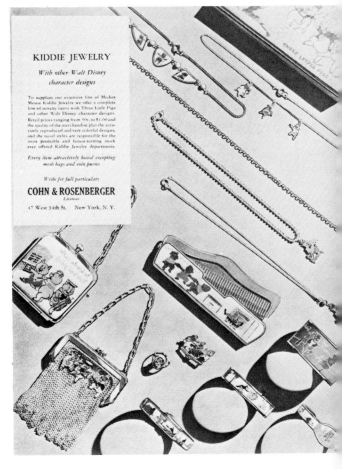

Items offered in 1936 by Brier Mfg. Co. of Providence, Rhode Island. Mickey Mouse, Minnie Mouse, Pluto, and Donald Duck are the featured characters on this firm's line of jewelry.

An expensive line of Disney character jewelry marketed in 1936 by Philip Reiter, Inc., of New York. The items pictured were handmade of gold and platinum, and some are bedecked with diamonds and other precious and semiprecious stones. The price range originally was from $10.00 to $150.00. Antique stores that specialize in jewelry are good places to find pieces like these.

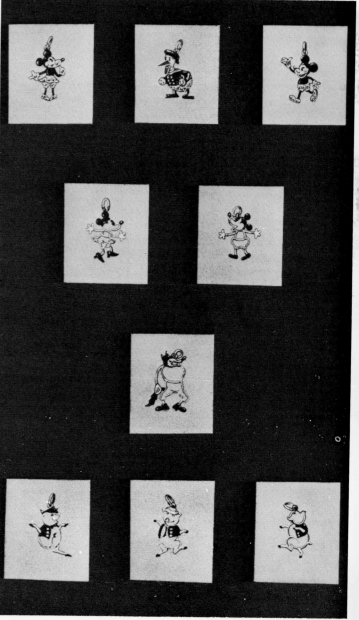

In 1938 Cartier, Inc., of New York offered this line of jewelry made of precious metals and bearing precious stones.

Rings, buttons, charm bracelets, and brooches made of plastics, composition, and enameled metals sold in 1938 by Brier Mfg. Co. of Providence, Rhode Island.

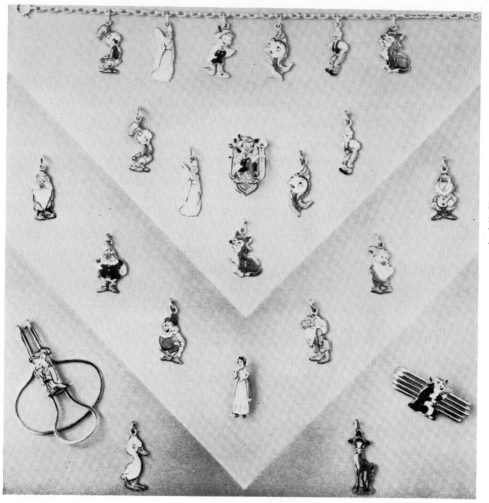

Disney character jewelry in gold-enamel and precious stones by the famous New York jeweler Cartier, Inc. This is the 1940 line.

Pinocchio jewelry made in 1940 by Brier Mfg. Co. of Providence, Rhode Island. This line of plastic jewelry retailed at prices not over 50¢.

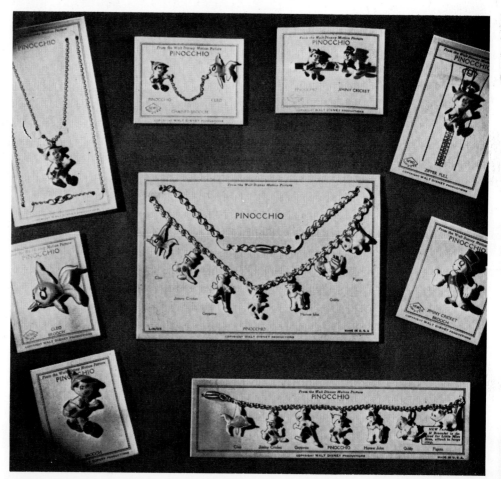

Multicolored enamel metal disks with overlays of characters from the Disney film *Pinocchio*. These items were made in 1940 by Speidel Corporation of Providence, Rhode Island.

A 1935 advertisement (page 4) from the Kay Kamen merchandise catalogue for Mickey Mouse savings banks by the Automatic Recording Safe Company of Chicago.

A 1934 advertisement for Mickey Mouse savings banks by the Zell Products Corporation of New York.

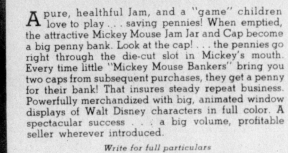

A 1935 advertisement for Mickey Mouse jam by the Glaser, Crandell Company of Chicago, Illinois. After the jam has been consumed, the jar becomes a coin bank. Around the shoulder of the jar likenesses of Mickey and Minnie Mouse are embossed in the glass. Coins are inserted through the lid. A specimen with the label intact would be worth more than one without it.

140

"Roly-Polys" and banks advertised in 1938 by the Crown Toy Mfg. Co., Inc., of Brooklyn, New York. The figural banks came complete with key and built-in lock.

11. Mickey Mouse Magazine(s)

It should be noted that "magazine" as used in this chapter refers to a periodical containing miscellaneous articles, stories, poems, gags, jokes, puzzles, games, and illustrations, as opposed to a "comic book," which is a periodical composed of comic strips. A collector who has a collection of Mickey Mouse magazines of the 1930s is apt to be a bit confused with his holdings. In addition to magazines being produced in Italy, France, and England, several were produced in the United States. Italian and French publications are not hard to identify, and the English version was called the *Mickey Mouse Weekly*. It is among the three domestic *Mickey Mouse Magazines* that there may be confusion.

The first *Mickey Mouse Magazine* was produced by Kay Kamen in 1933. Volume 1, number 1 was released in January of 1933; this series continued through volume 1, number 9—September 1933. The nine issues of this first magazine were distributed through department stores selling Disney character merchandise and at theaters showing Disney cartoons. Examples of this magazine are extremely difficult to obtain but certainly worth searching for by collectors who wish to have the first of a long line of magazines and comic books.

The second *Mickey Mouse Magazine* began in November 1933 and was edited by Hal Horne, who was also advertising director for United Artists. The second magazine was much like the first in appearance and format (gags, jokes, stories, puzzles, games, and the like), but was distributed nationally through dairies. The numbering system began all over again with the second magazine; thus, volume 1, number 1 is dated November 1933. This second magazine ran through volume 2, number 12, October 1935. Twenty-four issues of this second *Mickey Mouse Magazine* were produced in all. Space was left on the front and back covers of each magazine for the name of the local dairy which distributed it. As a result, collectors of these magazines can expect to find a number of different dairy names printed on the covers, unless the magazines are collected from the same primary source.

The third and final *Mickey Mouse Magazine* is by far the most attractive and desirable. This magazine was the brainchild of Hal Horne, editor of the second magazine. Early in 1935 Horne approached his friend Kay Kamen with the idea of becoming a licensee and publishing a "real" magazine, one that would be sold at newsstands and through subscriptions, not given away by stores, theaters, and dairies.

In addition to the many personal assets that

recommended Horne for the job, by 1935 he had the largest collection of jokes in the world. Horne had been a casual collector of jokes all during his checkered career as a newspaperman, head of publicity for the Boy Scouts, movie director, and radio scriptwriter. In 1931, he began to file them, his jokes into categories and properly file them, and by 1935 he had organized a staff to buy magazines and clip and classify the jokes within, as well as to copy others from files in the public library. It was partially because of his extensive joke file that Kamen hired Horne to edit the second *Mickey Mouse Magazine*. The file, again, helped Horne convince Kamen that he could produce the third magazine featuring Mickey Mouse.

The *New York Telegraph* for May 15, 1935, reported the birth of the new *Mickey Mouse Magazine*:

> The *Mickey Mouse Magazine* is what is called a quality publication. There are to be forty-four pages, all of them produced in four colors. There are to be stories and illustrations, concerning themselves with the adventures and misadventures of Mickey, Minnie, Donald Duck, Pluto Pup and other characters that, during the past six years, have flitted from the brain of Walt Disney. The publishers, basing their judgement upon a survey of motion picture audiences, declare that "adults will enjoy the book even more than children." The slogan with which the *Mickey Mouse Magazine* is being launched is "A Fun Book for Children to Read to Grown-ups."

The new magazine was very popular, and Roy reported to Hal Horne that, true to the slogan, his son spent an entire evening at a polo match reading the first issue and pestering his father by reading him the jokes. Walt was pleased too, and ordered six subscriptions for the Orthopaedic Hospital-School in Los Angeles, one of his favorite charities. When the famous movie star Mary Pickford saw the magazine, she made arrangements with Horne to purchase copies that were returned by newsstands. She then distributed the magazines to a number of hospitals she favored.

In a letter dated May 15, 1935, to Roy, Hal wrote:

> The Magazine goes on sale at the newsstands nationally today. This means that they will have made their appearance in every city of the coun-

try by the time you get this letter. . . . We have had a tremendous promotional campaign with tach cards, posters [both items prized collectors' items today], window displays, a barrage of publicity in the newspapers, special stories to magazines, radio plugs and what not, and a genuine interest has been aroused all over the country. Last week both Kay and I addressed two important gatherings. The first was a convention of the supervisors of the Interboro News Company—hundreds of men who supervise the trucks that sell to newsstands. This gathering turned into a tremendous clamor for more copies, all of them complaining that their respective allotments, based on 200,000-circulation, would hardly do. The same thing happened at the following convention of the heads of wholesale news companies, who came in from all over the East. They too maintained that 200,000 would hardly be sufficient for national sale and as a result of both these appeals I took a chance [this can be taken literally, because Horne seemed the sort to gamble] and ordered an additional run of 100,000, making the print order for 300,000 in all.

As previously stated, the magazine was popular, but Horne was too enthusiastic in his initial order. By October 1935 Horne was in financial trouble and probably beginning to realize that publishing a magazine was not as easy as he had anticipated. (Horne had resigned his job as advertising director for United Artists in July.) In a letter to Roy dated October 11, 1935, Kamen reported:

> The actual net sales on the twenty-five-cent issue is, at this time, 150,000. On the second issue (October), they expect 200,000 net. The print order for November is 300,000. The November issue will carry ten pages of advertising (paid for, but some at "special" prices [a policy neither Kamen nor the Disneys approved of]). They have already sold five pages for the December issue, and expect it to carry from ten to twenty pages of advertising. I had the entire Horne staff over here the other night for a pep meeting. Granger, of Australia [a good place for collectors to look for early issues of the magazine], wired an order in for 25,000 copies of the first issue and with the order came a draft for $750 (that was three cents a copy), so that was $750 like found to Hal. I am trying to sell the rest to Scott's Emulsion group for South America, or somebody like that. We have worked very closely with his organization, and, personally, I think the magazine might go over, provided Hal re-

mains conservative, although it is hard to keep him that way. I think the magazine is fundamentally right and am aware of what can and might happen, and you may be absolutely sure that I want to see him succeed, but that, if he doesn't, I have some ideas as to what we can do to continue the magazine.

By December, 1935, each issue was selling over a hundred thousand copies, but Horne had gotten off to such a poor start financially that he was unable to make the needed profit. He reported to Roy in a letter dated December 27, 1935, that "to date, it has cost me a terrific amount of heartaches and exactly $50,000, all of which seems such a crime when you consider that the magazine has been loved by those who have read it."

Horne continued to struggle to keep the magazine alive. On February 21, 1936, Roy wrote some good news to Horne.

We are more concerned now with saving you from a loss than with trying to get any revenue from the magazine. Therefore, you can accept this letter as evidence of our approval of your continuing with the magazine on a non-royalty basis to us, either by virtue of sales or advertising on royalties either due now or that may become due from now until December 31, 1936. . . . I have just received a long letter from Bill Levy, in London, this morning, advising me that his Mickey Mouse magazine [*Mickey Mouse Weekly*] there opened up to a complete sell-out

on the first issue of 375,000 copies, with an additional run of 25,000 being hurried off the press for further sales. The second addition is going to press at 450,000 copies.

The struggle for Horne continued until mid-1936, at which time he asked Kay Kamen to buy him out so that he could devote all of his energies to a career in the motion picture industry. Kamen reluctantly agreed. Both he and Roy had hoped that Horne would make a go of the magazine, and had helped Horne toward that end. At any rate, *Motion Picture Daily* of June 2, 1936, announced: "KAY KAMEN TO TAKE HAL HORNE MAGAZINE." The accompanying article read:

Kay Kamen, who handled Walt Disney's commercial enterprises, has closed a deal with Hal Horne and Cuneo Press whereby he will publish the *Mickey Mouse Magazine*, starting with the July issue, which goes to press this week. Horne has been publisher of the magazine since its first issue.

Thus, while Hal Horne did not make a financial success of the first "real" *Mickey Mouse Magazine*, he certainly contributed to the magazine's eventual success. As a result he will long be remembered by collectors as the man who gave the magazine life and provided them with nine very exciting issues. The following information may aid in the search:

TABLE 2

Mickey Mouse Magazine *Print Order, Newsstand Distribution, and Sales*

(May 1935 through June 1936)

ISSUE	PRINT ORDER	DISTRIBUTION	SALES
Summer 1935	300,000	294,274	147,751
October 1935	300,000	296,262	123,841
November 1935	300,000	294,709	134,681
December 1935	229,250	200,000	130,768
February 1936	232,000	201,500	117,859
March 1936	220,000	203,250	116,330
April 1936	205,000	200,000	108,500
May 1936	155,000	150,000	76,932
June 1936	154,015	150,000	104,000
TOTALS	2,095,265	1,989,995	1,060,662

Shortly after Kamen took over *Mickey Mouse Magazine*, the following article appeared in the August 1, 1936, issue of *Playthings*; it seems to summarize how Kamen was able to breathe life back into the dying magazine.

Rapidly approaching the end of its first year of operation, the Mickey Mouse Magazine has become an established publication on all newsstands. Hundreds of letters pour into the Kay Kamen office every day from children all over who either wish to subscribe or submit their contributions. The fact that this periodical is becoming a favorite in the home is indicated by constantly advancing circulation figures. The editorial make-up of the magazine permits the use of much material from the Mickey Mouse and Silly Symphony motion pictures. In addition, there are stories, jokes and featurettes, all employing the comical Disney characters. The book is growing in size each issue due to the increased interest of advertisers. Leading agencies state that it is very difficult for them to reach children with their message and that this Mickey Mouse Magazine fills a great gap in the field of juvenile publications. Formerly published by Hal Horne, who is now an associate producer for RKO, the magazine was taken over a few months ago by Kay Kamen, Ltd. The policy of having full illustrations on every page through-out the magazine will be continued and many new departments will be added. Many leading department stores carry the Mickey Mouse Magazine, not only in their magazine departments, but in other departments of the store where there is likely to be child traffic. During the camp season, it is reported that the newsstands in the Pennsylvania and Grand Central stations in New York ordered additional copies by the thousands and a similar situation was true at every railway terminus in the United States. It is interesting to note that a smiliar publication in England has now reached a total circulation of 600,000 per week. Although the American Mickey Mouse Magazine is a monthly, it is predicted that it will not be long before the same figure will be reached or surpassed in America.

Kamen did as the article stated, and *Mickey Mouse Magazine* survived through volume 5, number 12, September 1940. By 1940 the demand for a "magazine" had fallen off and the demand for a "comic book" had grown. Thus, in October of 1940 *Mickey Mouse Magazine* died and *Walt Disney's Comics and Stories* was born. (See Appendix B for a complete listing of domestic magazines issued by the Walt Disney organization over the years.)

Volume 1, number 2 (January 7, 1933) of *Topolino,* the Italian version of *Mickey Mouse Magazine.* Since Italy has long been the home of many Mickey Mouse fans, copies of this magazine should not be impossible to locate. The first issues were 13¾" x 10", but they have varied through the years. The magazine is still being published.

Cloth dolls designed by Charlotte Clark.

Proofs of two Sunday comic pages: Mickey Mouse from February 28, 1932, and Donald Duck from July 7, 1940.

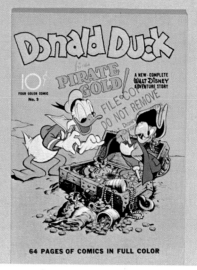

Selection of some of the most desirable of the Disney comic books.

A selection of early Mickey Mouse books.

Pop-up books published by Blue Ribbon Books in 1933.

A selection of activity books—cut-out and coloring, 1934–1942; published by Whitman and Saalfield.

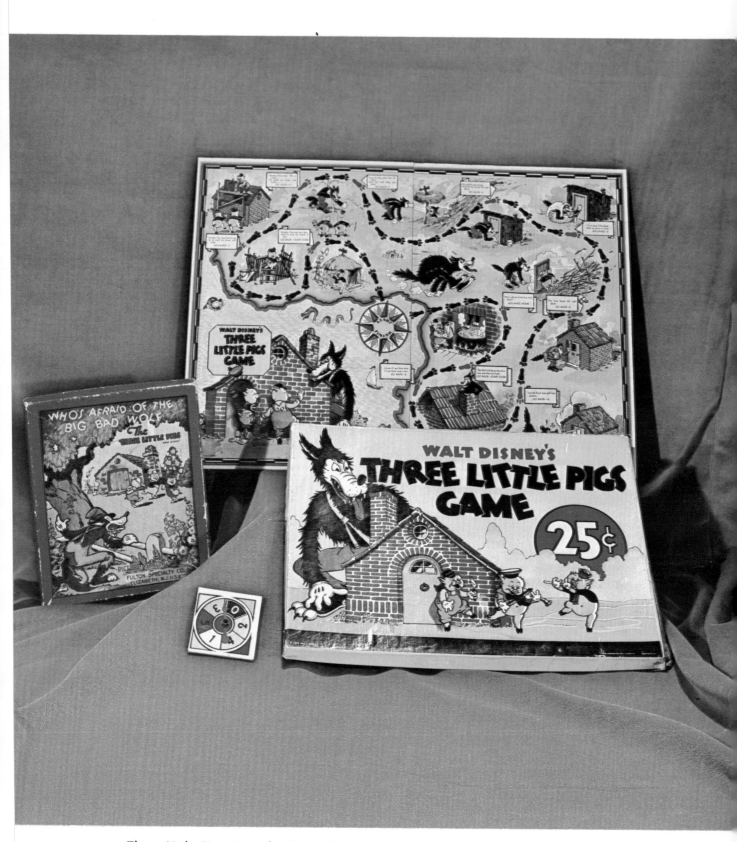

Three Little Pigs Game by Einson-Freeman and picture printing set by Fulton
Specialty Co., ca. 1933–1935.

A selection of sheet music, 1932–1939.

Three Little Pigs Game by Einson-Freeman and picture printing set by Fulton Specialty Co., ca. 1933–1935.

A display for Payne's Mickey Mouse chocolate bar from England, including the actual candy bar, from 1934.

A selection of Walt Disney Productions' Christmas cards (for 1935, 1938, 1939, 1958, 1959).

A selection of Hallmark (Hall Brothers) greeting cards, ca. 1932.

A selection of sheet music, 1932–1939.

A selection of Disney record albums: "Three Caballeros," "Saludos Amigos," "Treasure Island," "Bongo," and one of the first Disney records, "Mickey Mouse and Minnie's in Town" (1933).

Original poster for *Touchdown Mickey* (1932).

A few of the many styles of Disney character watches produced over the years. Note the two band styles of the first watch (top and bottom row).

Examples of early merchandise. Note the wooden Mickey Mouse (Borgfeldt), the rubber dwarfs, and the black rubber Mickey Mouse (Seiberling Latex Products).

A display of Mickey Mouse merchandise from the collection of the Walt Disney Archives.

Contemporary Disney character dolls made by Lars of Italy. Uncle Scrooge (*top left*), Pegleg Pete (*top right*), Goofy (*bottom left*), and Panchito from the film *The Three Caballeros* (*bottom right*).

The French version of *Mickey Mouse Magazine* was called *Le Journal de Mickey*. This is a photograph of volume 1, number 1, of the magazine; it was published on October 21, 1934. The French, like the Italians, have long been fans of Mickey Mouse, and as a result many collectibles can be found that are French in origin. This magazine started out as 16½" x 11¼". It is still being published today.

A complete set (perhaps the only one in existence) of the first *Mickey Mouse Magazine* from the Disney Archives. It begins with volume 1, number 1(January 1933) and ends with volume 1, number 9 (September 1933). This first magazine was produced by Kay Kamen and was given away in department stores and at theaters featuring Mickey Mouse cartoons. These magazines measure 7¼″ x 5¼″.

The second *Mickey Mouse Magazine* began with volume 1, number 1 (November 1933) and ran for 24 issues, or through volume 2, number 12 (October 1935). This photograph shows the first 12 issues of the magazine. The magazine was edited by Hal Horne and was produced for dairies all over the country. Note that each dairy distributing these magazines put its name just above the masthead.

This is a photograph of the second 12 issues of the second *Mickey Mouse Magazine,* which was edited by Hal Horne and ran from November 1933 to October 1935. At the very top of each magazine, the dairy distributing the publication stamped its name. These magazines were distributed nationally by dairies. They all measure 7¼″ x 5¼″.

The third *Mickey Mouse Magazine* was published by Hal Horne as a licensee of Kay Kamen. This third magazine was not a giveaway as the previous two had been; it was sold at newsstands for 10¢. The first issue, an oversized one (*left*) was the summer quarterly, which was produced in May of 1935. Hal Horne published the first 9 issues of the magazine (until June 1936). After that, Kay Kamen took over, and the magazine survived until September 1940; beginning in October 1940 it became *Walt Disney's Comics & Stories.*

A picture of the famous movie star Mary Pickford taken in June of 1930. She is holding a Charlotte Clark stuffed Mickey Mouse doll. In 1935 Mary Pickford, who had long been a devoted fan of Mickey Mouse, made arrangements with Hal Horne to purchase copies of *Mickey Mouse Magazine* that were returned by newsstands. She distributed them to children in various hospitals.

12. The Comic Book King

During the final years of the Depression, the popularity of comic books became widespread. They were an outgrowth of animated cartoons and newspaper comic strips. As 1940 approached, the Disneys and Kay Kamen began to realize that their *Mickey Mouse Magazine* was losing its following to the more popular comic books. At first it was thought that a solution would be to change the magazine's format, and during the early months of 1940 Kamen began to change the story magazine into a comic magazine. When the magazine's popularity did not revive, it was decided to make a complete change. Thus, *Mickey Mouse Magazine* ceased to be produced with volume 5, number 12, in September of 1940, and *Walt Disney's Comics and Stories* was first issued in October 1940, with volume 1, number 1. The new monthly series was published by Dell Publishing Company and has continued to be published over the years. While only 252,000 copies of *Walt Disney's Comics and Stories,* volume 1, number 1, were published, by August of 1942 the number had reached 1,000,000 copies per issue. By March of 1946 2,000,000 per issue were being published, and by August of 1951 3,000,000 were being published per issue. The peak was reached in September of 1952, when 3,115,000 were produced. In July of 1962 Dell stopped the publication of *Walt Disney's Comics and Stories,* but the series was continued as "Gold Key Comics." The switch to the name "Gold Key" was made because Western Printing and Lithographing decided to distribute the comic books they published instead of continuing to have Dell Publishing Company do

it. The major change introduced by Gold Key Comics was an elaborate numbering system. All *Walt Disney's Comics and Stories* after June 1962 featured a five-digit code number designating the title, followed by a three-digit code number designating the date. An example: 10114-405; the 10114 indicates *The Three Little Pigs* and the 405 indicates "May 1964."

Walt Disney's Comics and Stories was not, however, the first Disney comic book. In 1938 K. K. Publications produced an unnumbered black and white Donald Duck comic book with cardboard covers. (Some collectors classify this as a book rather than a comic book.) This was a limited offering, and as a result few examples exist today. In 1940, Dell Publishing Company produced a black and white comic book (number 16) which featured Donald Duck. In 1941 the same company published a black and white Donald Duck comic paint book (number 20). Both of these books are rare today and very valuable.

The fourth Disney comic book was published in February 1940 by the Dell Publishing Company, eight months before the same publisher issued the first *Walt Disney's Comics and Stories.* In 1939 Dell began a series of comic books called Dell Color Comics. This series was devoted to a wide variety of comic characters. The first Disney character used was Donald Duck, who appeared in February 1940 in Dell Color Comics number 4. Disney characters appeared irregularly in Dell Color Comics: Donald Duck was featured twenty-seven times from 1940 to 1952, between numbers 4 and 328. Mickey Mouse was featured twenty-seven times from 1941 to 1952, between numbers 16 and 334. There were other Disney characters featured as "one-shots," but several, including the two mentioned above, evolved into series of their own and were sold by subscription on a regular basis.

Other early one-shot comic books appearing in the Dell Color Comics series were: number 13, 1941, *The Reluctant Dragon* and number 17, 1941, *Dumbo*. By 1942 Dell Publishing Company had begun to use a four-color process in printing their comic books. The series was thus renamed Dell Four Color Comics. Number 12, 1942, was *Bambi*; number 19, 1943, was *Thumper*; number 30, 1943, was *Bambi's Children*; number 49, 1944, was *Snow White and the Seven Dwarfs*; number 71, 1945, was *The Three Caballeros*; number 92, also 1945, was *Pinocchio*.

Still other early Disney comic books include *Pluto*, which was featured in the 1943 Large Features Comic number 7. Throughout the years some comic books were produced as premiums for various commercial firms. Some of the early and most desirable giveaways include: *Comics by Walt Disney*, which was a Christmas giveaway for Firestone in 1943; *Walt Disney's Comics*, which was a Sears, Roebuck and Company giveaway in 1943; and *Donald Duck*, which was a giveaway used by a number of companies in 1945.

In addition, a number of series has been produced over the years. Some appeared on a regular basis and some did not; some consisted of many issues and some consisted of only a few. Many series have also been produced on a one-time-only basis and were primarily used as tie-ins for Disney films and/or television programs. There was also a not so popular series of "giant-size" comic books that first appeared in 1949 and sold for twenty-five cents each.

The list of Walt Disney comic books is extensive and is offered as Appendix C in this book. Comic book collecting has grown into a very large collecting specialization, and collectors of Disneyana should be prepared to pay from two dollars to over five hundred dollars for rare Disney comic books.

To create the many products of the Walt Disney organization a great number of artists were employed over the years. Involved in the making of Disney cartoons were the animators, Walt's largest group of artists. The various newspaper comic strips that have been published since the early 1930s also were created by a number of artists. A cursory examination of the chronology of newspaper comics, which appears in this book as Appendix A, will verify the variety of artists used. Their products were sold under contract to a syndicate, which in turn placed the comics in newspapers all over the world.

The artists who created the art for comic books were employed by the publisher licensed to produce the comic books. These artists usually worked in their own studios and sent their work, through the Disney studio for approval, to the publisher. Such was the case with Carl Barks, the "Comic Book King."

Many of the artists who drew the thousands of comic books that appeared on the market from the 1930s to the 1960s were fine artists—perhaps even great artists. Many comic book collectors, however, feel that Carl Barks has been the most inventive and painstaking, both in storyline and artwork. Some go so far as to claim that Barks's creations may be properly considered the most nearly complete crystallizations of comic art yet produced, and today there is a Carl Barks cult among collectors of comic books.

It is interesting to note that, like most of the artists who created and developed Disney characters, Barks never signed his work. In addition, during the years he actively drew Disney characters and others, his name was generally kept secret by the publishers. It was only after 1960 that many of his admirers learned his name and began to heap long-deserved attention upon him.

Carl Barks was born on March 27, 1901, in Merrill, Oregon. He received only an eighth-grade education. As a young man he tried being a cowboy, a logger, a printing press feeder, a steelworker, a chicken grower, and a carpenter, among other professions. In 1929 he was working in a railroad car shop as a riveter. He quit that job and began doing free-lance joke-writing as well as drawing. Although he had no formal training in either of these professions, he made a fair living.

In 1935 Barks went to work at the Disney studio as an "in-betweener" (drawing frames between action in animated cartoons) at twenty dollars a week. Within a few months he was transferred to the story department, where he helped write stories for the cartoons. His favorite character was Donald Duck.

Donald first appeared in 1934. Later, along with Pluto, he was given supporting roles in Mickey Mouse cartoons. By 1937 he was so popular he was starred in his first cartoon, *Don Donald*. Barks helped create the drawings for some of these early Donald Duck cartoons, until shortly after America's involvement in World War II in 1941. Early in 1942 Walt began planning a Donald Duck cartoon that was to be called *Donald Duck Finds Pirate Gold*. After Barks and others had completed the story, it was shelved because of war work that the Disney studio was doing. Barks and another Disney artist, Jack Hannah, volunteered to take the story and turn out a comic book version of it in their spare time. Each of the artists drew thirty-two of the sixty-four pages. The book was published by Dell Publishing Company as their Dell Four Color Comics number 9, *Donald Duck Finds Pirate Gold,* in 1942. This was one of the first Disney comic books to feature original material; until 1942 most Disney comic books were based on material previously used in cartoons and comic strips.

Since Carl Barks was not very happy working at the studio, he decided to quit before he was locked into his job (it was a common practice for men to be "frozen" at their work by the government during World War II). Barks decided to try farming but was called by the Whitman Publishing Company to draw a Donald Duck story about Donald protecting his victory garden from some crows. He illustrated the book, and it was published in April 1943. Whitman liked his work so well that it requested him to both write and draw another Donald Duck comic book, which was published in May 1943. For the next twenty-three years, until 1966, Barks wrote and drew Donald Duck comic books.

Barks worked in the studio of his San Jacinto, California, home for all those years. Since his retirement in 1966, Barks has been painting Donald Duck and other characters on canvas for his many fans. Recently one of his paintings sold at auction for $600. In 1943 Barks was paid $11.50 a page for the writing and $34.00 a page for the art. He produced about twenty-six pages a month, and worked about six to eight months in advance.

His work did not include coloring the drawings; they were colored at the publisher's.

Students of Carl Barks's work feel that 1949 was the year in which Barks did his best work. His best story was *Lost in the Andes* (Dell Color Comics number 223), which tells how Donald Duck and his nephews discover some square eggs. His best art, it is generally agreed, was done in stories featuring Uncle Scrooge in 1949. Scrooge was a character developed by Barks; he was first used in a 1947 Donald Duck comic book (Color number 179) one-shot entitled *Christmas on Bear Mountain*. It was not until his second appearance, however, in a 1948 Donald Duck comic book (Color number 189) called *The Old Castle's Secret*, that Scrooge was portrayed as a wealthy relative of Donald's.

Science fiction writers, cartoonists, comic book artists, and others who seem to have unlimited imaginations, often discuss or draw things that later become practical realities. Carl Barks was no exception. In 1964 a ship carrying 6,000 sheep sank in Kuwait Harbor near the Persian Gulf. It was estimated that it would take six months to salvage the vessel. Since the city of Kuwait pumped its drinking water from the harbor, it was essential to remove the decaying sheep from the water in a shorter period than six months. A Danish inventor, Karl Kryer, accomplished the task in six weeks by pumping expandable polystyrene foam into the sunken ship. When Kryer tried to patent his process, he discovered that a preliminary description had already been published, and as a result the process was unpatentable. In the May 1949 *Walt Disney's Comics and Stories* (number 104), Carl Barks had written and drawn a story in which Donald Duck and his nephews raise a sunken ship by pumping it full of Ping-Pong balls.

In 1960, six years before he officially severed his approximately thirty-year association with Donald Duck and his friends, Carl Barks reached his peak from a production standpoint. In that year he produced 358 pages of art, 249 pages of script, 15 covers, and 4 cover gags.

Without a doubt, the work of Carl Barks has done a great deal to enhance the popularity of many of Walt Disney's comic characters, and for that he truly does deserve the title of "Comic Book King."

The first issue of *Walt Disney's Comics and Stories* (formerly *Mickey Mouse Magazine*), which was published in October 1940. The first 30 issues of this comic book contain mostly reprints of *Donald Duck* and *Mickey Mouse* newspaper comic strips. Only 252,000 copies of this issue were published.

The second (*left*), third (*center*), and fourth (*right*) issues of *Walt Disney's Comics and Stories*, which commanded $250, $150, and $125 respectively on the collectors market today. The contents of these and all of the first 30 issues are reprints of *Donald Duck and Mickey Mouse* newspaper comic strips.

155

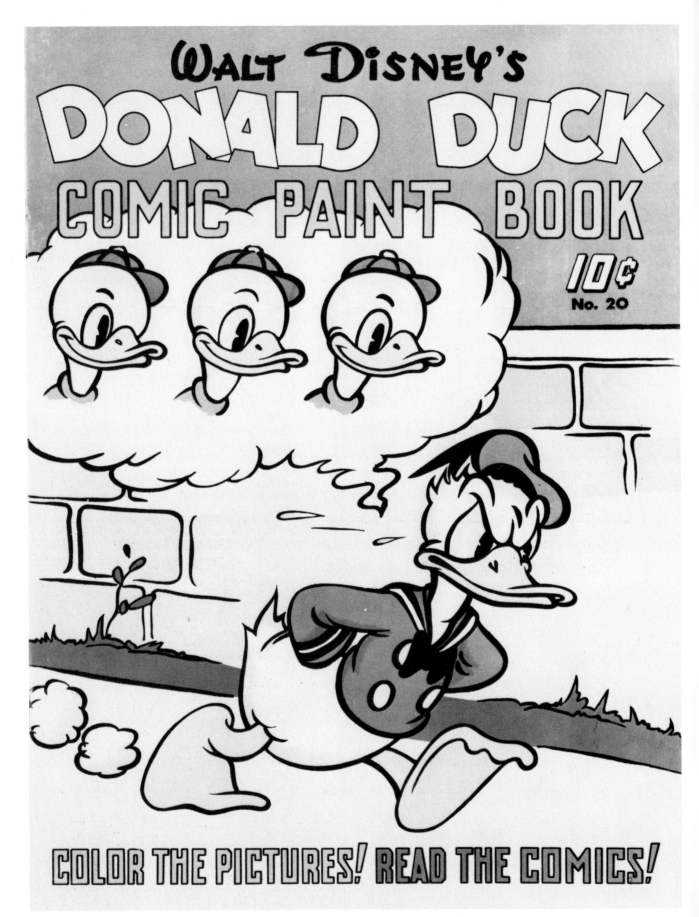

A black and white *Donald Duck Comic Paint Book* produced in 1941 by Dell Publishing Company. This book, when available, sells on the collectors market for approximately $250.

A miscellaneous selection of comic books featuring Walt Disney characters. These were all produced in the 1940s and are considered scarce and valuable by collectors.

A miscellaneous selection of giveaway comic books. These were produced as premiums for various commercial firms. The four at the top of the photograph are regular comic book size and were individual premiums, while the four at the bottom were given away as a set in the envelope pictured.

The first Walt Disney color comic—Dell Publishing Company, Issue No. 4, February 1940.
Copies of this issue currently sell for aproximately $350.

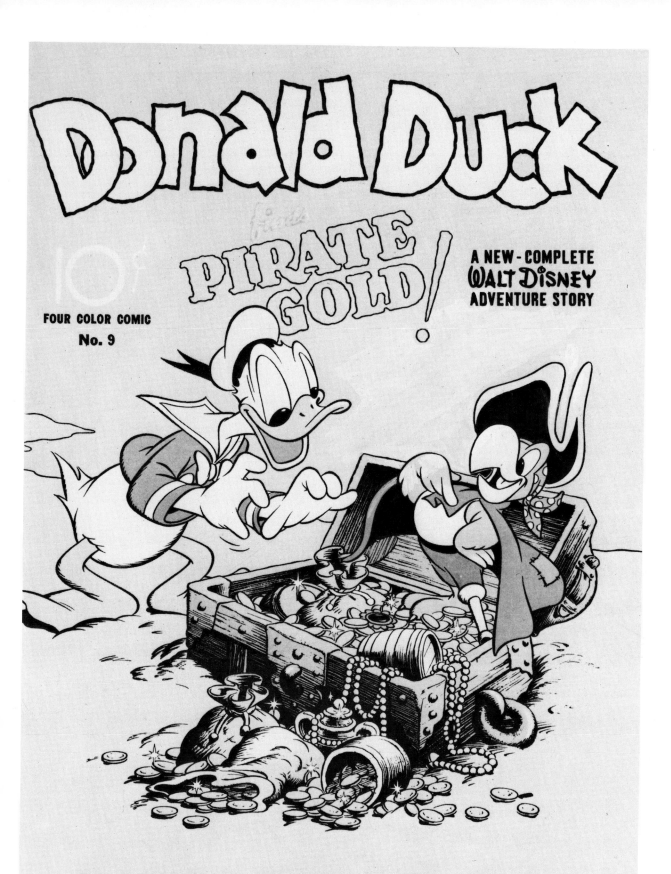

Dell Four Color Comic No. 9, 1942. This is the first comic featuring the artistry of Carl Barks.
Donald Duck Finds Pirate Gold currently sells for several hundred dollars.

A 1947 advertisement for *Walt Disney's Comics and Stories* published by K. K. (Kay Kamen) Publications, Inc., of Poughkeepsie, New York. The books were produced in Racine, Wisconsin, by Western Printing & Lithographing Co.

A 1947 advertisement for *Premium Comics* (giveaway) by Western Printing and Lithographing Co.

A 1947 advertisement by Dell Publishing Company of New York City for comic books. While Dell distributed these comic books, like most others, the actual books were printed in Poughkeepsie, New York, by Western Printing and Lithographing Co.

13. Books

During the past forty years hundreds of Disney books have been published. These books have been published to promote Disney films—almost every full-length feature has inspired at least one book, often a number—and to capitalize on the popularity of the Disney characters.

The first Disney book was called *Mickey Mouse Book* (subtitled *Hello, Everybody*) and was published in New York in 1930 by Bibo and Lang. This fifteen-page book was initially copyrighted "Walter E. Disney." Subsequent books have been copyrighted "Walt Disney Enterprises" and "Walt Disney Productions, Ltd.," until December 1938 and, after that date, "Walt Disney Productions." The story for the first book was written by Bobette Bibo, the eleven-year-old daughter of one of the co-publishers. Charlotte Clark, the woman who made the first Mickey Mouse stuffed dolls, sold the book for a short while along with her dolls. The book was a small venture, and a relatively small number was produced. Today the few that survive are eagerly sought by collectors.

In an effort to get more books about Mickey published, Roy wrote to a number of leading publishers and suggested that Mickey Mouse would be a good subject. Since it was during the Depression years, many replies were negative. David McKay Company, Publishers, of Philadelphia, however, had the foresight to take an interest in the comic character that within a few years would be world famous.

By September 1930, Roy had a manuscript prepared. A dummy book was made up and sent to the McKay company. In a letter dated September 16, 1930, from McKay, plans for the first McKay book began to materialize.

> We figure in order to get a large distribution of these books they should not retail for more than fifty cents per copy. This means that it would be impossible to use colored illustrations throughout the text. We would use a colored wrapper going all the way around the book and a paste-on in color on the front cover. The end papers could be done in color, but in the body of the book the illustrations would all have to be black and white in order to pay you a royalty and keep the cost so that it could be retailed at fifty cents per copy.

On December 23, 1930, Roy wrote the following letter to McKay. (Note the rejection of McKay's suggestion that the book be published in black and white.)

> Upon my return to the studio, I find the boys have all the drawings for the book, "THE ADVENTURES OF MICKEY MOUSE" made up, and are now making color schemes on photostatic copies of the entire number of sketches. This is being done in accordance with my brother's wishes that the book be put out entirely in colors, if possible. I will mail you tomorrow the drawings and color sketches for the front and back covers, together with sketches for the insides of these covers. I am doing this, thinking it might help you to speed up matters, as you suggested. I will see that the remainder

of the book follows along as soon as possible. I should like to hear from you if you have any further ideas with regard to the publication of the book. I am thinking, particularly, about your decision as to how much color would be practical to use. As I have said before, it is our wish to put the book out entirely in color, if practical and possible.

Walt and Roy were successful in convincing the David McKay Company to publish the book in full color and retail it for fifty cents. The book was released in 1931 and was a good seller for McKay until just before World War II. Since thousands of hardbound copies were sold in the approximately nine years that the book was in print, determined collectors should be able to locate a copy.

Besides being the first Disney book published and sold in great quantities, *The Adventures of Mickey Mouse* (Book 1) is interesting because it contains the first reference to Donald Duck. On the first page of the book the story begins:

> This story is about Mickey Mouse, who lives in a cozy nest under the floor of the old barn.
> And it is about his friend Minnie Mouse, whose home nest is safely hidden, soft and warm, somewhere in the chicken house.
> Mickey has many friends in the old barn and the barnyard, besides Minnie Mouse. There are Henry Horse and Carolyn Cow and Patricia Pig and *Donald Duck* [italics added].

It will be recalled that Donald Duck did not appear until 1934 in the Silly Symphony *The Wise Little Hen*.

By 1932 McKay had several Mickey Mouse books on the market. The titles included *The Adventures of Mickey Mouse* (Book 1), which was reported by *The Retail Bookseller* to be a best seller; *The Adventures of Mickey Mouse* (Book 2); *Mickey Mouse Movie Stories*, which featured two hundred illustrations and retailed for $1.50; and *Mickey Mouse* (Series 1), which was forty-six pages of reprinted newspaper comic strips that retailed for 25¢.

Word of the success of the David McKay Company with Mickey Mouse books spread rapidly, and soon publishers, some of whom had previously rejected the idea of a Mickey Mouse book, began to come to Walt and Roy for permission to feature Mickey Mouse and other Disney cartoon characters in books they proposed to publish.

The Saalfield Publishing Company of Akron, Ohio, produced the *Mickey Mouse Coloring Book* in 1931. This book was oversized, eleven inches by fifteen inches, with thirty pages of drawings and short captions. Part of the drawings were printed in appropriate colors to guide the user with crayon or paintbrush. The outlines were in black and white.

In 1933 Blue Ribbon Books, Inc., of New York City, introduced a series of pop-up books featuring Disney characters. The characters three-dimensionally popped up as the book pages were opened. The first four in the series were: *The Pop-up Mickey Mouse*, with twenty-seven pages; *The Pop-up Minnie Mouse*, with twenty-eight pages: *The Pop-up Silly Symphonies, containing Babes in the Woods and King Neptune*, with forty-eight pages; and *Mickey Mouse in King Arthur's Court*, with forty-eight pages. These pop-up books had the dual appeal of a book and a toy and became quite popular. Because of their unusual pop-up feature, they have become favorites among collectors.

Blue Ribbon Books added an even more refined novelty book to their line in 1934. It was titled the *Mickey Mouse Waddle Book*, "the story book with characters that come out and walk." It sold for one dollar. On November 11, 1934, the following review appeared in the *New York Herald Tribune*:

> The story in this volume is printed in large type with the regular Disney illustrations, on pages enough to make a story-book for very little children addicted to movie cartoons. Bound in with these pages are others of heavier paper, strong cardboard really, on which are large figures of the favorite animals of the Disney menagerie, punched out so that they may be slipped away from the page without cutting. Then, by folding not too difficult for father—who will by this time have taken a hand in the proceedings—the creatures assume three-dimensional vivacity; an inclined plane is then extracted from a pocket in the back of the book, folded to make a run-way, and the figures placed one by one at the top to see if they really will, as advertised, waddle

down the slope. There then ensues a breathless period while they don't. Then somebody with an extra twist for mechanics gets the idea of starting them, not by a push from the back but by poking the outstretched hand, nose or paw. They start, they move, they seem to feel the thrill of life along their somewhat ski-like legs. They do waddle. Also they are made so strongly they can be played with for some time after and if by reason of strong usage the brass joints show signs of loosing, slip a light rubber band around them. Begin with Pluto, he waddles so fast it encourages further effort. It will be seen that this reviewer is conscientious in dealing with books intrusted to her for report, even if it means extra work.

The *Waddle Book* is, perhaps, most sought after by collectors of Disneyana but it is also a favorite of collectors of "mechanical" books. Because of its removable parts, very few complete specimens have been found, and only a few unpunched books are known to exist at this time.

Another of the early publishers of Disney books, and the company that has produced more books than any other, is the Whitman Publishing Company of Racine, Wisconsin, now a subsidiary of Western Publishing Company. (Golden Press, which also has produced numerous Disney books over the years in its Little Golden Books and Big Golden Books series, is also now a subsidiary of Western Publishing Company. It should also be noted that Golden Books were published by both Simon and Schuster and Golden Press; in the mid-1950s Golden Press separated from Simon and Schuster and, subsequently, early Golden Books have been reprinted with the Golden Press imprint.) The Whitman Publishing Company has produced numerous series of books since the early 1930s, and many of them have featured Disney characters. The Big Little Books and the Better

Little Books were the most popular of the early series and consisted of many Disney subjects. Big Little Books featured several Disney titles that were used as premiums; for example, *Mickey Mouse, the Mail Pilot* (Big Little Book number 731) was given away by the American Oil Company and *Mickey Mouse Sails for Treasure Island* (Big Little Book number 750) was a premium for Kolynos Dental Cream.

Big Big Book, by Whitman Publishing, was a planned series that resulted in only one Disney book. Wee Little Books, produced in 1934 and 1935, were issued in sets of six. Set number 512 had six Mickey Mouse books in it. Each book was three and one-half inches by three inches, and contained forty pages of text and black and white illustrations. The six individual titles in the set were enclosed in a slip-case box one-half the height of the books. Complete sets with the container are scarce and highly desirable collectors' items.

Tall Comic Books, by Whitman, contained one Disney title: number 532, *Mickey's Dog Pluto*. The books in this small series were published in the early 1940s. They were eight and one-quarter inches by three and three-quarter inches and contained approximately two hundred pages of black and white illustrations.

In addition, the Whitman Publishing Company has produced a number of Disney story books over the years. There were also a number of Disney paint books and coloring sets (with crayons) published by this prolific firm.

Other publishers that have published significant numbers of Disney books include Grosset and Dunlap, Inc.; Random House, Inc., and D. C. Heath and Co. The books from these publishers and still others are presented alphabetically by title as Appendix D.

The first Disney book (*left*) was the *Mickey Mouse Book*, published in New York by Bibo and Lang. The book is 15 pages long and copyrighted by "Walter E. Disney." The second Disney book (*center*) is *The Adventures of Mickey Mouse, Book 1*, which was published by David McKay Co. of Philadelphia in 1931. The third book (*right*) is *Mickey Mouse, Series No. 1*, published by McKay in 1931. This book consisted of 46 pages of reprinted newspaper comic strips and sold for 25 ¢.

Mickey Mouse Coloring Books are
sold extensively in the leading
chain stores.

The ever increasing popularity of
these delightful coloring books is
shown by their sensationally large
sale all over the country.

...are 30 single
...in the Mickey
...e Coloring Book
...measuring 11 in.
...5 in.
...rawings are repro-
...d from originals by
...Disney.

Mickey Mouse Coloring Book, as advertised in the United
Artists campaign catalogue of 1932. The 11" x 15" book
had 30 pages and was published by the Saalfield Publishing
Co. of Akron, Ohio.

MICKEY MOUSE Coloring Book
the Children's Favorite

Mickey Mouse Coloring Books are splendid exploitation items for
the exhibitor. A contest among the children in your city under the
auspices of the theatre in cooperation with local dealers, newspapers, schools or juvenile organizations will stir up interest of great
advantage to your box office. This contest can be arranged by offering a prize or prizes to the child submitting the neatest and most
attractive coloring work in a Mickey Mouse Book.

These books have pages illustrating various escapades of Mickey
and Minnie. Part of the drawings are printed in appropriate
colors to guide the child in filling in with crayon or paint brush
the outlines in black and white. Here is an opportunity to organize exploitation stunts which will be educational and create good
will and patronage for your theatre. For additional information
communicate directly with:—

SAALFIELD PUBLISHING CO.
AKRON, OHIO

Page Nine

An advertisement showing the various Disney books that
were being published by the David McKay Co. of
Philadelphia. Note that two of the books are rated by *The
Retail Bookseller* as best selling books.

*Here is the book you
all have been waiting
for — The Story of
Mickey's Adventures.
Two books Left—dis-
play card.*

MICKEY MOUSE
BOOKS LEAD THE PARADE OF BEST SELLERS!

Mickey Mouse is close to a
child's heart long after his
frisky form has faded from
the screen. A Mickey Mouse
Book is a permanent com-
panion for children who want
to have their pal with them
always. For this reason
Mickey Mouse books move
quickly from the shelves.

The
RETAIL BOOKSELLER
Trade News for the Book Buyer

The Best Sellers
Ranking is based upon an actual count

Juveniles
1. THE ADVENTURES OF MICKEY
MOUSE, by Walt Disney,
May 19. (McKay) $0.50.
2. MICKEY MOUSE MOVIE
STORIES, by Walt Disney,
Dec. 5. (McKay) $1.50.
3. ANGUS AND THE CAT, by
Marjorie Flack. Oct. 29. (D.
D.) $1.00.
4. THE CHRIST CHILD, by Maud
and Miska Petersham. Nov.
5. (D. D.) $2.00.

Move Fast Off Shelves

Anticipation of a splendid public reception of these books has
been greatly exceeded by a realization of large sales volume.
Be sure that every book-seller in your town has a large quantity.

List of Titles and Retail Prices

MICKEY MOUSE. Illustrated Movie Stories. 200 illustrations. Large 12mo, cloth binding $1.50

ADVENTURES OF MICKEY MOUSE. By Walt Disney.
The story of Mickey's adventures, with 36 colored illustrations ....$ .50

THE ADVENTURES OF MICKEY MOUSE (Book 2).
With forty illustrations in full color ....$ .50

MICKEY MOUSE. Book I. Forty-six pages of the internationally syndicated comic strip. Special cover design
by Walt Disney. Bound in boards ....$ .25

Arrange Window Displays

Lively window and counter cards have been prepared, which
will attract crowds wherever they are displayed. Brilliantly colored jackets on these Mickey Mouse Books make them ideal
display material.

*Illustrated Movie Stories
— Eleven Scenarios —
Over 200 Illustrations.
Right—display card.*

Page Sixteen

Page 5 of the 1934 Kay Kamen merchandise catalogue, featuring an advertisement for "Mickey Mouse and Silly Symphony Books with and without Pop-up illustrations," published by Blue Ribbon Books, Inc., of New York.

An advertisement appearing on page 4 of the Kamen character merchandising catalogue for 1934 features the *Mickey Mouse Waddle Book*. This mechanical book had characters that could be punched out of the pages of the book, assembled, and made to "waddle" down the ramp that accompanied the book. These books are rare today, and only two unpunched examples are known to exist.

169

Disney books advertised by the David McKay Company in 1934.

Books sold in 1934 by the David McKay Company. The opened example shows reprinted newspaper comic strips, which were often used in the 1930s to make books.

Several types of books were published by the Whitman Publishing Company of Racine, Wisconsin, in 1934. "Big Little" books (*lower right*) are often sought by today's collectors.

1935 advertisement for Disney books published by the David McKay Company.

1935 advertisement for Disney books published by the David McKay Company.

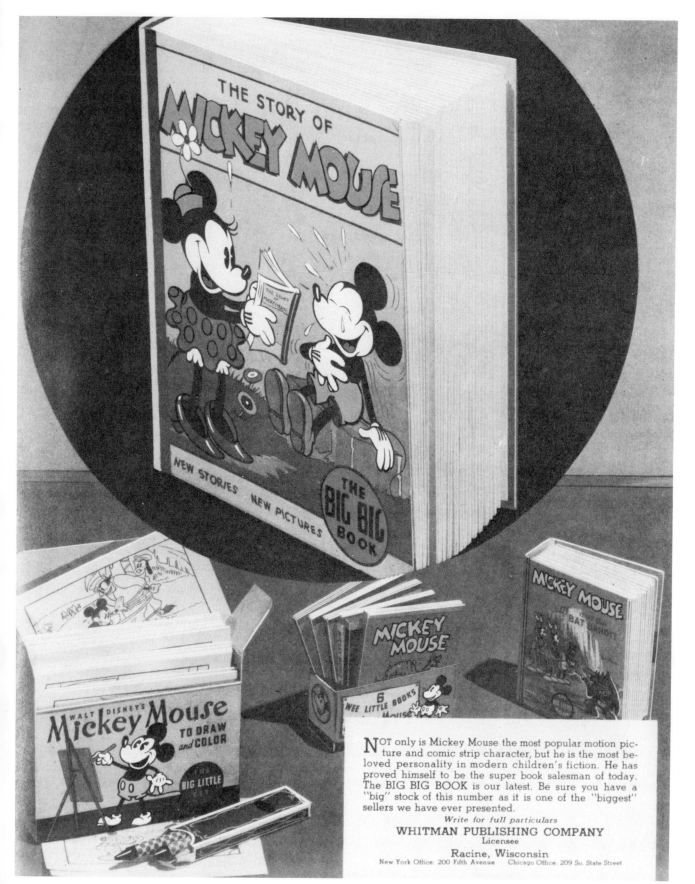

Page 73 of the merchandise catalogue for 1935, featuring *The Story of Mickey Mouse*, published by the Whitman Publishing Company of Racine, Wisconsin.

A selection of books sold in 1936 by the David McKay Company. *Who's Afraid of the Big Bad Wolf?* and *Little Red Riding Hood and The Big Bad Wolf* sold originally for 10¢ and the other books shown sold for 50¢ each in 1936.

176

More books advertised in 1936 by the David McKay Company of Philadelphia. *Mickey Mouse and His Horse Tanglefoot* and *Elmer Elephant* both sold for 50¢ originally, while the others shown went for $1.00 for three, along with an inflatable Mickey Mouse doll.

Mickey Mouse and Donald Duck story books, paint books, and scrapbooks for 1936. These were published by the Whitman Publishing Company. The Donald Duck book in the lower right-hand corner is the first Donald Duck book published.

David McKay Company books, as advertised in 1938. Some are reprints. The books sold for 25¢ to $1.00 each.

Books, games, and playing cards advertised by the Whitman Publishing Company in 1938.

179

Story books and cut-out books for 1938 by the Whitman
Publishing Company.

An advertisement for *Pinocchio* published in 1940 by
Grosset & Dunlap, Inc., of New York. The 56 page book
contains 39 drawings (15 in color) and sold originally for
50 ¢.

Pinocchio book published in 1940 by Random House, Inc., of New York. In addition to black and white drawings, this book contains 33 full color drawings. It sold originally for $1.00.

A selection of books published by the Whitman Publishing Company in 1940. These books ranged in size from the "Better Little Books" to the "Walt Disney Annual," and sold originally for 5¢ to 50¢.

Several books advertised in 1947 by Grosset & Dunlap, Inc.

Paint books, picture books, and games advertised in 1940
by the Whitman Publishing Company.

Books advertised in 1947 by D. C. Heath and Company of
Boston, Massachsetts. All of the books pictured originally
retailed for 84¢ to $1.08 each.

Books advertised in 1947 by Simon & Schuster, Inc. These
books are all part of the Little Golden Book series, which
sold originally for 25¢ each.

Big Golden Books and Giant Golden Books by Simon & Schuster, Inc., in 1947. They originally sold for $1.00 and $1.50 each.

These books were offered in 1949 by Grosset & Dunlap, Inc., for 50¢ each.

Children's books and a blackboard produced by the Whitman Publishing Company in 1947.

184

14. Collecting Original Disney Art

In 1935 the Academy of Motion Picture Arts and Sciences presented Walt with his fourth Academy Award. The film was called *The Tortoise and the Hare,* and it was declared the best cartoon production of 1934. Toby Tortoise and Max Hare both were introduced in this film. In 1936 *Three Orphan Kittens* won Walt another Academy Award, for the best cartoon production of 1935. Again, in 1937 *The Country Cousin* was pronounced the best cartoon short subject of 1936, and Walt was presented with his sixth Academy Award.

By 1934 Walt had decided to make a feature-length animated film. While Max Fleischer had produced a long cartoon called *Einstein's Theory of Relativity,* it was generally accepted that an audience would not tolerate ninety-minute cartoons. Walt's idea was not to produce a cartoon but an animated feature film that would successfully compete with the live-action features being produced by the other studios. Since film rental fees were based on running time, the idea was a good one from an economic point of view if the cost of producing the film was not excessive. To Walt, while the economic possibilities were appealing, the possible improvement of his product was the most important aspect of his plan.

Interestingly, the story that Walt selected for his first feature-length animated film was *Snow White and the Seven Dwarfs,* the subject of the first film he had ever seen; as a boy, he had seen a silent version in Kansas City.

Walt realized that to sell the public on a feature-length animated film he would have to produce an even better product than he had created in the past. With that in mind, he decided to experiment with a new camera method that would produce a real illusion of depth. Until that time an animated character was painted on celluloid and photographed against a flat background. The new plan was to develop a "multiplane" camera, which would be able to photograph simultaneously several layers of animation and a background. The layers would be separated in such a way that the effect of depth was created as the camera was moved in for close-up shots.

The multiplane camera was developed and tested in the cartoon *The Old Mill.* The technique was so successful that Walt received two Academy Awards in 1938, one for the best cartoon short subject of 1937 and another one for the design and application of the multiplane camera.

The success of the multiplane camera came in time for it to be employed in *Snow White and the Seven Dwarfs,* but not extensively. Even so, the scenes shot with the new camera added a great deal to Walt's first feature-length film. In 1936 and 1937 when this film was being produced, approximately a thousand people were employed at the Disney studio, and most were directly involved with its production.

On December 21, 1937, after $1,480,000 had been expended, *Snow White and the Seven Dwarfs* premiered at the Carthay Circle Theater in Hollywood. The film was an immediate success and grossed over $8,500,000 world-wide. (Subsequent reissues in 1943, 1952, 1956, and 1967 grossed a total of nearly $30,000,000 on a world-wide basis.) After the debts were paid, a profit of approximately $3,000,000 was realized. The profit was used to build a new home for Walt Disney Productions. On September 29, 1938, Walt Disney Productions, Ltd., Walt Disney Enterprises, and Liled Realty & Investment Company, Ltd., were consolidated to form Walt Disney Enterprises, and three months later the name was changed to Walt Disney Productions. The new studio in Burbank was completed and occupied by May 6, 1940.

In 1939 Walt received two more Academy Awards, one for the best cartoon short subject of 1938, *Ferdinand the Bull*, the other for *Snow White and the Seven Dwarfs*.

By 1938 Mickey Mouse, the Three Little Pigs and the Big Bad Wolf, Donald Duck, Pluto, and Snow White and the Seven Dwarfs were the very popular subjects of millions of dollars worth of character merchandise. By mid-year Guthrie Sayle Courvoisier, the owner of a very exclusive fine arts gallery in San Francisco, had convinced Walt and Roy that the original watercolors on celluloid that were used in the *Snow White and the Seven Dwarfs* film were valuable original works of art and that they could be sold through art galleries all over the world. Thus, on July 19, 1938, a contract between Courvoisier Galleries and the Disneys was signed, which made Guthrie Courvoisier the sole representative for marketing original Disney art.

Guthrie Courvoisier, at the time he signed the contract, was no stranger to the art business. His father, Ephraim B. Courvoisier, had established the gallery in 1905, and Guthrie became the president of the corporation in 1934, after his father retired. A June 17, 1938, report submitted to the Disneys regarding Courvoisier indicated that he "is considered the leading art connoisseur on the Pacific Coast. . . . [He] retails expensively priced picture frames, prints, oils, and other art objects." In the same report it was stated that Courvoisier's "clientele is largely wealthier art collectors and residents of the Pacific Coast."

Before Courvoisier convinced Walt and Roy to allow him to be the sole representative for marketing original Disney art, he discussed his idea with Kay Kamen. Kamen thought the idea of marketing original Disney art a good one, and he began to make plans to license Courvoisier *and others* to do so. Kamen even obtained some of the original Snow White material and convinced a St. Louis department store, Stix, Baer & Fuller, to take some on consignment for a test of the market. Thus, the first sale of painted celluloids—or "cels," as they are now more commonly called—was not by the Courvoisier Galleries.

When Courvoisier learned that Kamen was test marketing cels in a department store, he wrote a letter to Kamen, with copies to Walt and Roy, politely protesting department store sales. The letter, dated April 18, 1938, reads in part:

> I feel that there is a better opportunity to sell these celluloids through the channels provided by the fine art market than in a commercial way, such as through department stores. I believe that more sales can be effected this way and that Mr. Disney's reputation as an artist of great importance will at the same time be maintained. The position he now holds in this respect is outstanding. Through my own business I have come to know many museum directors, most of the important art dealers of America and a great host of collectors and people interested in art. They have not only been amused by the Walt Disney animated cartoons, but have often expressed a great respect for Mr. Disney as an artist of profound ability in the same sense as a great painter or composer. Proof of this may be found in the recent scheduling of the exhibition of celluloids at the Museum of Modern Art in New York. This was official recognition that Mr. Disney has actually created a new and distinct artistic expression which will rank his name with the great artists of this age. And not only that, but I believe a larger business can be built on the basis of art than by merely selling the celluloids as pictures which are amusing or suitable for children's rooms. They are after all not ordinary prints but original paintings from the hands of the Disney artists themselves, and as such open up a whole new field for their sale.

Courvoisier further pointed out in the same letter that

This is a field of tremendous importance, holding out extraordinary sales possibilities. It is a field that cannot be touched however if the pictures should be cheapened in any way. If kept on a high plane, a few of the possibilities can be enumerated as follows: (1) Purchase by the serious collectors of America as original, integral parts of a great artist's work. (2) Purchase by all the museums for their permanent collections for the same reason. (3) Hanging in the New York and San Francisco World Fairs with the leading American artists. (4) Sale through the best interior decorators as decorative groups on the walls of smartly done homes and apartments. (5) Purchase by the well-to-do social set of large and small communities. (6) Purchase by schools for their art departments. (7) Purchase by libraries and institutions. (8) Creation of the same markets for celluloids of future productions.

As a result of that letter, Kamen was asked to stop the department store sales, and a contract was made with Courvoisier. Since Kamen's contract was for character merchandise licensing and did not mention original art, the Courvoisier contract did not include Kamen. Roy explained the Disney position to Kamen in a letter dated June 15, 1938, which reads in part:

The entire presentation, atmosphere and build-up and exploitation approach from the department store angle is wrong, if we are to accomplish making this material a subject of recognized art, suitable for collection purposes. We have made up our minds to approach this entirely on a consignment basis, through this man, Courvoisier. He, in turn, will be a dealer sponsoring the art material from Disney pictures, much as any art dealer would sponsor the art work of an individual artist. Personally, I am convinced that this is the proper approach to this problem. It is a method of handling that will give it a better build-up, greater art value and prestige, and of a more lasting nature.

Kamen accepted the decision gracefully and even helped Courvoisier to promote the cels.

Even before the contract was signed, Courvoisier, operating on a verbal agreement with the Disneys, began to promote the cels. On June 17, 1938, in a letter to Roy, he reported that he had sold an order of the Snow White cels to the Honolulu Academy of Arts and the Colorado Springs Museum for exhibits and permanent placement in their collection. In a July 28, 1938, letter Courvoisier reported another precontract sale. This time it was to the San Francisco Museum. In the same letter, he also reported that the first shipment of cels (approximately fourteen hundred) had arrived and was being processed. On August 5, 1938, Courvoisier wrote to Roy that the California State Library had purchased a number of cels for their permanent collection and, like the other institutions who had made presale purchases, expressed an interest in obtaining cels from future Disney productions as they were released.

Also in the August 5, 1938, letter, Courvoisier described his experiments with pricing:

You will be interested to hear about the sales response to date. I have been experimenting with a few people and collectors and without half trying have sold approximately sixty-five celluloids at prices from five dollars to thirty-five dollars—and one for fifty dollars! This one was #142—Snow White with the animals looking through the window. I am going to try to get seventy-five dollars for similar ones in the East. There are a few other items that I am going to try at fifty dollars.

Early in August of 1938, Courvoisier released the news of his contract with the Disneys and the impending public sale of the original Disney art. Newspapers all over the country ran articles informing their readers of the newsworthy event. A typical article, from the August 10, 1938, Hartford (Connecticut) Times read:

The Walt Disney Studios have signed a contract with the Courvoisier Art Galleries of San Francisco for the world-wide distribution of original art work not only from "Snow White and the Seven Dwarfs" but from future Disney productions and short subjects as well.

The pictures, mounted by Disney artists especially for this commercial distribution, consist of the painted celluloids which are photographed to create the finished productions.

Although approximately 475,000 paintings were photographed to create the feature-length "Snow White," only some 7,000 of them will be put on sale, as only the most suitable were selected and the others destroyed. Those destroyed were, in general, parts of action sequences where the figures did not show up to advantage when viewed as separate units.

Through the Courvoisier Galleries, these originals will be distributed to one outstanding art gallery in each principal city in the world.

The studios entered into the contract because of the overwhelming demand for the celluloids not only from the general public, but from museums and art collectors as well.

Present plans call for them to go on sale in September. Future art work to be placed on sale include original paintings from "Pinocchio" and "Bambi" the next two Disney full-length productions.

Collectors should note that each *Snow White* cel marketed by Courvoisier Galleries was identified with a sticker on the back which read, "This is an original painting on celluloid from the Walt Disney Studios, actually used in the filming of 'Snow White and the Seven Dwarfs!' Only a very limited number have been selected to be placed on the market. Walt Disney [printed]." Later texts of Courvoisier stickers read differently. The few cels sold in St. Louis by Kay Kamen were not identified; small numbers that were given away by the Disneys before the Courvoisier contract were also not identified, except that a very few were authographed by Walt—needless to say, cels of this latter group are more valuable than the others.

The very exclusive Julien Levy Galleries in New York City opened their 1938 season on September 15 with an exhibit of Disney cels. On opening day this gallery sold sixty-three cels at a total of $1,345. Soon other exhibits were opened. The Toledo (Ohio) Museum and London's Leicester Galleries added prestige to the project by purchasing and displaying cels. By the end of 1938, Guthrie Courvoisier had kept his word, and cels were being displayed and sold in major cities all over the world.

The newspaper reviews of the various exhibits were excellent and gave assurance of a continuing market for Disney cels as true pieces of fine art. The review that appeared in the October 4, 1938, issue of the *Philadelphia Record* was typical:

> They took down the immortal picture of Whistler's "Mother" from its time-honored spot on the walls of the Charles Sessler Galleries . . . yesterday, and in its place they hung a portrait of—DOPEY! Down came the Rembrandts, the Durers and the works of other old masters. And up went the picture of Grumpy being doused in the watering trough, a scene showing Sneezy and Dopey dancing with Snow White, the turtle rolling down the steps and other now famous scenes from Walt Disney's "Snow White and the Seven Dwarfs."
>
> It was the opening of the first showing and sale of original watercolors on celluloid used in the Disney production, which started simultaneously in fifteen cities in the United States. And the children who tried to get a glimpse of the Disney exhibition were crowded out by the grownups, collectors and museum scouts, who bought nearly 200 of the 275 pictures in the first few hours after the showing began. "This is the most amazing sale we've had in twenty odd years I've been in business," Sessler beamed as his clerk took down and wrapped picture after picture. "The highest priced pictures were sold first," Sessler said. Most of them were bought by well known art connoisseurs in Philadelphia, who pledged Sessler to anonymity. A group were purchased by the Metropolitan Museum of New York and by Mrs. H. P. Whitney's Museum of Modern Art.
>
> The collectors also placed orders for originals from Disney's forthcoming productions, "Ferdinand the Bull" and "Pinocchio." The most popular celluloids were those of the heroine Snow White, while those of the animals were second. Happy's picture was greatest in demand in the dwarf sequences, with Dopey running a close second.

During 1938 the sale of original Disney art was limited to cels from *Snow White and the Seven Dwarfs*, but by February of 1939 it was decided that other types of original art would be released to Courvoisier for sale. The art was divided into the following four categories in the order of relative value and importance: (1) genuine original *backgrounds* from the picture, with or without celluloids of characters from action of the theme superimposed thereon; (2) *story sketches*, which are made just after the film's discussion period— these are placed side by side in succession, telling the story in rough form; (3) original *animation drawings* done by the head animators to show basic movement of the characters—others are made by in-betweeners, who make the many drawings necessary to create the illusion of movement between the basic drawings of the head animators; and (4) the original *celluloids*, which are made by tracing on celluloid the animation drawings and painting them on the opposite side

from which they will be photographed or viewed as art.

The following is a listing of the art that was sent or being prepared to be sent to Courvoisier Galleries as of March 7, 1939:

TABLE 3

Art Sent or Being Prepared for Courvoisier Galleries as of March 7, 1939

FILM	BACKGROUNDS	STORY SKETCHES	ANIMATION DRAWINGS	CELLULOIDS
Snow White	150	206	500	8,136
Ferdinand the Bull	35	20	500	1,340
The Ugly Duckling	0	0	0	900
The Practical Pig	0	0	0	198
Brave Little Tailor	0	0	0	300
Wynken, Blynken and Nod	0	0	0	297
Donald's Penguin	0	0	0	600
The Beach Picnic	0	0	0	500
The Pointer	0	0	0	300
Donald's Golf Game	0	0	0	500

In the original contract with Guthrie Courvoisier, the Disneys were responsible for the matting of cels and other activities necessary before the original art was suitable for sale to the public. As a result, Roy had to hire people to do the work and purchase the materials necessary to do the job. The following is a brief financial report submitted to Roy on April 21, 1939, representing the sale of approximately 6,000 of the approximately 11,000 pieces of art that had been prepared for sale. A total of $28,311.28 had been received from Courvoisier; the Disney payroll for the project was $8,400.80; and the cost of materials was $4,573.45. The latter two expenses subtracted from the total received left a profit of $15,337.03 for the Disney studio.

It was further reported that the *Snow White* cel set-ups cost an average of $2.13 each, and that the average income to the studio was $5.16 each. Twenty people were employed to prepare the art for Courvoisier at the time.

After reading and studying the above report, Roy decided that after the release of the original art from *Pinocchio* (the film was released on February 7, 1940), they would ask Courvoisier to assume the responsibility of preparing the art.

Courvoisier agreed and all art released after *Pinocchio* was prepared by Courvoisier Galleries.

The following is a listing of the art from *Pinocchio* prepared by the Disney group for marketing: Backgrounds, 259; story sketches, 276; animated drawings, 951; and celluloids, 6,311. In addition to the above, a small number of art painted onto *glass* was released through Courvoisier. While the newly perfected multiplane camera had been used in *Snow White and the Seven Dwarfs* to great advantage, it was extensively used in *Pinocchio*, and it is with multiplane shots that the glass was used—all paintings but the bottom one were painted on glass with oil paint. (Actually, most experts agree that *Pinocchio* was Walt's most technically brilliant film. Much of the unsurpassed technical excellence in the film was because of the multiplane camera, which was very expensive to use. One multiplane scene in *Pinocchio* that lasted only a few seconds cost $45,000 to produce; in today's money, that would amount to approximately $200,000). The few pieces of original art on glass that have reached the collector market over the years are more valuable than the art done on celluloid.

By mid-1939 Guthrie Courvoisier was overwhelmed with requests for original Disney art, which he could not completely supply. As a result he approached Kay Kamen about obtaining a license to produce lithographed prints of Disney art. It was his plan to market the prints through department stores much in the way Kamen had marketed the cels originally. Courvoisier reasoned that such a release of prints would relieve the demand for original art to a level that was within his and the studio's ability to supply.

Kamen granted Courvoisier the license, and by September 1939 the Whitman Publishing Company had produced the 8-inch by 10-inch lithographed prints and their accompanying cellophane-windowed envelopes. Thus armed with a good supply of prints, Courvoisier hired a number of young salesmen to promote them in department stores all over the United States. One of these salesmen, Harry "Bud" Barber, recalled the experience in a 1973 interview this way: "The first time out we sold enough prints and were well received . . . but the second time out we had more fun than we made money, the stores just weren't buying." The project collapsed after a year, and in June of 1940 Courvoisier made the remaining 10,326 prints available to Roy and Kay Kamen at cost (5¢ a piece). Kamen promoted some as a favor to Courvoisier, and Roy bought the remainder to give away as promotional items.

Apparently, while the public would purchase original art it would not buy prints in quantities sufficient to make it a paying proposition. The failure of the prints did not dampen Courvoisier's enthusiasm in selling original Disney art. In September of 1940 he proudly sent the following list to Walt and Roy:

THE FOLLOWING MUSEUMS HAVE
ACQUIRED WALT DISNEY ORIGINALS
FOR THEIR PERMANENT COLLECTIONS

Metropolitan Museum of Art, New York.
Museum of Modern Art (Film Library), New York, N. Y.
Cleveland Museum of Art, Cleveland, Ohio.
Toledo Museum of Art, Toledo, Ohio.
San Francisco Museum of Art, San Francisco, Calif.
California State Library, Sacramento, Calif.
Honolulu Academy of Art, Honolulu, T. H.
Faulkner Memorial Art Galleries, Santa Barbara, Calif.

Colorado Springs Fine Arts Center, Colorado Springs, Colo.
Vassar College Museum, Poughkeepsie, New York.
De Young Memorial Museum, San Francisco, Calif.
Trenton Museum of Art, Trenton, New Jersey.
Seattle Museum of Art, Seattle, Washington.
Boise Art Association, Boise, Idaho.
Dallas Museum of Art, Dallas, Texas.
Museum of Arts, Great Falls, Montana.
Trenton Public Library, Trenton, New Jersey.
William Rockhill Nelson Gallery, Kansas City, Mo.
Phillips Memorial Gallery, Washington, D. C.
Albright Art Gallery, Buffalo, New York.
Abilene Museum of Fine Arts, Abilene, Texas.
Fort Wayne Art School and Museum, Fort Wayne, Indiana.
Illinois State Museum, Springfield, Illinois.
San Diego Fine Arts Gallery, San Diego, California.
Saugatuck Art Gallery, Saugatuck, Michigan.

Although Courvoisier closed his gallery in 1942 in order to manufacture plastic parts for military aircraft, he continued to act as the Disneys' sole representative for marketing original Disney art until September 30, 1946. By then the demand had fallen off quite a bit, so it was mutually agreed that Walt Disney Productions would market their own original art. Guthrie Courvoisier died on December 9, 1966. Original art, mostly in the form of handpainted cels, was periodically released by Walt Disney Productions from 1946 until 1955.

In 1955, when Disneyland opened, regular marketing of original Disney art resumed. The shop in the park where most of the art was sold was called the "Art Corner." While the Art Corner sold a variety of character merchandising items, cels were one of its biggest attractions. In a 1956 Art Corner catalogue can be found the following listing:

WALT DISNEY ORIGINAL CELLULOID DRAWINGS: Walt Disney "originals," are hand inked and painted in full vivid color, and mounted on heavy colored 9 in. x 12 in. matboard ready for framing. Not copies, transfers, or duplicates of any kind, but the actual hand-drawn art work used in photographing a recent Walt Disney picture. These beautiful pictures are a most appropriate souvenir of Disneyland.

Ideal for children's rooms. Now available are Lady and Tramp and some other characters from this feature. Also Goofy, Donald Duck, Chip and Dale, Humphrey the Bear, and Jiminy Cricket, from recent Disney pictures. $1.47 complete with souvenir mailing envelope.

Original cels continued to be sold at Disneyland until the early 1970s for films produced up through *The Aristocats*.

Late in 1973, reminiscent of the Courvoisier days, original Disney art was once again being shown and sold at fine art galleries. Cels from Disney's *Robin Hood* were the feature of a Disneyana exhibit at the prestigious Bernard Danen-berg Galleries in New York and at the Circle Gallery in Los Angeles. Instead of commanding $1.47 as they did in 1956 at the Art Corner in Disneyland, the 1973 prices were "$75.00 and up, framed."

Just as all art sold by Courvoisier was iden-tified with a sticker on the back, so has been all art issued since. The stickers vary over the years, so collectors generally rely on the subject matter of the art to aid in dating their finds rather than sticker information. As one art critic wrote in the September 25, 1938, *Sacramento* (California) *Union*, "No one can doubt that it is serious art or predict its seemingly limitless future."

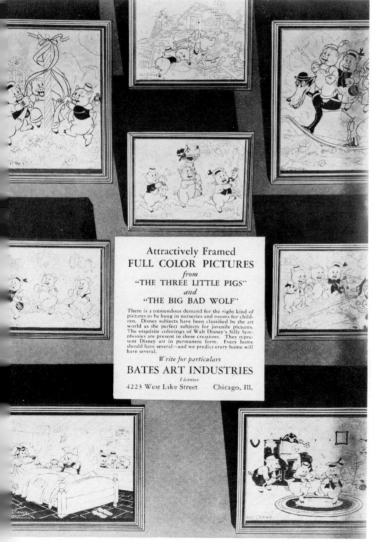

Page 8 of the 1934 Kay Kamen character merchandise catalogue featuring full color pictures of the characters from the Disney film *Three Little Pigs*.

191

Wall plaques advertised in 1936, and made by Kerk Guild, Inc.

Framed pictures sold in 1938 by Artisto, Inc., of New York City. Each picture came with an "antiqued" frame in a box and retailed for 39¢.

Animation drawings and celluloids from the Disney film *Ferdinand the Bull* on display and for sale in 1939 at Courvoisier Galleries in San Francisco.

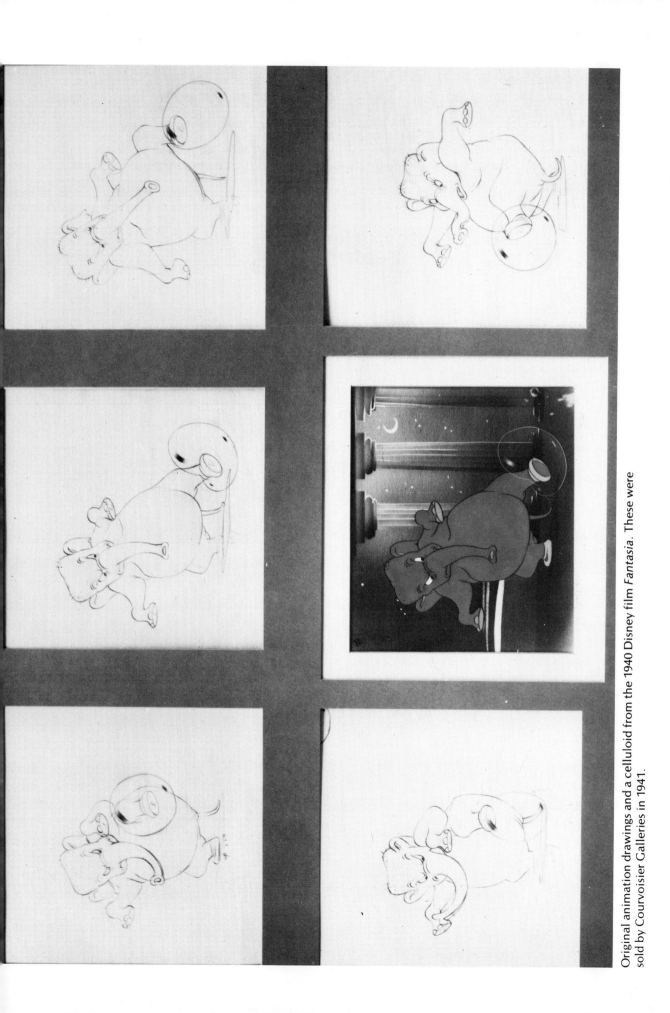

Original animation drawings and a celluloid from the 1940 Disney film *Fantasia*. These were sold by Courvoisier Galleries in 1941.

Original story sketches from *Fantasia*. Courvoisier Galleries of San Francisco sold these in 1941.

Walt Disney prints made by a six-color process. The prints measure 8″ x 10″ and originally came in an envelope, complete with mats, wood frames, and glass, along with a story about each print. These were sold by Courvoisier Galleries for $1.00 to $1.50.

Decalomania transfers made in 1940 by the Meyercord Company of Chicago, Illinois. They came in three sizes: 7½″ high, 2½″ high, and a 1½″ high. Frequently the larger transfers were put on some form of cardboard backing and framed.

Lithographed prints by the New York Graphic Society. These full color prints from the feature-length animated Disney film *Snow White and the Seven Dwarfs* and *Bambi* were advertised in 1947, and came in three sizes: 20″ x 24″ for $4.00; 15″ x 18″ for $2.00; and 10″ x 12″ for $1.00. The prints could also be ordered with special freplex frames without glass.

15. Photo-Chronology Three

Binoculars and electric scissors (1947) by the Royal American Corporation of Chicago, Illinois.

Donald Duck camera (1947) by the Herbert George Company of Chicago, Illinois. The camera is made of plastic and uses standard 127 film.

Mickey Mouse
MOVIE PROJECTORS
with screen and
Mickey Mouse Films!

There's going to be excitement in every
neighborhood when the children of
America see the New Mickey Mouse
Projector. We offer this marvelous promotional feature at a promotional price.
The moment you announce it, there will
be a new sales record established by your
toy department!

Write for full particulars

KEYSTONE MFG. CO.
Licensee

288 A Street, Boston, Mass.
New York Office: 200 Fifth Avenue

A 1934 advertisement for a Mickey Mouse movie projector by the Keystone Mfg. Co. of
Boston, Massachusetts.

Model E-18 Mickey Mouse Projector

Size: 9½ x 6¼ x 12 inches high when spool is in place. Equipped with 50-ft. capacity, with rewind for standard lengths 16 mm. film. Furnished with one empty spool. Simple threading—automatic framer. Ventilation: Air circulating through the top vents and side vents on the lamp house from the bottom. Size of picture: Up to 18 x 22 inches at a distance of 8 feet from screen. Finished: Decorated in green with Mickey Mouse illustrations on each side. Packed individually in printed corrugated carton, six per shipping carton. Weight when packed for shipment, 56 lbs. to the dozen.

Write for full particulars

KEYSTONE MFG. CO.

Licensee

288 A Street, Boston, Mass.
New York Office: 200 Fifth Avenue

A 1935 advertisement for a Mickey Mouse movie projector by the Keystone Mfg. Co.

A "Talkie Jecktor" made by Movie Jecktor Co., Inc., of New York in 1935.

Mickey Mouse 16mm films sold in 1936 for home use.

A Mickey Mouse viewer and 13 filmstrips made by Craftsmen's Guild of Hollywood, California, in 1946.

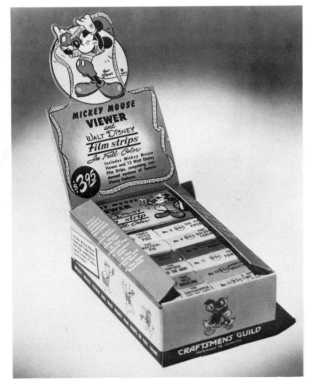

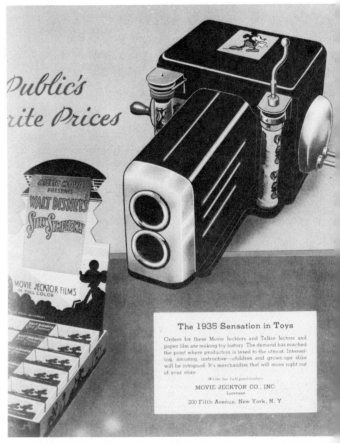

A 1935 advertisement for "Movie Jecktor" by Movie Jecktor Co. Inc. Six Silly Symphony films were available for the machine.

An advertisement for the Mickey Mouse viewer and slides by Craftsmen's Guild.

An advertisement from a 1944 issue of *Playthings Magazine* promoting a viewer and 6 series (10 each) of Disney slides.

Mickey Mouse viewer and filmstrips as advertised in 1947. This viewer retailed for $1.00 and the film strips for 25¢ each.

Color slides sold in 1947 by Hollywood Film Enterprises, Inc., of Hollywood, California. The picture is of 3 sets of 10 each: *The Three Caballeros, Snow White and the Seven Dwarfs,* and *The Three Little Pigs.* The slides are 35mm, 2" x 2", and retailed for $1.95 per set.

Metal Mickey Mouse table lamps and shades (*top*), sewing kit (*lower left*), and yarn holder (*lower right*) of 1935 by Soreng-Manegold Company of Chicago, Illinois.

Christmas tree lights featuring Disney characters. Made in 1936 by Noma Electric Company of New York.

Disney character lamps and shades of 1936 by Soreng-Manegold Company of Chicago, Illinois.

Disney character "Kiddy-Lites" of 1938 by Micro-Lite Company, Inc., of New York. The lamps are battery-operated and retailed at 25¢ to 29¢, including bulb and battery.

1938 lamps (La Mode Studios, Inc., New York) and lamp shades (Doris Lamp Shades Co., Inc., New York) featuring Disney characters.

Bookends, lamps, and night lights made by La Mode Studios, Inc., of New York in 1938 of "Modeware [plastic-composition] or of wood."

1940 Pinocchio wall and table lamps by Flexo Products Corporation of Chicago, Illinois. Lamp bases and plaques are made of "thermo plastic wood fiber simulating hand-carved wood." Lamps also featured matching parchment shades.

Ceramic table lamps (1947) by the Railley Corporation of Cleveland, Ohio.

Wall lamps (1947) made by the Railley Corporation.

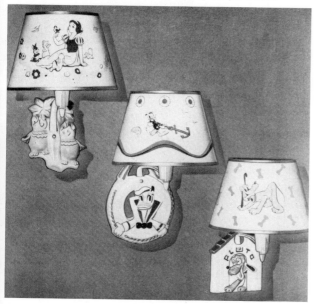

Character flashlights of 1936 made by U.S. Electric Mfg. Corp. of New York. The flashlights came with red, green, and white colored disks and two batteries, and sold for 49¢ to 59¢.

16. The Insignia Years

Daisy Duck was introduced in the 1937 film *Don Donald*. She was not actually called "Daisy," however, until she appeared in *Mr. Duck Steps Out*, which was released in 1940. Donald Duck's famous nephews, Huey, Louie, and Dewey, were first introduced in 1938 in the film *Donald's Nephews*. In 1940, in *Bone Trouble*, Butch (the bulldog) was born. All of these characters have been featured on merchandising items to some degree.

Walt received his eleventh Academy Award in 1940 for *The Ugly Duckling*, which was declared the best cartoon short subject of 1939. In 1941 Walt was indirectly honored by the Academy of Motion Picture Arts and Sciences: Academy Awards were presented to Disney employees for the music in *Pinocchio*. Leigh Harline and Ned Washington received the Award for "When You Wish upon a Star," which was named the best song, and Leigh Harline, Paul J. Smith, and Ned Washington received the Award for the best original musical score.

On April 2, 1940, Walt Disney Productions "went public," as it is called in the financial world, with the initial issuance of 155,000 shares of 6 percent cumulative convertible preferred stock, which had a par value of twenty-five dollars per share. Until then Walt and his wife, Lillian, had owned 60 percent of the business, and Roy and his wife, Edna, owned the remaining 40 percent.

The Disneys did not want to offer stock to the public, but they were in debt approximately $4.5 million. They had used the profits from *Snow White and the Seven Dwarfs* to build the new Burbank studio. *Pinocchio* had cost over $2 million to produce. Revenue from overseas had been cut off because of the war in Europe. The sale of stock helped pay their debts and allow the studio to continue the planning and production of several feature-length films.

Because Mickey Mouse was rapidly being replaced as Walt's most popular character by Donald Duck, Walt decided to star Mickey in a film tentatively called *The Sorcerer's Apprentice*, a story that was based on a poem written by Goethe and orchestrated in 1897 by Paul Dukas. Walt hired the famous conductor Leopold Stokowski and the Philadelphia Orchestra. The resulting film was, of course, *Fantasia*. On November 13, 1940, after Walt had expended over $2 million producing it, the film was released. Unfortunately, like *Pinocchio*, it was not initially a financial success. In 1944, when it was released a second time, it was more appreciated. Today it is considered one of Walt's greatest films.

With two not so profitable films in a row, Walt quickly went to work on a feature-length animated film about an elephant. *Dumbo* was released on October 23, 1941, and became a very successful film. In addition, it had cost only $800,000 to produce.

In 1942 Walt received another Academy Award, this time for "outstanding contribution to the advancement of the use of sound in motion pictures through the production of 'Fantasia.'" He received, that same year, a second Academy Award for the best cartoon short subject of 1941. The award-winning cartoon was *Lend a Paw*, which featured Pluto. Leopold Stokowski also won an Academy Award for his part in making *Fantasia*. Frank Churchill and Oliver Wallace were given an Academy Award for the best original score, which was the result of their efforts on *Dumbo*.

On June 20, 1941, the first live-action Disney film was released—*The Reluctant Dragon*. While it is not considered by most film critics as one of the Disney greats, it is at least historically interesting. The film showed, through a tour of the Disney studio, how cartoons were made. The film was done in black and white until the tour reached the multiplane camera department and then, as the actors entered, the film became color.

Shortly after *The Reluctant Dragon* was released, the United States government requested that Walt make a goodwill tour of South America to cement better relations with several countries there. On August 17, 1941, Walt, his wife, and eighteen cartoonists, musicians, photographers, and writers began the requested trip. In addition to creating goodwill, Walt and his crew gathered enough material during the six-week tour to eventually produce (in 1943) a film called *Saludos Amigos*.

On December 8, 1941, the day the United States declared war on Japan, seven hundred soldiers belonging to the anti-aircraft forces around Los Angeles were moved into the Disney studio. They took over some of the facilities and were billeted there for eight months. On the same day the troops arrived at the studio, Walt became even more involved in World War II, he received a call from the navy asking him to produce what was to be the first of a long list of films for the armed services.

The completion and release of *Bambi* on August 13, 1942, marked the end of the era of expansion for Walt Disney Productions that began in the early 1930s and peaked in 1940. Until the end of World War II the Disney studio was busy with mostly war work.

Shortly before the outbreak of World War II, Walt received what was to be the first of many requests for his artists to create insignia for the fighting services. Such insignia, once created, were used to decorate tanks, ships, and airplanes.

The first insignia, created in 1940, was for the U.S. "Mosquito Fleet." This was the group who manned the P.T. boats that launched torpedoes at sixty miles per hour. This first emblem pictured a mosquito astride a torpedo being hurtled toward its objective.

Throughout the war Walt complied with such requests, and over two thousand emblems were created. Roy once estimated that it cost about twenty-five dollars to create the average insignia. There was never a charge, however; the Disneys felt that it was their duty to fill such simple requests. Requests were received from every branch of service in combat, support, training, and civilian defense of this country, as well as from our allies.

It is interesting to note that the first insignia to feature a Disney character had nothing to do with World War II. Early in 1933 Walt received a request from an aviation squadron of naval reserves headquartered at Floyd Bennett Field in New York to use Mickey Mouse on their new emblem. Walt gave his permission, and the new emblem was created. It featured Mickey Mouse, armed with a trident and a bomb and astride a duck, driving down past the Statue of Liberty. Undoubtedly, shoulder patches and other items bearing this first insignia featuring a Disney character are extremely rare and valuable.

Of the insignia created during World War II by the Disney staff, over four hundred featured Donald Duck. Donald's personality made him the natural favorite of wartime good luck pieces. Donald was presented riding torpedoes and bombs, destroying submarines, carrying mines, aiding the wounded, and doing a host of things to help end the war.

Pluto was second in the line of favorite Disney characters featured on insignia. The most famous of the Disney characters, Mickey Mouse, was least favored as the feature of insignia, possibly because Mickey was not often portrayed as a fighter in Disney cartoons.

The Seven Dwarfs, individually and collectively, and Dumbo were popular insignia subjects. A number of fighting fetishes for the Marines featured Butch the Bulldog doing various things of a military nature. Even timid and allegedly submissive characters, such as Flower the Skunk, Thumper the Rabbit, and Ferdinand the Bull, became the stars of military emblems of faith. Jiminy Cricket, the conscience of Pinocchio, was appropriately selected to be on the insignia of the Chaplains' Corps; he served on other emblems as well. Flower the Skunk appeared on the insignia of a unit of the Chemical Corps. The Disney villains were also requested to do duty on the graphic boasts of prowess and invincibility; a number of outfits had the Big Bad Wolf or the horrid witch from *Snow White* as their animated mascot.

While Disney characters were most often requested, Walt's artists filled requests for bears, lions, tigers, eagles, mermaids, and many others. Among the most famous of the World War II military organizations to carry Disney-created insignia were the Flying Tigers, China Air Service, Eagle Squadron, the Seabees, and the Alaskan Command.

The Disney pictorial mascots were credited with having been exceptional morale building factors. After the requested emblems were created, they were sent to the War Department for approval; only a very few were ever rejected, and those were accepted after slight modification. All in all, the artists working for Walt performed a great service by providing insignia.

Collectors can expect to find Disney-created insignia on shoulder patches, lapel buttons, decals, pin-back buttons, decorated mugs and glasses, wall plaques, and a host of other items. Often the Disney-created insignia are overlooked by collectors if they do not feature one or more of the famous animated characters.

On January 1, 1943, Walt Disney Productions released its most popular wartime cartoon, *Der Fuehrer's Face*. Donald Duck was the star of this film, which was designed, like others Walt produced during the war, to help sell United States War Bonds. In 1943, Walt received an Academy Award for *Der Fuehrer's Face*; it was acclaimed as the best cartoon short subject of 1942–1943.

From a military standpoint, Walt's single most important wartime film was probably *Victory through Air Power*, which was based on a bestselling book by the recognized air strategist Major Alexander de Seversky. This film was released on July 17, 1943. Also released the same year (February 19) was *Saludos Amigos*, which was based on material gathered by Walt and his associates during their six-week goodwill tour of Argentina, Peru, Chile, and Brazil in 1941. On February 3, 1945, a similar film, *The Three Caballeros*, was released. Although these two films were aimed at the South American market, they were even more successful in the United States. These two films, in fact, were the most important commercial releases of the war years.

In 1945, when World War II came to an end, the Disneys were faced with the massive job of rebuilding their business. Equaling and surpassing the years of *Snow White and the Seven Dwarfs*, *Pinocchio*, *Fantasia*, *Dumbo* and *Bambi* was no little undertaking.

The following are examples of some of the over 2,000 insignia created during World War II by Disney artists. Such insignia appeared on shoulder patches, lapel buttons, decals, pin-back buttons, decorated mugs and glasses, and wall plaques. They are all collector's items.

U.S. Naval Reserve Aviation Base.

North American Aviation, Inc.—Flight Test Department, Inglewood, California.

Civil Air Patrol, 18th Patrol Force, Falmouth, Massachusetts.

70th Station Hospital—Fort Lewis, Washington.

2nd Reconnaissance Squadron, Fresno, California.

63rd Submarine Base, St. Thomas, the Virgin Islands.

Company K, 3rd Battalion, 4th Regiment, Minnesota Defense.

H.M.M.T.C. 62—Royal Naval Volunteer Reserve, London, England.

36th Military Police—Fort Lawton, Washington.

Second Scout Company, Second Marine Division—San Diego, California.

Parachute Corps—Free French, South Africa.

H.M.S. Oxlip—London, England.

Royal Canadian Air Force, Marine Section—Bella Bella, British Columbia.

U.S.S. Piedmont (AD17)—Tampa, Florida.

22nd Field Hospital—Camp White, Oregon.

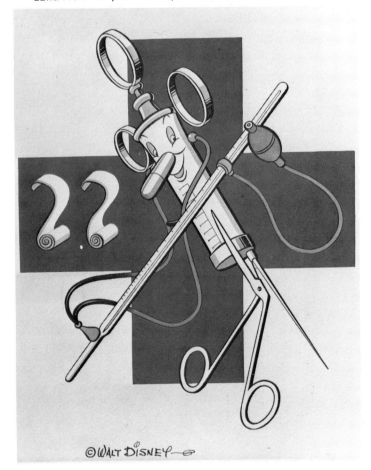

© WALT DISNEY

Division Chaplain Office, 13th Armored Division—Cam Beale, California.

16th Bombardment Wing—Bowman Field, Kentucky.

Mine Division-19, U.S.S. Howard.

44th Pursuit Squadron—Wheeler Field, Hawaii.

63rd Signal Battalion—Camp Claiborne, Louisiana.

© WALT DISNEY

Motor Gun Boat #51—London, England.

17. Photo-Chronology Four

A Mickey Mouse velocipede (tricycle) made in 1934 by the Colson Company of Elyria, Ohio. Perhaps the most interesting feature of this tricycle are the pedals, which are made to resemble Mickey's legs and feet. This firm manufactured Disney character merchandise for only one year, so examples of this item are rare and quite valuable.

Rubber toys by the Sun Rubber Company of Barberton, Ohio. These toys sold originally for 59¢ each.

Mickey Mouse wind-up toys advertised in 1936 by Joseph Schneider, Inc., of New York. The featured toy is a "Rideeo"—the cars go round and round with flashing lights as music is played on the record in the center. The accompanying race cars are driven by Mickey Mouse and Donald Duck.

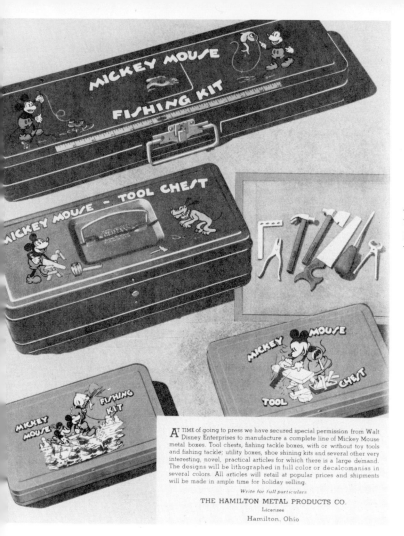

A 1935 advertisement for Mickey Mouse tool chests and fishing kit. These very colorful items were made by the Hamilton Metal Products Company of Hamilton, Ohio. The boxes were sold with and without contents.

Mickey Mouse fishing kits (1936) by the Hamilton Metal Products Company. Boxes were sold originally with and without tackle.

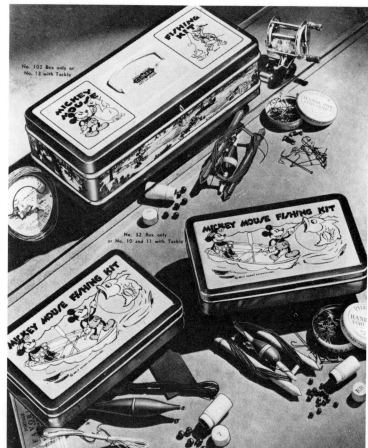

Mickey Mouse tool chests (1936) by the Hamilton Metal Products Company. Boxes were sold with and without tools.

Pull toys and toy telephones as advertised in 1934 by the N. N. Hill Brass Company of East Hampton, Connecticut.

A 1935 advertisement for toys marketed by the George Borgfeldt Corporation of New York.

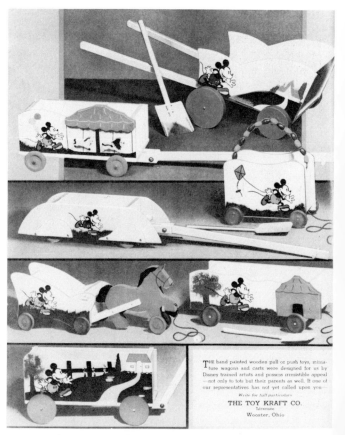

A 1935 advertisement for push and pull toys by the Toy Kraft Company of Wooster, Ohio.

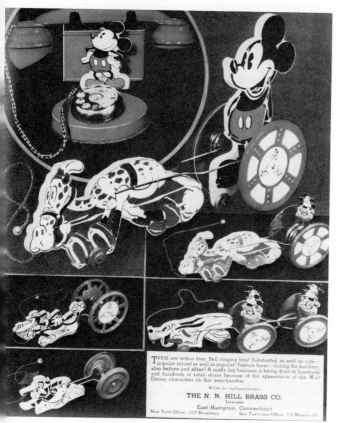

A selection of pull toys and a Mickey Mouse toy telephone as advertised in 1935 by the N. N. Hill Brass Company of East Hampton, Connecticut.

Pull toys (1936) by Fisher-Price Toys, Inc., of East Aurora, New York.

A selection of push and pull toys advertised in 1936 by Fisher-Price Toys, Inc.

Disney character pull toys advertised in 1936 by the N. N. Hill Brass Company of East Hampton, Connecticut.

Pull toys (1936) by the N. N. Hill Brass Company.

Pull toys and telephones (1938) by the N. N. Hill Brass Company of East Hampton, Connecticut.

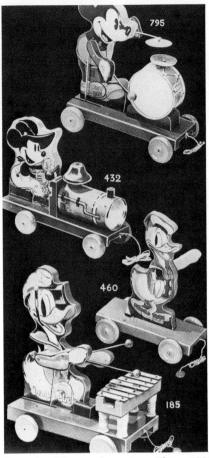

Pull toys featuring Disney characters. These 1938 toys were manufactured by Fisher-Price Toys, Inc., of East Aurora, New York.

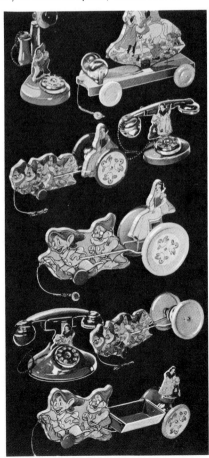

Pull toys and telephones (1938) by the N. N. Hill Brass Company.

Action and pull toys (1940) by Fisher Price Toys, Inc., of East Aurora, New York. These toys sold originally for 25¢ to 50¢ each.

Chime and action toys (1940) by the N. N. Hill Brass Company of East Hampton, Connecticut.

Handmade figures (1940) by the Bert B. Barry Furniture Mart of Chicago, Illinois. All are designed after the Disney character of Pinocchio.

A 1935 advertisement for a mechanical pull toy by Fisher-Price Toys, Inc., of East Aurora, New York.

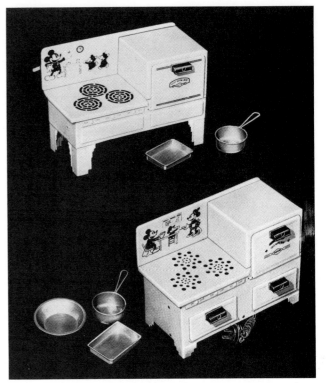

Mickey stoves (1936) by the Metal Ware Corporation of Two Rivers, Wisconsin. These stoves sold for 50¢ to $1.00.

Mickey Mouse popcorn poppers (1936) made by the Empire Products Corporation of Two Rivers, Wisconsin.

Wind-up toys (1938) by Louis Marx & Co. of New York. The featured characters are Dopey (*top*) and Ferdinand the Bull (*bottom*).

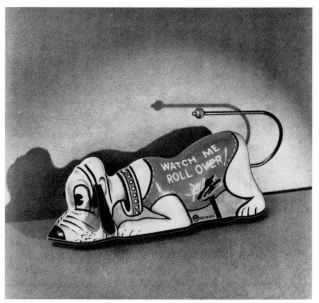

Wind-up action Pluto toy (1947) by Louis Marx & Co., Inc.

A selection of Louis Marx & Company (New York) wind-up action toys as advertised in 1940. These toys retailed for 25¢ to 59¢ each.

A Donald Duck and Goofy wind-up action toy by Louis Marx & Co., Inc. This 1947 toy features Donald Duck playing a drum while Goofy dances.

A tumbling Mickey Mouse toy (1947) by the Marks Brothers Company of Boston, Massachusetts. The toy is manipulated by squeezing the sticks together at the base. This toy sold originally for 10¢.

Plastic Disney character toys (1947) by Precision Specialties, Inc., of Los Angeles, California.

Toy washing machines manufactured by Precision Specialties, Inc., in 1950.

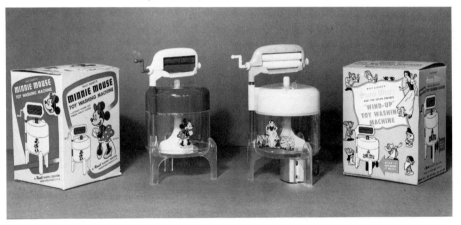

Mechanical Disney character toys (1949) by Mavco, Inc., of New York. These plastic toys have a wind-up motor built in. *Left to right:* Donald Duck, 6¾" tall, $1.00; Mickey Mouse, 6¾" tall, $1.49; and Donald Duck, 5¾" tall, $1.00.

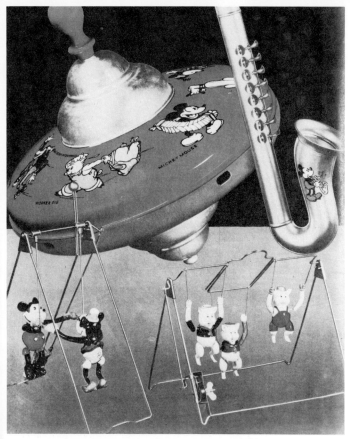

Toys marketed in 1935 by the George Borgfeldt
Corporation of New York.

Mickey Mouse musical instruments (1936) by Noble &
Cooley Company of Granville, Massachusetts.

A 1934 advertisement for Mickey Mouse rubber balls by
the Seiberling Latex Products Company of Akron, Ohio.
The balls were produced in sizes from 4″ to 8″.

Mickey Mouse musical toy instrument marketed in 1936 by
the George Borgfeldt Corporation of New York.

MICKEY MOUSE RUBBER
BALLS
(Sponge Rubber and Inflated)

SEIBERLING LATEX PRODUCTS CO.
Licensee
Akron, Ohio   New York Office, 354 Fourth Ave.

Disney character rubber balls (1949) by the Eagle Rubber Company, Inc., of Ashland, Ohio. The balls were made in 4″, 5″, and 6″ sizes.

A 1934 advertisement for paint, crayon, and sewing sets by the Marks Brothers Company of Boston, Massachusetts.

A variety of print sets as advertised in 1935 by the Fulton Specialty Company of Elizabeth, New Jersey.

Crayon and paint set of 1940 by Transogram Company, Inc., of New York. The crayon boxes are made of lithographed metal, as are the paint boxes.

A ring toss game featuring the animated star of Walt Disney's *Pinocchio*. This 25¢ toy was made by the De-Ward Novelty Company, Inc., of Angola, New York in 1940.

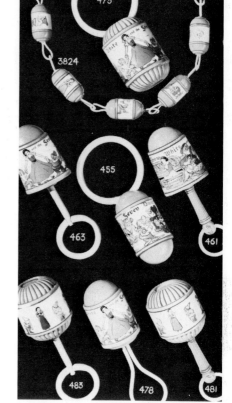

Celluloid baby rattles (1938) by the Amloid Company of Lodi, New Jersey.

Celluloid baby rattles (1940) by the Amloid Company. These two toys retailed for 10¢ each.

A 1934 advertisement for target games and "Bagatelle Sets" featuring Mickey Mouse. These were made by the Marks Brothers Company of Boston.

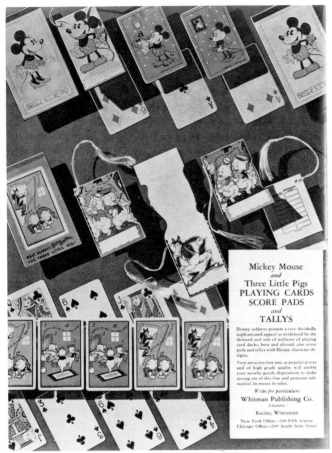

A 1934 advertisement for playing cards, score pads, and tallies by the Whitman Publishing Company of Racine, Wisconsin.

A 1934 advertisement for toys and puzzles with Mickey Mouse and the Three Little Pigs. These were products of the Marks Brothers Company of Boston.

A 1935 advertisement for a "Mickey Mouse Bubble Buster" by Kilgore Mfg. Co. of Westerville, Ohio.

A 1935 advertisement for a battery-operated "Mickey Mouse Funny Facts" game by the Einson-Freeman Publishing Corporation of New York.

A page from the 1935 merchandise catalogue by Kay Kamen advertising cards, games, and the like produced by the Whitman Publishing Company of Racine, Wisconsin.

Page 23 of the 1935 Kay Kamen character merchandise catalogue advertising Disney character blocks by the Halsam Products Company of Chicago, Illinois.

Mickey Mouse cards and games for 1936 by the Whitman Publishing Company.

Snow White and the Seven Dwarfs target game of 1938 by the American Toy Works of New York.

A selection of games (1940) by Parker Brothers, Inc., of Salem, Massachusetts.

Games featuring Disney characters made in 1940 by the Milton Bradley Company of Springfield, Massachusetts.

Games advertised in 1940 by the American Toy Works of New York.

A "Library of Card Games" (1947) by the Russell Manufacturing Company of Leicester, Massachusetts.

Wooden inlay puzzles (1947) by the Judy Company of Minneapolis, Minnesota. This firm made 12 different Disney character puzzles, which sold for $1.25 each.

Two types of jigsaw puzzles by the Jaymar Specialty Company of Brooklyn, New York. Regular puzzles (*left*) contain 300 interlocking pieces and measure 14" x 22" when put together; they sold for 29¢. The "Kiddies" puzzles (*right*) came with large pieces and retailed originally for $1.00 per box of four. These were marketed in 1947.

18. The End of an Era

Make Mine Music was the first postwar feature-length Disney film. In reality, it consisted of a series of short films tied together. It was released on August 15, 1946. Another film, *Song of the South*, was released on November 12, 1946, and was based on the famous Joel Chandler Harris stories of *Uncle Remus*. This film was mostly live action, but it featured three animated Br'er Rabbit stories. In 1948 the film earned three Disney employees two Academy Awards. Allie Wrubel and Ray Gilbert were presented an Award for the best song, "Zip-a-Dee-Doo-Dah," and James Baskett won an Award for his portrayal of Uncle Remus.

On May 27, 1947, another pieced-together film was released, called *Melody Time*. Still another, *Fun and Fancy Free*, was released on September 27, 1948. Then on October 5, 1949, Walt completed and released *The Adventures of Ichabod and Mr. Toad*. The film consisted of two episodes, one based on Kenneth Grahame's *The Wind in the Willows* and the other based on Washington Irving's *The Legend of Sleepy Hollow*. Earlier in the same year the live-action film *So Dear to My Heart* was released on January 19, 1949.

Along with feature-length films, Walt was still producing cartoons. The most popular character was, however, no longer Mickey Mouse. Donald Duck had superseded Mickey as Walt's animated cartoon star. (Mickey had evolved from star to straight man to supporting player; today he serves mostly as a corporate symbol.) Along with Don-ald, Goofy was a popular favorite. It took Goofy a long time to become a star—he was first introduced in the 1932 cartoon *Mickey's Revue*. Two other Disney cartoon stars of the late 1940s were the pesky chipmunks, Chip and Dale. While they first appeared in *Private Pluto* in 1943, they were not named until they became stars in the 1947 film, *Chip 'n Dale*. Pluto was still a favorite too, and he along with the others continued to star in Disney cartoons until 1956, when Walt Disney Productions stopped making cartoon shorts.

With the advent of feature-length animated films, earnings from character merchandise increased sharply. For example, earnings in the first nine months after *Snow White* was released were over $57,000 more than for the whole year of 1937.

With the advent of World War II, there was a drop in income from merchandise initially, because manufacturing was curtailed and raw materials diverted to the war effort. This was a temporary situation, and by the end of 1942 merchandising income slowly began to increase. It is safe to assume that while there was a slight income increase during the war years, it was small compared to what it would have been had more materials and manufacturers been available. The merchandise catalogues, a luxury of nonwar years, were discontinued between the 1940–1941 issue and the one for 1947–1948.

After World War II, the Disney character merchandising business began to return to nor-

236

mal. It took a year or so for conditions to clear up to the point where sufficient raw materials were available in the United States. In foreign countries, because of destruction, it took longer for the Disney merchandising business to get back to normal. England is a good example. Johnsons of Hendon, Ltd., a firm that had been successfully marketing the Johnson Disney Toy Projection Lantern before the war, did not get back into the projector business until 1947. They were not able to catch up with the demand for their postwar Disney Film Strip Projector for several years. Lewis Knight, Ltd., makers of balloons, had similar difficulties in obtaining the necessary rubber for their products.

Chad Valley, a firm that produced a wide variety of toys before the war, was still recovering in 1949. While this firm was able to resume production of some of their Disney character toys that did not require raw materials needed for more essential things in 1946, they did not reintroduce such best sellers as the Roly Poly Toys and the ABC Blocks until 1949.

William Ellis & Co., Ltd., a jigsaw puzzle manufacturer, was destroyed by enemy action in 1940, and most of their valuable sketches and models were lost. Still, after the war the leaders of this firm renewed their contracts and by 1948 were doing a limited business. By 1949, when more raw materials were available, they began to produce Welcom Big-Piece jigsaw puzzles, and these fifty-piece puzzles have been big sellers ever since. Welcom puzzles of the prewar years are very desirable collectors' items and, since they were exported, it is possible for collectors in many countries to locate early examples.

J.U.W. Spear & Sons, Ltd., in 1941 switched from manufacturing games to producing bombs and machine gun parts. After turning out millions of bombs and gun parts, they returned to game and toy manufacturing. One of this firm's biggest postwar toys was the humming top featuring Disney characters.

In England, as in other countries, some firms did not recover from the war, but there were new licensees to take their places. Projects (Coventry), Ltd., was one of the postwar newcomers to Disney character merchandise. This firm produced a fine line of character dolls that are already being collected—especially the movable models.

Perhaps the most exciting of the postwar English firms producing Disney merchandise was Blalmers Glass Fabrications, Ltd., of Watford. This firm began producing Disney characters in glass in 1949. Their glass figures were all handmade in clear glass and decorated with a variety of colors. The workmanship was such that they were gathered by glass collectors as soon as they were released. Since the figures were exported, collectors in other countries have the opportunity of locating specimens. Collectors of Disneyana competing with glass collectors for these fine glass figures find that higher prices are one result of their mutual interest.

In mid-1948, when Kay Kamen's contract came up for renewal, preliminary reports showed that over 2,000 articles bearing the imprint or image of the Disney characters were being turned out and distributed by 150 firms in America and by another 500 in Europe and the rest of the world. It was obvious from the report that successful world-wide development of this enormous business was too great for Kay Kamen to handle alone.

Thus, early in October of 1948, Kamen was given a seven-year contract that limited his territory to the Americas, or as Kamen put it, "My territory reaches from the Isthmus of Panama to Hudson Bay." Walt Disney Productions took over the management of all foreign character merchandising under the overall supervision of Roy Disney, with Oliver B. Johnston, who had long served as studio liaison with Kamen, in direct charge.

O. B. Johnston was born in Ireland in 1901 and received his college education at Salesian College in England, the National University of Ireland in Dublin, and George Washington University in Washington, D.C. From 1926 to 1928 he was an English teacher at Peking French College in Peking, China. While in China he met and married Marion Percival Firor. Johnston joined the Disneys in 1934 and was associated with character merchandising initially and on and off over the years, except from 1943 to 1945, when he served in the United States Army.

On October 28, 1949, Kay Kamen and his wife,

the former Kate Arlene Goldstein, were on an Air France Constellation flying from Paris to New York. The plane strayed from its course in bad weather and crashed into the side of 3,500-foot Mount Algarvia in the northeast section of Sao Miguel Island. The plane was only 90 miles from Santa Maria, the Azores, where it was to refuel. All thirty-seven passengers and eleven crewmen were killed. Kay was fifty-seven at the time of the fatal crash, and his wife was forty-two. Thus a year to the month after signing a new seven-year contract with Walt Disney Productions, Kay Kamen's brilliant career was over. With his death, after seventeen years of innovative leadership in the Disney character merchandising business, came the end of an era.

With Kay Kamen gone, the entire character merchandising business became the responsibility of Walt Disney Productions. It was at this point that the Character Merchandising Division was created.

The popularity of the Disney characters in Italy has almost become a legend. Character merchandise from that country has been extensive since the 1930s. Today the trend continues. The following photographs picture only a few of the many items from Italy. Some of them are exported to this country, but many are not. Fork, knife, and spoon set featuring Mickey Mouse, Pluto, and Donald Duck respectively. The set is silverplated and coated with enamel. It was made by Ganci.

A miscellaneous selection of plastic playing cards made by Plasticards of Italy.

Wall and floor tiles in ceramic by Bardelli of Italy. These tiles were exported.

Six wall or floor tiles by Bardelli.

240

Four Disney character ceramic tiles by Bardelli.

A Donald Duck pedal car by Ampaglass of Italy. This item was exported to the United States as well as being sold in Italy and nearby countries.

Commemorative coins by Cocepa of Italy. These coins were made in gold, silver, and bronze.

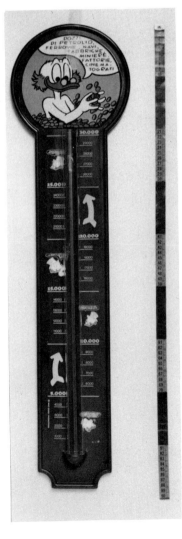

18-17.
A plastic money-meter by Paraphernalia of Italy. This was not made for export and could probably be found in any quantity only in Italy.

Pluto (*top*) and Joe Carioca (*right*), stuffed dolls by Lars of
Italy.

19. Photo-Chronology Five

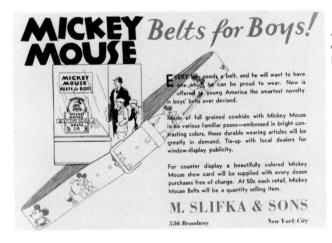

A 1932 advertisement for Mickey Mouse belts. These early character belts were manufactured by M. Slifka & Sons of New York.

A 1934 advertisement for Disney character belts by the Hickok Mfg. Co., Inc., of Rochester, New York.

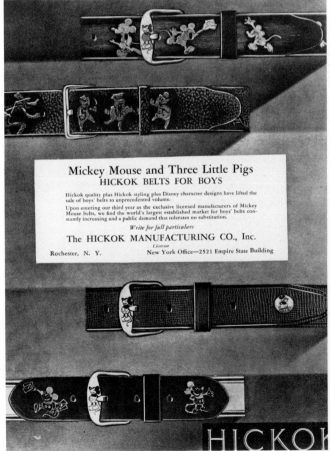

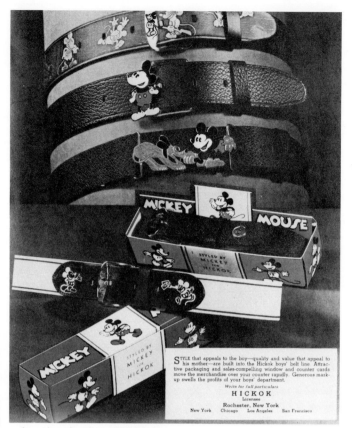

Belts advertised in 1935 by the Hickok Mfg. Co., Inc.
Hickok reissued some of their belts and suspenders using
the early Mickey in the early 1970s.

A selection of Disney character belts marketed in 1936 by
the Hickok Mfg. Co., Inc. The unusual package is also
collectible.

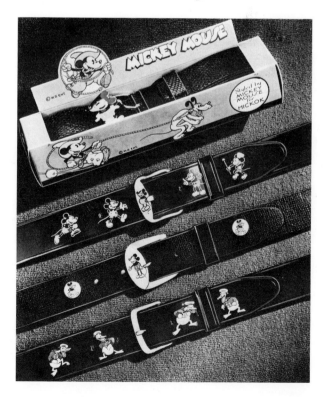

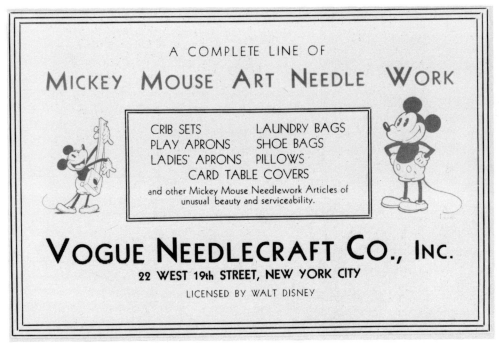

A COMPLETE LINE OF

MICKEY MOUSE ART NEEDLE WORK

CRIB SETS LAUNDRY BAGS
PLAY APRONS SHOE BAGS
LADIES' APRONS PILLOWS
CARD TABLE COVERS

and other Mickey Mouse Needlework Articles of
unusual beauty and serviceability.

VOGUE NEEDLECRAFT CO., INC.

22 WEST 19th STREET, NEW YORK CITY

LICENSED BY WALT DISNEY

A 1932 advertisement for crib sets, play aprons, card table
covers, laundry bags, shoe bags, and pillows featuring
Mickey Mouse.

The All-Star

MICKEY MOUSE

Cast of Characters
by HICKORY

★

A 1934 advertisement for a number of Mickey Mouse
products produced by A. Stein & Company of New York.

BABY PANTS . . . Pure gum rubber with printed Mickey Mouse pattern.

CRIB SHEETS . . . Heavy pure gum rubber, metal grommets and Mickey Mouse design.

BIBS . . . Gum rubber made with Mickey Mouse or Three Little Pigs design.

RUBBER APRONS . . . Children's, Misses', Ladies' in a variety of styles decorated with Mickey Mouse pattern.

PLAY SUITS . . . Percale with printed Mickey Mouse design. Pantie gum rubber lined.

BRIDGE TABLE COVERS . . . Gum rubber, Mickey Mouse decorated.

RAIN CAPE, BERET, BAG . . . for children — Cape with collar has Three Little Pigs pattern, Bag and Beret match.

BATHING CAPS . . . Juvenile — Durable rubber with Mickey Mouse print.

ELASTICS . . . Mickey Mouse printed, and plain elastics packed with Mickey Mouse buttons.

CHILDREN'S HOSE SUPPORTERS . . . Finest quality mercerized lisle elastic — special Mickey Mouse buckles. Metal Mickey Mouse button with each pair.

BABY GARTERS . . . Satin, daintily ornamented. Each on Mickey Mouse card in individual Mickey Mouse box.

CHILDREN'S SOCK GARTERS . . . Fine quality plain and printed ⅜" elastics packed on card with metal Mickey Mouse button.

CHILDREN'S WAISTS . . . Body and skeleton styles. Each with Mickey Mouse metal button.

LADIES' FANCY RIBBON GARTERS . . . Made with satin ribbon and satin bow decorated with Mickey Mouse characters.

LADIES' ADJUSTABLE GARTERS . . . Honeycomb elastic printed with alternating Mickey and Minnie Mouse figures.

COMBINATION HOLIDAY GIFT SETS . . . For Boys and Girls in a wide variety of novel items with strong juvenile appeal.

★

PRODUCED BY A. STEIN & COMPANY

NEW YORK	CHICAGO	TORONTO
330 W. 34th St.	1143 W. Congress St.	Peter & Mercer Sts.

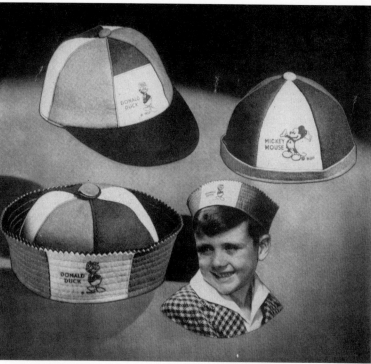

Hats and caps sold in 1947 by the Cali-Fame Hat Company of Los Angeles, California. Characters featured on these hats include Mickey Mouse, Donald Duck, Pluto, Jiminy Cricket, Dumbo, Figaro, the Big Bad Wolf, Joe Carioca, Bambi, and Minnie Mouse.

A Mickey Mouse stocking cap manufactured in 1947 by the Reliable Knitting Works of Milwaukee, Wisconsin. The ad, in the form of a post card, is a collector's item.

Masquerade costumes advertised in 1947 by Ben Cooper, Inc., of New York. These Disney character costumes retailed for $2.98 and $3.98.

A Mickey Mouse costume manufactured by Gertrude Cornell of Blairstown, New Jersey. These costumes were generally sold to stores, theaters, and the like for commercial use—for $135.00 each.

A 1932 advertisement for Mickey Mouse and Minnie Mouse purses by Herz and Kory of New York. These are among the earliest character merchandising items made for Disney characters.

Mickey *and* Minnie Mouse
CHILDRENS BAGS

The Newest Selling Sensation

Handbags that every girl will be proud to carry. Leathers of exquisite finish in an unusual range of colors. Modish shapes convenient to carry, and capable of holding every accessory required by the stylish little lady. Distinction is achieved by the stamp of the familiar shapes of either Mickey or Minnie Mouse on the bag or in the form of simulated ivory ornament.

Every showman knows that his feminine audience is most important to the box office. Mothers are sensitive to the appeal of smart children's apparel. Capitalize on the potential publicity value of creating the vogue of Mickey Mouse Handbags.

Tie Up with Radio Broadcasts and Newspapers

Every radio station in the country has broadcasts of the newest fashions. Be sure that your local station carries mention of your theatre with the news of these Mickey Mouse Handbags. Retailers will want to assist in these campaigns because it means new records on the sales chart. Here is a natural tie-up to increase your feminine patronage!

HERZ and KORY

1239 BROADWAY   NEW YORK CITY

248

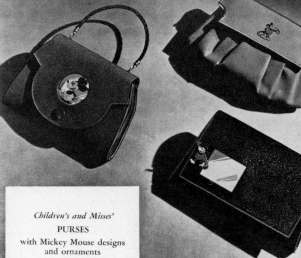

A 1934 advertisement for Disney character purses by King Innovations, Inc., of New York. These rather durable purses have survived in good numbers and are frequently offered for sale on the collector's market.

A 1935 advertisement for Mickey Mouse purses. The purses were made by King Innovations, Inc.

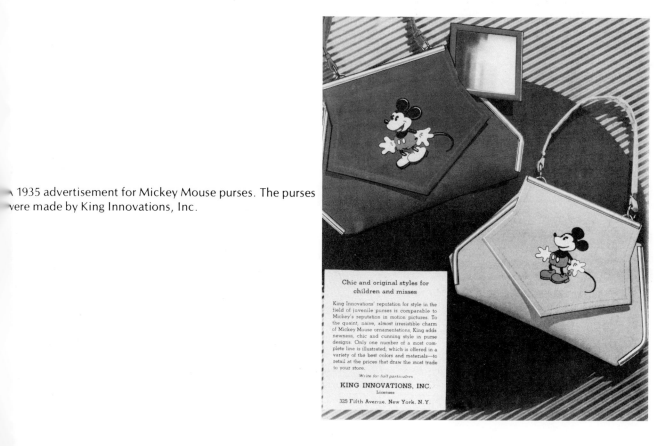

20. Character Merchandising Division

At the end of World War II, Walt was faced with two basic problems: he had to quickly produce a number of films that would earn enough money to keep the studio financially solvent, and he had to produce animated films of the quality of the late 1930s and early 1940s. By 1949 Walt was not only producing a regular stream of films that were doing well, but also, he was in full production on two feature-length animated films, *Cinderella* and *Alice in Wonderland*.

The Disney films were the basis of many of the firm's ancillary activities, and growth in these areas depended heavily on the success of the films. The tragic death of Kay Kamen in 1949 forced a major change in merchandising, that is, the creation of the Character Merchandising Division, which was responsible for merchandising on a world-wide basis. Oliver B. Johnston was an able leader and soon was running the new division smoothly.

On May 4, 1949, *Seal Island*, Walt's first True-Life Adventure film, was released. It became successful, however, only after Walt convinced the film distributors that his innovative film was salable. Reminiscent of the time Walt made the first Silly Symphony, he had to arrange for a short run of *Seal Island* on his own. The film was first shown in a Pasadena, California, theater. Walt not only proved to the distributors, by the attendance records of that first showing, that his new nature film was saleable, but also that he was still one of the foremost innovators in the motion picture

industry. Later, he was presented with an Academy Award for *Seal Island*, which was declared the best two-reel short subject film of 1948. That was the twenty-third Academy Award that Walt, Walt Disney Productions, or studio employees had earned.

Seal Island had little direct effect on the character merchandising business. In fact, until the mid-1950s live-action films were not a significant factor in character merchandising.

On February 15, 1950, *Cinderella* was released. This was Walt's first feature-length animated film since the war. Not only was it a box office success —it grossed over four million dollars its first run— but also it inspired a great deal of merchandise. Collectors newly interested in Disneyana frequently find prewar Disney items not only difficult to locate but also expensive; as a result, many begin with *Cinderella* items and build a contemporary collection.

Five months after *Cinderella* came Walt's first completely live-action feature. On July 19, 1950, *Treasure Island* was released. Because money earned by Walt Disney Productions in England at the time had to be spent there, *Treasure Island* and some subsequent films were made to use up the blocked funds. While this film was not an especially successful one financially, it inspired collectible character merchandise.

Alice in Wonderland premiered on July 28, 1951. Just as Walt had used the profits from *Snow White and the Seven Dwarfs* to further develop his business in the late 1930s, he used the profits from *Cinderella* to produce—at a cost of three million dollars—*Alice in Wonderland*. While the film inspired a great deal of character merchandise, it did not do very well from a box office standpoint.

Another live-action film, *The Story of Robin Hood*, was made in England and released a year later. The next feature-length animated film, *Peter Pan*, was released on February 5, 1953. The Character Merchandising Division licensed a number of manufacturers to produce Peter Pan, Captain Hook, and Tinker Bell items. Just thirteen days later, on February 18, 1953, *The Alaskan Eskimo*, the first in a series of People and Places films, was shown. On July 23, 1953, still another English-made film, *The Sword and the Rose*, was released. This live-action picture was commemorated on character merchandise.

By late 1953 Walt Disney Productions decided to distribute its own films. The Buena Vista Distribution Company was formed for this purpose. To aid collectors in identifying and dating certain collectibles (posters, stills, and the like) which are marked with the name of the film distributors, the following table is presented:

TABLE 4

Disney Film Distributors, 1923–Present

YEARS	DISTRIBUTOR
1923–27	Winkler
1927–28	Universal
1928–29	Celebrity Productions
1929–32	Columbia
1932–37	United Artists
1937–53*	RKO
1953–present	Buena Vista

The first film distributed by the new Buena Vista Distribution Company was a True-Life Adventure film called *The Living Desert*. This film was released on November 10, 1953, and unlike previous True-Life Adventure films, was feature length. While the Disney True-Life Adventure series was not responsible for any appreciable amount of collectible character merchandise, it

* *Victory Through Air Power* was distributed by United Artists.

did collect a number of Academy Awards for Walt. In 1949, 1951, 1952, 1953, and 1954, *Seal Island*, *In Beaver Valley*, *Nature's Half Acre*, *Water Birds*, and *Bear Country* were honored by the Academy of Motion Picture Arts and Sciences for the best two-reel short subjects. *The Living Desert* won an Award, in 1954, for the best documentary feature of 1953; that same year, *The Alaskan Eskimo* won an Award for the best documentary short subject of 1953. Walt's fourth Academy Award in 1954 was for *Toot, Whistle, Plunk & Boom*, which was selected as the best cartoon short subject of 1953. *The Vanishing Prairie* came out on August 17, 1954, and in 1955 it, too, earned Walt an Academy Award for the best documentary feature.

On December 23, 1954, *20,000 Leagues Under the Sea* was released. This film was probably Walt's most ambitious live-action feature, and the public received it with great enthusiasm. Some character merchandise was produced, but because it was a live-action presentation, related merchandise was issued on a rather limited basis. The film earned two Academy Awards in 1955: one for the best achievement with special effects of 1954, and one (to John Meehan and Emile Kuri) for the best achievement in art and set decoration of 1954.

On June 16, 1955, after four million dollars and over three years of work, *Lady and the Tramp* was released. This feature-length animated film, the first since *Peter Pan*, was a significant one for character merchandise. The animated stars, Lady and Tramp, were featured on a number of items that are fast becoming favorites of collectors of Disneyana.

In the first six years of the Character Merchandising Division, O. B. Johnston initiated a number of changes. In the earlier days of Disney merchandising, manufacturers waited until a character became popular before they obtained a license to use the character on merchandise. Because it took several months to work out contract details, produce the new item, sell it to store buyers, and fill orders through jobbers and distributors, new merchandising items were six months or so getting on the market. Johnston reasoned that it would not only be better for the merchandising business but also would help with film promotion if character merchandise could be in the stores by the time the films were released. He further reasoned that the publicity department could increase merchandise sales by including information about new character merchandise in the prerelease advertising campaign. As a result, a campaign to convince licensees and prospective licensees of the benefits to them of being in the marketplace with merchandise at the time each film was released was initiated.

Because of the past commercial successes of Disney character merchandise, the campaign to presell characters was a success. By 1955, the studio was providing the Character Merchandising Division's art department in New York City with material as early as one year before the release of a new film. As a result, the merchandise salesmen were able to easily promote new character merchandise, and the New York merchandise artists were able to help manufacturers in plenty of time to allow the new merchandise to be in the stores at or before the time a new film was released.

Another change initiated by the Character Merchandising Division was to arrange tie-in advertising campaigns in connection with new films. For some of the new films, as many as six firms that advertised on a national basis were allowed to use characters from the new films in their newspaper and magazine advertisements. This activity was limited to new characters; the more established characters, such as Mickey Mouse, Donald Duck, Pluto, Goofy, Chip and Dale, and so forth, were not used in such promotions. Such national exposure of new characters helped sell not only the new films but the new character merchandise as well.

As Walt Disney Productions began to produce television shows on a regular basis, and after Disneyland became a reality, and, more recently, after Walt Disney World was opened, the Character Merchandising Division expanded to include them in its promotions of new merchandise.

As it did in the days of Kay Kamen, most of the direct selling of licenses and assisting of manufacturers was accomplished from the New York office. The information that allowed the New York office to operate was, of course, supplied by the Disney studio in Burbank, California. Information, photographs, art, and other materials pertinent to the merchandising business were sent to the New York and other offices at least every two weeks.

In 1955 the New York office of the Character Merchandising Division was managed by Vincent H. Jefferds. There were six salesmen and a staff of artists. Because of its geographical location, the New York office and its representatives were able to maintain a close contact with the centers of the toy, clothing, and novelty trades.

After contracts were signed between Walt Disney Productions and manufacturers, the facilities of the New York office were made available to the licensees. The art department worked with the manufacturers' production staff in preparing the most appropriate applications of the Disney characters for the manufacturers' articles. The artists created artwork for the manufacturers in the authentic Disney style, and oftentimes they even developed ideas for new articles that could be adapted to the manufacturers' production methods and line of products. After the production of merchandise was under way, the New York office offered manufacturers promotional and publicity services. Information and photographs of the manufacturers' Disney character merchandise were prepared and mailed to the appropriate buyer of every important department store in the United States, to the central buying offices of chain stores, to buying agencies, and to buying service editors of national trade publications and magazines of ordinary circulation. In addition, the New York office worked with licensees and large stores to stage special promotions—for example, Easter, back-to-school, and Christmas; this assistance was in the form of displays, newspaper advertising, and the like.

In the early 1950s the Character Merchandising Division supervised an extensive food licensing program, but with the advent of the Disney television programs it was felt that such licensed products would conflict with the sponsors. It was thus decided to reduce the licensing of food producers. By 1955 only three major food producer accounts remained; a citrus juice account, a cookie account, and a bakery account. A number of the more durable remains of the food-producer era are excellent examples of Disneyana. Collectors of such items should note that Donald Duck was almost always the subject of the food merchandise and that cans, boxes, bottles, and the like featuring other characters are unusual and very desirable.

While in 1951 there were three character merchandising offices in the United States and eighteen full-time Disney merchandising representatives covering twenty-three countries abroad, by 1962 there were twenty-nine merchandising offices. These offices licensed seven hundred manufacturers in forty countries. In 1966 it was reported that eighty million pieces of Disney character merchandise were sold.

The Character Merchandising Division reported, in 1970, a dramatic resurgence in the popularity of "mod" Mickey Mouse merchandise among teenagers and young adults. As it is stated in the 1970 *Annual Report*:

> Although this was also the biggest year in history for our regular line of the more contemporary Mickey Mouse juvenile merchandise, the biggest story rests with the "camp" Mickey Mouse items—those which feature the original design of Mickey as he appeared in *Steamboat Willie* and other early Disney cartoons.

In May of 1972, the Los Angeles offices of the prestigious London art auctioneers Sotheby Parke-Bernet held a first-time-on-record auction of Disney artifacts. This auction enhanced the respectability of collecting Disneyana, and the more than 170 items auctioned commanded a total price of almost $15,000. Many of these Disney items came from the private collection of the heirs of the late Kay Kamen. To give the reader an idea of the current value of Disney memorabilia, some of the items auctioned are listed and the selling prices are recorded in this book as Appendix G.

Not only did the Sotheby Parke-Bernet auction legitimatize the hobby of collecting Disney memorabilia, but it indirectly honored the character merchandise produced under the guidance of Kay Kamen, Oliver B. Johnston, Vincent H. Jefferds (who took over the leadership of the Character Merchandising Division in 1972 after Johnston retired), and William H. G. "Pete" Smith (who took Jefferds's position as head of the New York office and who is currently director of Character Merchandising for the United States).

Today, under Jefferds's leadership, the Character Merchandising Division continues to produce Disney character merchandise that becomes collectible almost as soon as it is released. The fact that contemporary character merchandise is considered collectible is indicative of a growing hobby, and a compliment to Jefferds and the others who, through numerous innovation, have put the Character Merchandising Division in a position of being able to be unusually highly selective about the companies licensed and the merchandise produced.

An early poster proclaiming that a Mickey Mouse cartoon will be shown "Here Today!"

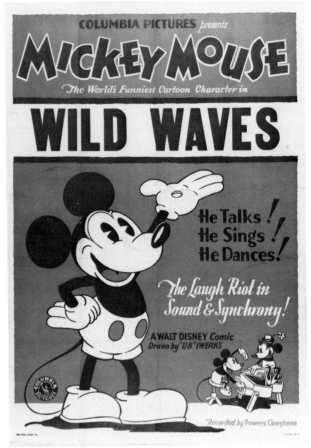

A 1929 lobby poster announcing the Mickey Mouse cartoon *Wild Waves*. Note that this is a standard poster and that the specific film was printed on after the poster was made. Columbia Pictures, distributors of Disney cartoons at the time, had these general-use posters printed by the Otis Litho Co. It is interesting, also, to note that there is a joint credit: "A Walt Disney Comic Drawn by 'UB' IWERKS."

Two general-use theater lobby posters used in 1931 to promote Mickey Mouse cartoons. These posters were done for Columbia Pictures Corporation by the Morgan Litho Company. (The specific film titles were printed on the poster in the space provided.)

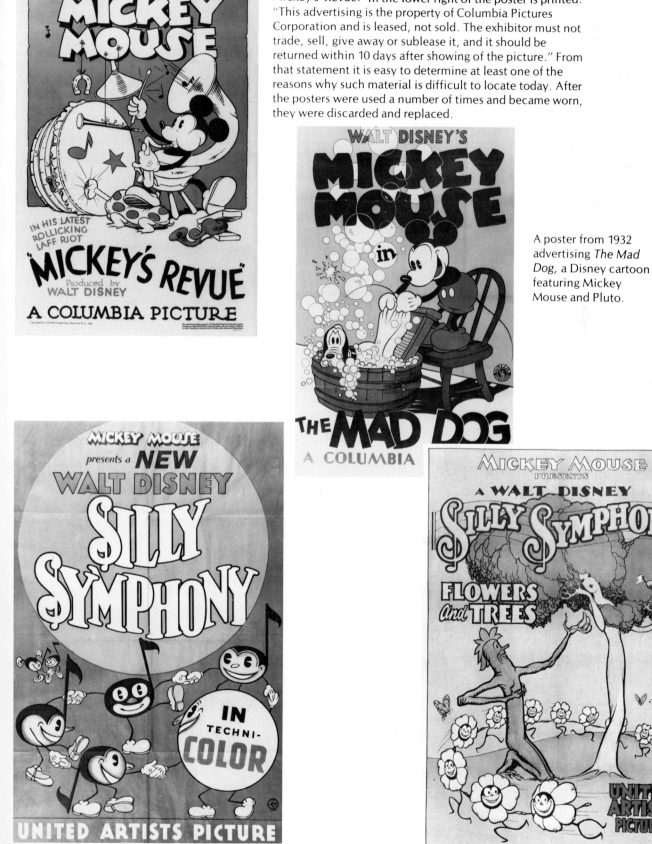

A 1932 theater lobby poster advertising the Disney cartoon *Mickey's Revue*. In the lower right of the poster is printed: "This advertising is the property of Columbia Pictures Corporation and is leased, not sold. The exhibitor must not trade, sell, give away or sublease it, and it should be returned within 10 days after showing of the picture." From that statement it is easy to determine at least one of the reasons why such material is difficult to locate today. After the posters were used a number of times and became worn, they were discarded and replaced.

A poster from 1932 advertising *The Mad Dog,* a Disney cartoon featuring Mickey Mouse and Pluto.

This is a general-use poster of the 1932–33 period. Since no specific film was mentioned, such posters could be used over and over again for films in the Disney Silly Symphony series.

A 1932 lobby poster advertising the Walt Disney Silly Symphony *Flowers and Trees,* the first Disney film produced in Technicolor.

This is a 1932 poster for the Mickey Mouse cartoon *Trader Mickey*. A few reproductions were created recently for advertising purposes by the artists of Walt Disney Productions.

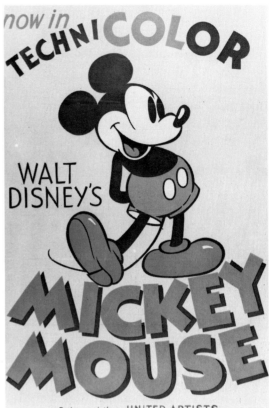

A mid-1930s general-use theater lobby poster advertising Mickey Mouse cartoons in Technicolor. Such posters were frequently used with other posters citing the specific film being shown. This poster was printed by Tooker-Moore Lithograph Co., Inc., of New York City.

A 1937 lobby poster advertising *Snow White and the Seven Dwarfs,* Disney's first feature-length animated film.

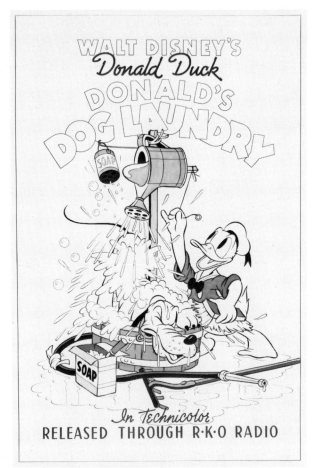

A 1940 poster advertising *Donald's Dog Laundry,* a Disney cartoon featuring Donald Duck.

A 1941 theater lobby poster advertising the classic film *Fantasia,* and music conducted by Stokowski.

This poster was used in 1943 to advertise the Disney film *Victory through Air Power.*

A 1949 poster used to promote the True Life Adventure film *Seal Island.*

During World War II, Disney artists created (free of charge) numerous posters to help with the war effort. This is a poster made to help sell war bonds. It was requested by the state of Connecticut.

A poster made during World War II for the United Service Organization (USO). This poster was designed so that it could be reused and was most likely hung on a bulletin board at the USO facility.

This clever poster was made during World War II by Disney artists to warn of the dangers of walking around outside the "net."

A World War II poster made by the Disney artists to warn soldiers not to "tramp or cut shrubbery near your position."

A poster made during World War II by Disney artists. This poster warns soldiers, "Don't park truck on [the] sunny side of [the] street." Because most of these posters were used overseas they are difficult to locate now, and when examples are found they are generally sold on the collector's market for rather large sums of money.

A 1942 still for the Disney film *Bambi*.

"Stills" are 8" x 10" photographs generally showing a scene from a film. They are used in displays at theaters, and in magazines and newspapers to advertise a film. While stills are generally returned to the distributor after being used, many have not been and are collected today. This is an early example of a Disney still that was used ca. 1932–37.

This still advertises the 1943 Disney film *Der Fuehrer's Face*.

An early 1930s box that was made to contain Mickey Mouse Comic Cookies. Such packages are scarce and hard to find.

Candy is one of the food products endorsed by Disney characters. Pictured here is a box of figural chocolates and three Mickey Mouse Rave candy bars. All were made by the Comet Candy Company of Brooklyn, New York.

A photograph of Walt Disney holding a loaf of Donald Duck Bread. The wrappers, as well as the cardboard cut-outs of Snow White and the Seven Dwarfs, are collectible items.

Various packages of Donald Duck Rice.

1949 Donald Duck Coffee cans are very durable items and much sought after by today's collectors. This product was made by the Goyer Coffee Company of Greenville, Mississippi.

21. Sheet Music and Song Folios

Since November 18, 1928, when the first fully synchronized sound cartoon, *Steamboat Willie*, was released, music has been an integral part of Disney films. The same has been true of Disney television programs. In addition, other activities engaged in by the Disneys have resulted in important popular music; in fact, the *first* Disney song appeared in the *first* Disney book: *Mickey Mouse Book* (New York: Bibo & Lang, 1930). The song was entitled, "Mickey Mouse (You Cute Little Feller)."

Songs that have reached high degrees of popularity began in 1933 with "Who's Afraid of the Big Bad Wolf?" from the Silly Symphony *Three Little Pigs* and include "Some Day My Prince Will Come," "Whistle while You Work," and "Heigh-Ho," all from the 1937 feature *Snow White and the Seven Dwarfs*; "When You Wish upon a Star," from the feature *Pinocchio*, which came out in 1940; "You Belong to My Heart," from the 1945 film *The Three Caballeros*; "Zip-a-Dee-Doo-Dah," from *Song of the South*, a 1946 film; "Bibbidi-Bobbidi-Boo" and "A Dream Is a Wish Your Heart Makes," both from the 1950 feature *Cinderella*; "Chim Chim Cher-ee," "A Spoonful of Sugar," and "Supercalifragilisticexpialidocious," all from *Mary Poppins*, the Disney hit of 1964; "Ballad of Davy Crockett," from the 1954 television program "Davy Crockett"; and "It's a Small World" from the Disney exhibit at the 1964 New York World's Fair.

Three of the most popular songs from Disney films were given Academy Awards by the Academy of Motion Picture Arts and Sciences. These songs were: "When You Wish upon a Star" (1940), "Zip-a-Dee-Doo-Dah" (1946), and "Chim Chim Cher-ee" (1964).

Royalties to the Disneys for their music were not especially impressive until the late 1930s, when the music from *Snow White and the Seven Dwarfs* became very popular.

The tremendous increase in revenue for Walt Disney Productions from music royalties in 1938–39 started a trend. In fact, music became such an important part of the Disneys' business that in October of 1949 the Walt Disney Music Company was formed. Until the formation of this company, which was a wholly owned subsidiary of Walt Disney Productions, the Disneys depended on various music publishers to produce the many songs that the Disney films and other activities had made popular.

The earliest publishers of Disney music included Villa Moret Music Publishers and Irving Caesar, Inc., but with those and a few other exceptions, the Disney songs through *Dumbo* (1940) were published by Bourne Music Publishers (formerly Irving Berlin, Inc.); through *Bambi* (1942) by Broadcast Music Company; through *Make Mine Music* (1946) by Southern Music Publishing Company, Inc.; and through *So Dear to My Heart* (1949) by Anne-Rachel Music (formerly Santly-Joy Music Publishing Company).

By forming the Walt Disney Music Company in 1949 (and later Wonderland Music), it was possible to retain full control of music copyrights and secure maximum benefit from the exploitation of the music contained in Disney films. Collectors of Disney sheet music should be aware that the activities of the Walt Disney Music Company are not limited to just Disney-inspired music. For example, by 1951 the company's catalogue contained such unrelated hits as "Mule Train," "No Other Love," "My Destiny," "Would I Love You," "Once," and "Shrimp Boats."

The sheet music and song folios that collectors gather are most conveniently organized into three categories: (1) songs from *films*—the largest category; (2) songs from *television* productions; and (3) songs from *other activities*. An extensive listing of the published Disney music is offered in this work as Appendix E.

A miscellaneous selection of sheet music mostly from the 1930s. *Top* (*left to right*) "Minnie's Yoo Hoo!"—1930; "What! No Mickey Mouse?"—1932; "Who's Afraid of the Big Bad Wolf?"—1933; *bottom* (*left to right*) "Mickey Mouse's Birthday Party"—1936; "Whistle While You Work—1938; "When You Wish upon a Star" from the 1940 film *Pinocchio*.

A miscellaneous selection of sheet music. *Top* (*left to right*) "Der Fuehrer's Face"—1942; "Zip-A-Dee-Doo-Dah" —1946; "Mickey Mouse March"—1955; "The Ballad of Davy Crockett"—1954; "Once upon a Dream"—1952; and "Chim Chim Cher-ee"—1963.

This is a 1935 advertisement for a song folio produced by the Irving Berlin Company, Inc., of New York.

A 1940 advertisement by Irving Berlin, Inc., for sheet music and song books featuring music from the Disney films.

A selection of sheet music advertised in 1947 by Bourne, Inc., of New York and Broadcast Music, Inc., also of New York.

In 1947 Santly-Joy, Inc., of New York published these
song sheets featuring music from *Song of the South* and
Fun and Fancy Free.

Southern Music Publishing Co., Inc., of New York
published these pieces of sheet music in 1947. The songs
are from *The Three Caballeros, Make Mine Music,* and
Saludos Amigos.

22. Photo-Chronology Six

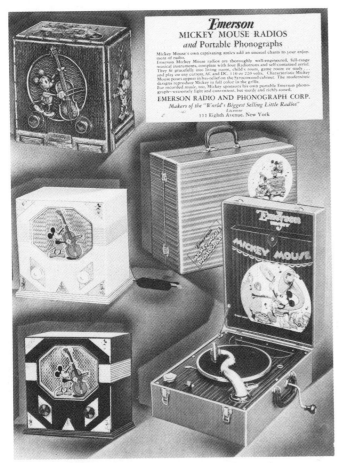

Radios and record players have long been favored items with collectors. These three Mickey Mouse radios and a Mickey Mouse portable phonograph are products of the Emerson Radio and Phonograph Corporation of New York in 1934.

Mickey Mouse radios were such a popular item in the 1930s that the Emerson Radio and Phonograph Corporation continued to manufacture them for a number of years with little or no changes. This is an advertisement used in 1936 and 1937 to promote the four-tube Mickey Mouse Radio. The knobs are different from those of earlier models.

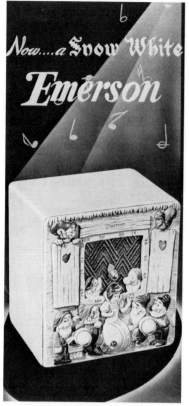

This is a 1938-39 advertisement photograph of a Snow White and Seven Dwarfs radio. This radio was manufactured by the Emerson Radio and Phonograph Corporation.

Phonograph records are avidly collected by many people; collectors of Disney memorabilia must compete with record collectors when trying to gather some of the recordings of music from Disney films. Here are three records by Frank Luther and his orchestra, produced by the RCA Victor Company, Inc., of Camden, New Jersey, in 1934. These are thought to be the first Disney records.

This is a selection of records (sold individually or in sets) produced in 1938 by the RCA Victor Company,

1947 record albums featuring music from *Song of the South* (*Tales of Uncle Remus*) with the original cast, plus Johnny Mercer and the Pied Pipers and *Fun and Fancy Free* (*Mickey and the Beanstalk*). Both were produced by Capitol Records, Inc., of Hollywood, California.

This photograph includes eight Disney albums produced by Decca Distributing Corporation of New York in 1947. They are: *Saludos Amigos* (3 records); *The Three Caballeros* (3 records); *Snow White and the Seven Dwarfs* (4 records); *Pinocchio* (4 records); *Alice in Wonderland* (3 records); *The Happy Prince* (2 records); *Cinderella* (3 records); and *Rip Van Winkle* (2 records). The last three albums feature Walt Disney art, but the music was not part of any Disney films at that time.

Five albums produced in 1947 by RCA Victor, Inc., of Camden, New Jersey. *Three Little Pigs* (1 record); *Snow White and the Seven Dwarfs* (3 records); *Pinocchio* (3 records); *Dumbo* (3 records); and *Peter and the Wolf* (2 records). All are original sound track recordings except *Peter and the Wolf*.

A 1949 advertisement for record albums published by Capitol Records, Inc., of Hollywood, California. These records are 78 RPM 10″ records, which were typical for the time, but the albums were also produced in 7″ 45 RPM discs. The albums pictured are *Tales of Uncle Remus* (3 records); *So Dear to My Heart* (original music arranged and conducted by Billy May); *Mickey and the Beanstalk* (3 records), with a 20-page full-colored Record Reader; and "Little Toot" (single record), from the film *Melody Time* featuring Don Wilson and the Starlighters. Other records of the time by the same company are: "Three Little Pigs"; "Grasshopper and the Ants"; "Mr. Toad."

An advertisement used in 1949 to promote the RCA record album *Dumbo,* which has illustrations and was narrated by Shirley Temple. It is a 3-record album, and was part of the RCA's Little Nipper series, which included some of the records already pictured plus *Pecos Bill* (3 records); *Johnny Appleseed* (3 records); and *Bambi* (3 records). All records in this series were sold in either 10″ 78 RPM or 7″ 45 RPM discs.

Children's records produced by Simon and Schuster, Inc., of New York in 1949. These small records were sold originally for 25¢ each and featured music by the Mitchell Miller Orchestra and singing by the Sandpiper Quartet.

This photograph shows four of the records from the 1940 film *Pinocchio.* They were produced by Simon and Schuster, Inc.

23. Copyright © Walt Disney Productions

In the August 9, 1971, issue of *Time* magazine (page 16) there appeared a short article entitled "The Disney Fetish," which reported one of the Disney organization's latest copyright infringement problems. Specifically, the article discussed an unauthorized series of offensive posters featuring a number of the Disney characters. The article reported:

> The Disney lawyers were unamused. They filed suit in Chicago federal court against eighteen defendants, including local shopkeepers and two distributors, charging copyright infringements, trade disparagement and other offenses.

The Disney organization has been involved in numerous cases of copyright infringements over the years, and by now, with many past decisions in its favor setting legal precedent, the organization has little difficulty stopping those who would violate its copyrights.

Ever since Walt lost his popular cartoon character Oswald the Lucky Rabbit in 1928 because of a contract flaw, he very carefully protected his properties legally. Everything produced by the Disney organization since the late 1920s has been copyrighted or in some other way protected. Of course having things properly protected has not stopped the occasional violator, and, as a result, collectors of Disneyana will undoubtedly have some items in their collection that were produced without the proper permission. The lack of the standard copyright notice on an article is an indi-

cation that the item may have been unauthorized. To some collectors, however, the distinction between authorized and unauthorized items is not a matter of concern.

In an interview on the subject of copyright infringements Roy stated, "We have never fought for money. We have always turned our back on things of this kind, 'Let's go ahead constructively and work on something fresh.' We never were rag-pickers trying to get money out of a situation." Speaking more specifically about an early filmmaker who copied Mickey Mouse and was successfully sued by the Disneys, Roy said:

> We just stopped him. That's all we were out to do. We didn't ask any damages. We even let him finish marketing his pictures. We wanted to establish our right. That's what we were after. To establish a copyright like that is a big thing and that's an important thing to do.

Today that attitude has changed, and when Walt Disney Productions goes to court to protect its copyrights it asks for damages. Otherwise, potential infringers would believe they could infringe Disney's copyrights without much financial injury to themselves.

It is hard to pick out any one case as *the* one that firmly established in the minds of potential infringers the Disneys' right to license their copyrighted characters to manufacture. Perhaps the 1934 case of "Walter E. Disney, Walt Disney Productions, Ltd., and Walt Disney Enterprises against the United Biscuit Company of America, Sawyer Biscuit Company, and the Chicago Carton Company" was the significant case. At any rate, it was an important litigation and one of the early ones. The suit to stop the use, in connection with the manufacture and sale of animal crackers, of the name "Mickie" Mouse, and the representation of Mickey Mouse, the Three Little Pigs, the Big Bad Wolf, and other fanciful characters created by Walt Disney, was filed on July 31, 1934, in the United States District Court for the Northern District of Illinois, Eastern Division.

Gunther Lessing, the chief legal counsel for the Disney organization for many years, gathered numerous pieces of evidence that Mickey Mouse was the artistic creation of Walt Disney and was used in films, books, and comic strips produced by him. In addition, evidence was offered that the Silly Symphony cartoons were introduced by Mickey Mouse and that the Three Little Pigs, the Big Bad Wolf, Minnie Mouse, Horace Horse-collar, Clarabelle Cow, Pluto the Pup, Pegleg Pete, and other unnamed characters were also the artistic creation of Walt Disney. With the evidence presented was proof that the name Mickey Mouse had been registered for trademark as far back as September 18, 1928.

The Disney attorneys then charged, on behalf of Walt Disney and the Disney organization, that the biscuit companies and the carton manufacturer were making, offering for sale, and selling animal crackers imitating Disney characters, and putting illustrations of Disney characters on packages containing the crackers.

An affidavit signed by Roy was offered to support the contention that the animated characters being used by the defendants were the legal property of the Disney organization. He swore that he was a co-partner with Walt when they produced the first group of Mickey Mouse and Silly Symphony motion pictures and that several thousand prints of Disney films had been distributed throughout the world. He also swore that they employed approximately 170 persons to make cartoons and approximately another 30 people in related work. He indicated that the Disney organization produced about one motion picture every two weeks and that it produced a comic strip that was published daily throughout the world; the goodwill and value of the films he estimated to be worth $5,000,000, the comic strip $50,000, and the books $100,000. He swore, in addition, that more than $200,000 had been spent in publicizing their work. He even explained that Walt had, by that time, been the recipient of three Academy Awards; won decorations from Cuba, Argentina, England, and Italy; and that the College Art Association, a branch of the Carnegie Foundation, had exhibited the works of Walt as "distinct creations and works of art of merit and originality."

The case took only four months to litigate and was settled in favor of Walt and the Disney organization when neither the United Biscuit Company of America, the Sawyer Biscuit Company, nor the Chicago Carton Company replied to the charges.

As previously mentioned, in the world of collectors there does not seem to be much concern about whether a collectible item is one authorized or not authorized by the Disney organization. The lack of concern is most likely rooted in the lack of knowledge on the part of collectors about such matters; the vast majority of collectors of Disneyana just take it for granted that the character merchandise and other things they gather are *all* Disney collectibles. And, for that matter, who is to say that unauthorized items featuring the Disney characters are not examples of Disneyana? As the popularity of collecting Disneyana continues to grow, however, there are bound to be more collectors who will at least try to separate their collections into "authorized" and "unauthorized" sections.

While today it is hard to imagine a manufacturer so naïve as to think he could produce Disney character merchandise without permission, in the early days there were some domestic and many foreign manufacturers who did not think they needed permission to copy the Disney characters and put them on toys, novelties, and the like. Firms such as the biscuit companies and carton manufacturer successfully sued by Disney in 1934 obviously knew they were infringing on the Disney copyrights—the fact that they spelled Mickey "Mickie" would support that contention.

Charlotte Clark—the woman who made the first Mickey Mouse stuffed dolls—on the other hand, did not realize she needed permission to make the dolls. The unthinking manufacturers generally obtained a license or stopped production when notified by the Disney legal staff of their mistake; others were, and still are, taken to court and stopped.

Finally, collectors should realize that unauthorized Disney artifacts will frequently be found in lesser quantity than authorized ones; because of this, prices for unauthorized items will sometimes be higher than for the more plentiful authorized items.

A copy of trademark #273,817, dated August 12, 1930, for Mickey Mouse in animated form. Walt applied for this trademark on June 5, 1929.

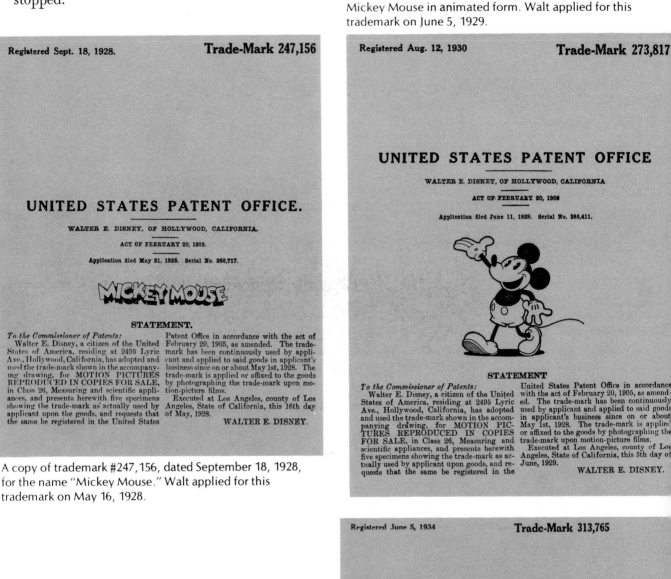

Registered Sept. 18, 1928.

Trade-Mark 247,156

UNITED STATES PATENT OFFICE.

WALTER E. DISNEY, OF HOLLYWOOD, CALIFORNIA.

ACT OF FEBRUARY 20, 1905.

Application filed May 21, 1928. Serial No. 266,717.

MICKEY MOUSE

STATEMENT.

To the Commissioner of Patents:
Walter E. Disney, a citizen of the United States of America, residing at 2495 Lyric Ave., Hollywood, California, has adopted and used the trade-mark shown in the accompanying drawing, for MOTION PICTURES REPRODUCED IN COPIES FOR SALE, in Class 26, Measuring and scientific appliances, and presents herewith five specimens showing the trade-mark as actually used by applicant upon the goods, and requests that the same be registered in the United States

Patent Office in accordance with the act of February 20, 1905, as amended. The trade-mark has been continuously used by applicant and applied to said goods in applicant's business since on or about May 1st, 1928. The trade-mark is applied or affixed to the goods by photographing the trade-mark upon motion-picture films.
Executed at Los Angeles, county of Los Angeles, State of California, this 16th day of May, 1928.

WALTER E. DISNEY.

Registered Aug. 12, 1930

Trade-Mark 273,817

UNITED STATES PATENT OFFICE

WALTER E. DISNEY, OF HOLLYWOOD, CALIFORNIA

ACT OF FEBRUARY 20, 1905

Application filed June 11, 1929. Serial No. 285,411.

STATEMENT

To the Commissioner of Patents:
Walter E. Disney, a citizen of the United States of America, residing at 2495 Lyric Ave., Hollywood, California, has adopted and used the trade-mark shown in the accompanying drawing, for MOTION PICTURES REPRODUCED IN COPIES FOR SALE, in Class 26, Measuring and scientific appliances, and presents herewith five specimens showing the trade-mark as actually used by applicant upon goods, and requests that the same be registered in the

United States Patent Office in accordance with the act of February 20, 1905, as amended. The trade-mark has been continuously used by applicant and applied to said goods in applicant's business since on or about May 1st, 1928. The trade-mark is applied or affixed to the goods by photographing the trade-mark upon motion-picture films.
Executed at Los Angeles, county of Los Angeles, State of California, this 5th day of June, 1929.

WALTER E. DISNEY.

A copy of trademark #247,156, dated September 18, 1928, for the name "Mickey Mouse." Walt applied for this trademark on May 16, 1928.

A copy of trademark #313,765, dated June 5, 1934, for the symbol used to identify "Walt Disney Productions, Ltd." Walt applied for this trademark on February 12, 1934.

Registered June 5, 1934

Trade-Mark 313,765

UNITED STATES PATENT OFFICE

Walt Disney Productions, Ltd., Hollywood, Calif.

Act of February 20, 1905

Application February 12, 1934, Serial No. 347,272

MICKEY MOUSE

STATEMENT

To the Commissioner of Patents:
Walt Disney Productions, Ltd., a corporation duly organized under the laws of the State of California, and located at Hollywood, California, and doing business at 2719 Hyperion Street, Hollywood, California, has adopted and used the trade-mark shown in the accompanying drawing, for BOOKS AND NEWSPAPER CARTOON STRIPS, in Class 38, Prints and publications, and presents herewith five specimens showing the trade-mark as actually used by applicant upon the goods, and requests that the same be registered in the United States Patent Office in accordance with the act of February 20, 1905. The trade-mark has been

continuously used and applied to said goods in applicant's business since January 27, 1930. The trade-mark is applied or affixed to the goods by being printed thereon.
The undersigned hereby appoints Fulton Brylawski, whose postal address is 1331 G Street, N. W., Washington, D. C., its attorney to prosecute this application for registration, with full powers of substitution and revocation, and to make alterations and amendments therein, to receive the certificate, and to transact all business in the Patent Office connected therewith.
WALT DISNEY PRODUCTIONS, LTD.,
By WALTER E. DISNEY.

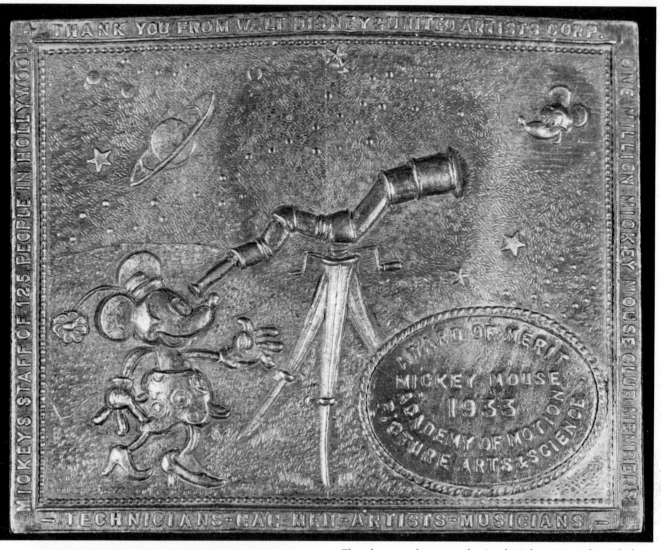

The obverse of an unauthorized Mickey Mouse brass belt buckle. While all the embossed lettering is designed to give the impression that the buckle was made in the 1930s, the buckle was actually manufactured in England in 1973. The exact manufacturing origin of this piece is as yet unknown.

The reverse of the brass belt buckle made in England in 1973. Again, the stamping on this side of the buckle is designed to give the impression that the buckle is old and made in the 1930s—more specifically, 1933.

The obverse (*left*) and the reverse (*right*) of a circular brass belt buckle. The embossed lettering, "Mickey Mouse 1937 Hollywood Cal. U.S.A." on the obverse and the stamped lettering, "Sun Rubber Co USA A Disney Product California USA" on the reverse are designed to give the impression that the belt buckle is old and made in 1937 by the Sun Rubber Company. The buckle is not old. It began to appear on the market in 1971. A check of records reveals that the Sun Rubber Company never made belt buckles.

276

The school supplies and stationery featured are a variety of writing tablets (*left*) and notebook paper (*top right*) and Three Little Pigs stationery (*bottom right*), produced by the Powers Paper Company of Springfield, Massachusetts, in 1934.

Notebooks (*left*), tablets (*right*), and Mickey Mouse stationery produced by the Powers Paper Company in 1934.

A variety of stationery, notebook paper, writing tablets, and notebooks advertised in 1936 by the Powers Paper Company.

Writing tablets (8" x 10") made in 1940 by the Western Tablet and Stationery Corporation of St. Joseph, Missouri.

This selection of stationery and greeting cards was made by the White and Wyckoff Manufacturing Company of Holyoke, Massachusetts, in 1938. According to an advertisement this firm was offering "Walt Disney character note paper wrapped in cellophane with colorful bands or in special gift boxes; combination sets of note paper an an assortment of toy balloons; school stationery including writing tablets of various sizes, composition books, loose leaf fillers, and a 'Dopey' note book; distinctive Walt Disney character greeting cards and the sensational new novelty talking card" (*upper right*).

A sampling of some of the stationery used over the years by Walt Disney Productions and its related enterprises. While it is very difficult for collectors to obtain unused stationery, it is not so difficult to locate letters written on the various stationery.

A miscellaneous selection of the official film stationery of Walt Disney Productions. For almost every film that is produced, a special letterhead is created for the film's promotion. This stationery is almost always very colorful and visually appealing.

A selection of film stationery and examples of the stationery of the second Mickey Mouse Club and the Mouse Factory.

Three examples of "hustlegram" letterheads used by the Character Merchandising Division of Walt Disney Productions. A "hustlegram" is the equivalent of a memorandum.

A 1932 advertisement for Mickey Mouse greeting cards produced by Hall Brothers of Kansas City, Missouri.

Page 22 of the 1934 character merchandising catalogue, featuring a selection of Mickey Mouse and Three Little Pigs greeting cards by Hall Brothers.

These Disney character valentines of the 1940–41 period were produced by the Paper Novelty Manufacturing Company of New York. Those with moving parts are more valuable that those without.

A selection of greeting cards sold in 1947 by Hall Brothers, Inc. of Kansas City, Missouri.

Greeting cards of 1947 produced by Hall Brothers, Inc.

Each year Walt Disney Productions has a special Christmas card printed. This is a miscellaneous selection of the cards used over the years.

An advertisement for Mickey Mouse fountain pens. These pens were made by the Inkograph Company, Inc., of New York in 1935, and they retailed for $1.00. The boxes in which the pens were packed are also collector's items.

Pens and pencils by the Inkograph Company, Inc., promoted in 1936. Note the "Fountain Feed Pen" in the lower right of the photograph.

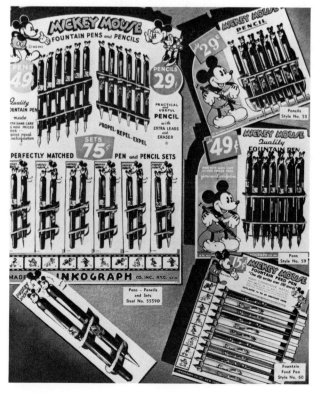

This is a 1932 advertisement for seven different Mickey Mouse pencil boxes. The boxes were manufactured by the Joseph Dixon Crucible Company of Jersey City, New Jersey.

"Mickey Mouse Pencils and Pencil Box Novelties," as advertised in 1934 by the Joseph Dixon Crucible Company.

284

1936 pencil boxes by the Joseph Dixon Crucible Company.

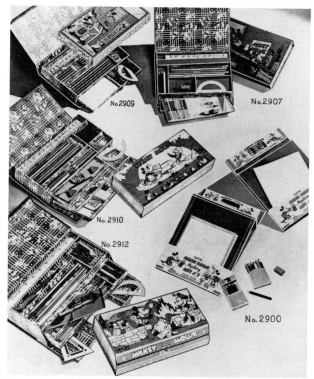

More pencil boxes and a "Mickey Mouse Mystery Art Set" made in 1936 by the Joseph Dixon Crucible Company.

Mickey Mouse, Donald Duck, and Pluto pencils made in 1949 by Hassenfeld Brothers, Inc., of Pawtucket, Rhode Island. The pencils came in solid colors and pin-striped.

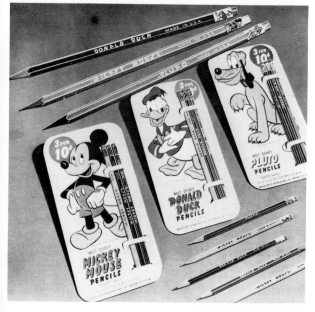

Pencil sharpeners and thermometers advertised in 1940.
These were made by Plastic Novelties, Inc.

An assortment of pencil sharpeners
and napkin rings made in 1938 by
Plastic Novelties, Inc., of New York.

Pencil sharpeners advertised in 1947 by
Plastic Novelties, Inc.

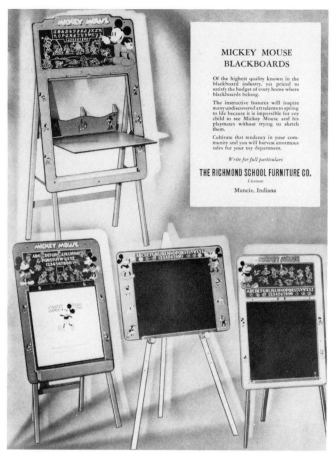

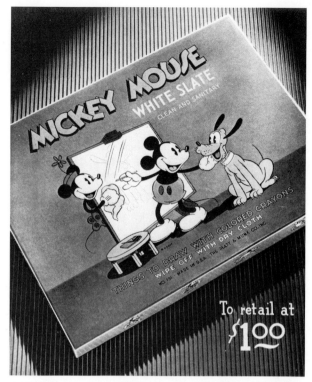

A Mickey Mouse "White Slate" advertised in 1936. The white slate came with specially prepared colored crayons that wipe off with a dry cloth. This was made by the Platt & Munk Company, Inc., of New York.

A 1934 advertisement for Mickey Mouse blackboards made by the Richmond School Furniture Company of Muncie, Indiana.

Disney character blackboards made in 1947 by the Barricks Manufacturing Company of Chicago, Illinois. These and others made by the firm came in 12 styles and sizes and sold originally for $1.00 to $10.95 each.

25. Television Collectibles

When, on Christmas Day in 1950, the first Disney television show was aired, it was not the Disneys' first encounter with the medium. As early as the 1930s Walt had allowed Mickey Mouse cartoons to be used in tests of television transmitting equipment. Since all of their film contracts during those early years had clauses retaining television rights, it is logical to assume that Walt and Roy were in some way planning for a future that took television into account. That is something some of the other studios and many film stars of the time overlooked and later regretted. In the late 1940s, when most other studios were selling their old films to television to recoup losses sustained in failing theater attendance, Walt and Roy refused to succumb to the short-term advantages of such a course of action and again displayed foresight for their future role in television.

At any rate, "One Hour in Wonderland," the first Disney television show, which was sponsored by The Coca-Cola Company, got excellent ratings; and Walt was asked to do a similar show during the holiday season the following year. The second one, "The Walt Disney Christmas Show," also received excellent ratings. Walt had refused offers to produce a regular series of television programs and only agreed to the annual shows because he could do them on his own terms, which meant, at the time, that there would be a commercial announcement only at the beginning and ending of the shows.

By the mid-1950s, Walt was ready to build his famous Disneyland theme park but was having some difficulty raising the necessary money. The American Broadcasting Company offered to make a substantial investment in the park in exchange for a Disney television series. Walt found the proposition appealing and agreed to do his first series of television programs. He decided the programs would be called "Disneyland." In addition to gaining him a large investor in the new park, Walt reasoned, the regular television programs would afford him an excellent promotional vehicle for Disney films and the new park. Thus, in keeping with the format of the new park, the television shows were divided into categories: Adventureland, Fantasyland, Frontierland, and Tomorrowland. There were cartoons, *True-Life Adventure* nature films, multi-episode adventures, announcements on the progress of Disneyland, and some of the old Disney films the Disneys had wisely not sold earlier to television.

The first program of the Disneyland series was shown on October 27, 1954. The hit of the season, however, was a trilogy of Davy Crockett shows: "Davy Crockett, Indian Fighter" (December 15, 1954); "Davy Crockett Goes to Congress" (January 26, 1955); and "Davy Crockett at the Alamo" (February 23, 1955). Originally the idea was to produce a series of shows on American folk heroes such as Johnny Appleseed, Daniel Boone, Big Foot Wallace, and Davy Crockett. For no reason in particular, Davy Crockett was selected as the subject of the first show in the series.

The filming for the three planned television shows about Davy Crockett was shot in Tennessee. After the crew returned from location and discovered they had not shot enough footage for three sixty-minute shows, some sketches of Davy's life were drawn and added to the films to make them the required length. Walt felt that the sketches were dull by themselves, so he asked Tom Blackburn, who had written the scripts, to write a song to go with them. Blackburn got together with George Bruns, a composer, and in approximately twenty minutes they wrote "The Ballad of Davy Crockett." Like the television shows, the song was a big hit. In fact, in just sheet music alone three-quarters of a million copies were sold. In record form, "The Ballad of Davy Crockett," in this country, sold over ten million; four million were twenty-five cent records. Numerous record companies produced their versions of the song, and almost all sold well.

In 1954, before he was selected to star as Davy Crockett, Fess Parker was a little-known actor who previously had worked in science fiction films. By the time the third Davy Crockett show was shown on television in the spring of 1955, Parker was the idol of an estimated fifty-two million television viewers. He toured the United States and a number of foreign countries as Davy Crockett and earned enormous amounts of money. For example, he was paid fifty thousand dollars for a ten-day tour of Australia and ten thousand dollars for a one-day appearance at a baseball game in Baltimore.

For collectors, the phenomenal sale of Davy Crockett merchandise is of importance. By June of 1955, or about six months after the first Davy Crockett show was shown on television, more than one hundred million dollars worth of Davy Crockett character merchandise had been made and sold. Of the hundreds of different items of Davy Crockett merchandise, the coonskin hats were probably the most popular. A collector could specialize in just Davy Crockett items alone.

While the television programs were transmitted in black and white, they were filmed in color. After they were used on television they were re-edited and strung together to make a feature-length film, *Davy Crockett, King of the Wild Frontier,* which was released to theaters on May 25, 1955.

The death of Davy Crockett at the Alamo in the third television program and at the end of the film shown in theaters drew more than fifteen thousand letters of protest a week, for months. The Disneys had no intention of stopping the series, however, with Davy's death. They could not proceed in a chronological way, so they went backwards and filmed two more episodes of Davy Crockett legends. "Davy Crockett's Keelboat Race" was shown on November 16, 1955, and "Davy Crockett and the River Pirates" was aired on December 14, 1955. Both of these television shows were put together and released through theaters as *Davy Crockett and the River Pirates* on July 18, 1956.

By the end of 1956 the Davy Crockett fad had run its course after having grossed nearly $150 million dollars for the Disneys. Fess Parker stayed with Walt Disney Productions for two more years (he was under a seven-year contract, 1954–61), playing parts in such films as *Westward Ho the Wagons* (1956), *Old Yeller* (1957), and *The Light in the Forest* (1958). In August of 1958, by mutual agreement, Parker was released from his two thousand dollar a week contract.

In October of 1955, when Fess Parker was at the height of his popularity as Davy Crockett on the weekly Disneyland series, Walt started his "Mickey Mouse Club" programs. This was a series of daily telecasts that were shown on American Broadcasting Company stations Mondays through Fridays from 5:00 to 6:00 P.M. The "Mickey Mouse Club" was produced as a one-hour show for the first two years (1955–57) and then became a half-hour program for the second two-year period (1957–59).

The "Disneyland" and "Mickey Mouse Club" programs were so popular that in 1957 Walt introduced another show, "Zorro," a half-hour, once-a-week series that ran for two years (1957–59). Like Davy Crockett, Zorro inspired a great deal of character merchandise, which has since become collectible. The live-action Zorro series consisted of thirty-nine episodes based on a fictional book originally published in 1919. Guy Williams played the part of Zorro in the Disney television series. Williams was following in the footsteps of two great film stars, Douglas Fairbanks, Sr., and Tyrone Power, each of whom had played Zorro in earlier motion pictures.

The Zorro stories were written about the period in the early 1800s when Spanish California was ruled by a military dictatorship. Zorro's dual identity as a spineless intellectual during the day and a masked avenger at night, which enabled him "to aid the oppressed and punish the unjust," was a difficult role to play, but Guy Williams did an excellent job for the Disneys. As a result, Williams quickly became one of the most popular television personalities in the United States. The Zorro series was so popular that it enjoyed one of the highest ratings ever recorded at the time and was reported to have reached thirty-five million viewers each week during its two-year run.

Among the most popular of the character merchandise associated with the Zorro series were hats, masks, swords, and capes. In addition there were hundreds of pieces of merchandise which carried the picture of Zorro; all, of course, are collectors' items today.

The "Disneyland" show became "Walt Disney Presents" for the 1958–59 television season and was moved from Wednesday to Friday evenings.

The show was moved from Friday to Sunday nights for the 1960–61 season.

In the fall of 1961, the program was moved from the American Broadcasting Company network to the National Broadcasting Company network. Because of the network change and the fact that the programs were being transmitted in color, the show became "Walt Disney's Wonderful World of Color." That name was retained until the 1969–70 season when the name was once again changed, this time to the "Wonderful World of Disney."

In general, the Disney television programs have not provided the inspiration for a great deal of character merchandise. That generalization, however, must exclude the "Davy Crockett," "Zorro," and "Mickey Mouse Club" shows. Those three programs captured the imagination of the public in such a way as to lead to the mass production and purchase of hundreds of pieces of character merchandise.

Fess Parker (*right*), the star of the Disney films and television shows about Davy Crockett, posing with Vincent Jefferds (*left*) of the Character Merchandising Division in the late 1950s. Behind them are examples of much of the character merchandise that was generated by the popularity of the Davy Crockett shows.

An official Davy Crockett Indian fighter hat made by the
Welded Plastics Corporation of New York.

An official Davy Crockett "Western Prairie Wagon." This
wagon was made by the Liberty National Corporation of
New York.

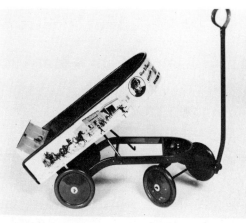

An "exact replica" of the original Davy Crockett guitar. The instrument was made by Peter Puppet Playthings, Inc., of Brooklyn, New York. It came with nylon strings, a plastic pick and fret, and a rope holder, and was packaged in a corrugated suitcase.

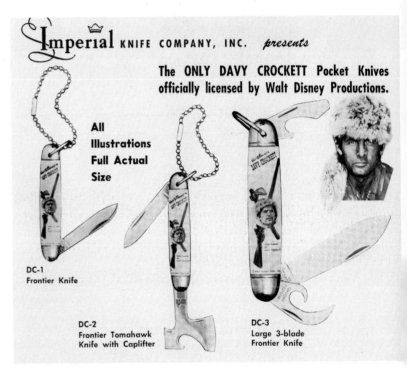

A selection of Disney Davy Crockett pocket knives made by the Imperial Knife Company, Inc.

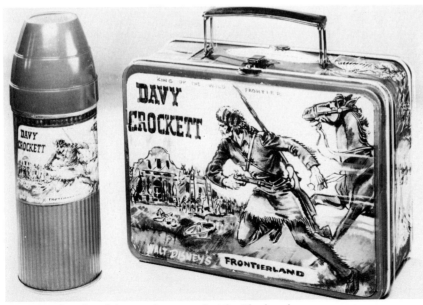

Davy Crockett lunch box and vacuum bottle. The lunch box features a nickel-plated steel handle; the box itself is made of steel. These two items were produced by the Liberty National Corporation of New York.

A Zorro hat with a fold-down mask. This was made by the Bailey Company of Los Angeles, California.

An advertisement for a Zorro target game and water pistol made by the Knickerbocker Plastic Company, Inc., of North Hollywood, California.

An advertisement for a Zorro whip set (mask, whip, ring, lariat) made in 1959 by M. Shimmel Sons of New York.

26. The Second Mickey Mouse Club

The second Mickey Mouse Club premiered on October 3, 1955, on the American Broadcasting Company network. For two years the show was a daily (Monday through Friday) one-hour program that was telecast from 5:00 to 6:00 P.M. For the second two years, the show was a half-hour presentation. All of the programs were black and white.

Although the series ended in 1958, it was reissued in syndication as a half-hour program from 1962 through 1965. Even as a reissued program, it was one of the most popular children's programs of its day. During the 1962–65 period, the show was aired on an average of eighty-eight stations in this country and numerous stations in foreign countries. The audio portions were translated into Spanish, French, German, Italian, and Japanese. Because of this foreign exposure, Disney character merchandise of many types enjoyed large sales in foreign countries and inspired collecting activities abroad. Collecting Disneyana had been popular in foreign lands since the 1930s; but the "Mickey Mouse Club" telecasts served to inspire further collecting. The following table illustrates the extent to which foreign countries were exposed to the popular Mickey Mouse Club series.

TABLE 5

"Mickey Mouse Club" in Foreign Countries

COUNTRY	NUMBER OF YEARS BROADCAST
Australia	14
Austria	1
Belgium	2½
Canada	8⅓
Chile	3
Columbia	1¼
Equador	1
Finland	2
France	9
Italy	7
Japan	3
Mexico	4½
Panama	1
Peru	1
Switzerland	5½
Uruguay	1
Venezuela	1

As already mentioned, the "Mickey Mouse Club" was one of the most popular children's shows on television. During the three-year period from 1955 to 1958, over 350,000 pieces of fan mail were received. Annette Funicello, the most popular of the young stars on the show, received between 3,000 and 6,000 letters each month.

Because of the show's popularity, a quarterly magazine was created. This periodical, *Walt Disney's Mickey Mouse Club Magazine,* had a peak circulation of four hundred thousand for two years. The name was changed in mid-1957 to *Walt Disney's Magazine* and it was issued bimonthly; and for three years subscriptions held at three hundred thousand. When, in the fourth year, circulation dropped to one hundred thousand, the magazine was discontinued. Each of the twenty-two issues that were published is a collectible today, and, as is almost always the case, not many were saved by subscribers; so collectors have to search diligently to locate the few that are available.

In addition to the magazine, the "Mickey Mouse Club" show and its characters inspired three hardbound books (see Appendix D), two of which were titled *Mickey Mouse Club Annual* and one, *Walt Disney's Big Book.* Also, the live-action serials from the third segment of the programs inspired comic books (see Appendix C)—seven one-shot comic magazines and seven series of comic books—and a number of fiction books. There were also thirty-six "Mickey Mouse Club" editions of Little Golden Books, eleven coloring books, and nineteen cut-out or paper doll books—Annette Funicello was featured in fifteen of these.

An integral part of the "Mickey Mouse Club" programs was music. Eight albums were produced to capitalize on the popularity of the "Mickey Mouse Club" shows: *The Musical Highlights from the Mickey Mouse Club T.V. Show, Twenty-Seven New Songs from the Mickey Mouse Club T.V. Shows, We're the Mousekeeters, Walt Disney's Song Fest, Songs from the Mickey Mouse Club Serials, Annette and Songs from Disney Serials,* and *Sleeping Beauty by Darlene Gillespie.* In addition, some individual songs from the albums were made into single records. All of these records were produced by Disneyland Record Co., a record company owned by Walt Disney Productions. These records, as well as all other Disney records, are considered excellent collectors' items.

In addition to the magazines, hardbound books, comic books, and records mentioned above, there was an abundance of Mickey Mouse Club character merchandise produced during the time the show was aired. By February of 1956, only five months after the "Mickey Mouse Club" show premiered, thirty-eight companies were involved in the designing, creating, promoting, and selling of character merchandise inspired by the programs.

Mickey Mouse's head became the copyrighted insignia for the club, the Mouseketeers, and other things associated with the television show. While the basic design of the insignia was specific, it was varied according to its special function on merchandise.

Among the most popular items, which are prized collectibles today, were hats, T-shirts, records, record players, balloons, and "mousegetars." Posters, streamers, banners, logos, insignia, emblems, and so forth used by the firms providing and marketing Mickey Mouse Club merchandise were also made. Examples of the special stationery designed for and used by the Mouseketeers to answer fan mail are also very popular among collectors of Disneyana. Examples of advertisements based on the "Mickey Mouse Club" show, such as those which appeared regularly in *Women's Wear Daily,* are also sought by collectors.

One of the most successful features of the "Mickey Mouse Club" show, and one which stimulated the sale of a great deal of merchandise, was the Talent Round-Up. This feature began in 1956 and inspired a national search for talent. Department stores, markets, and the like sponsored talent shows across the nation. Each child auditioned received a Certificate of Talent (collectible today), and local winners won store merchandise as prizes. The best of the winners were flown to Hollywood to make guest appearances on the show.

In 1962, when the "Mickey Mouse Club" show went into syndication, over five hundred thousand Mickey Mouse hats had been sold. The number of manufacturers producing Mickey Mouse Club merchandise had climbed from the original thirty-eight in 1956 to seventy-five. The syndicated show had an estimated daily audience of twelve million children and was shown on sixty-five television stations, which covered over 62 percent of the market. A survey taken at a national manufacturers' Toy Fair revealed that Mickey Mouse Club merchandise rated first or second in sixty-seven of eighty-two general markets.

Because of the lapse in time, the medium involved, and other variables, it is difficult to compare the first and second Mickey Mouse Clubs. Both were extremely popular, for a time successful, and, most importantly to the readers of this book, both were responsible for inspiring what are considered today a number of collectors' items.

The following is a partial listing of some of the collectibles related to the "Mickey Mouse Club" television show. The most obvious omission is a listing of the hundreds of pieces of character merchandise that were produced and marketed in the name of the "Mickey Mouse Club" show.

TABLE 6

Selective List of Recordings and Publications Inspired by the Second Mickey Mouse Club

TITLE	DATE	ITEM
Annette	1956	Cut-out doll portfolio
Annette	1958	Cut-out doll portfolio
Annette	1960	Cut-out doll portfolio
Annette	1961	Coloring book
Annette	1962	Coloring book
Annette	1963	Coloring book
Annette	1963	Cut-out book
Annette: A Clue to the Mystery of the Missing Necklace	1958	Comic
Annette and Songs from Disney Serials	1958	Recording
Annette and the Mystery at Smuggler's Cove	1963	Book
Annette: Desert Inn Mystery	1961	Book
Annette in Hawaii	1961	Doll portfolio
Annette: Mystery at Moonstone Bay	1962	Boxed paper doll
Annette: Sierra Summer	1960	Book
Annette's Life Story	1960	Comic
Bongo	1957	Little Golden Book (Mickey Mouse edition)
Cinderella's Friends	1956	Little Golden Book (Mickey Mouse edition)
Clint and Mac	1958	Comic
Corky and White Shadow	1956	Comic
Corky and White Shadow	1956	One-shot comic magazine
Davy Crockett's Keelboat Race	1955	Little Golden Book (Mickey Mouse edition)
Disneyland on the Air	1955	Little Golden Book (Mickey Mouse edition)
Donald Duck and the Mouseketeers	1956	Little Golden Book (Mickey Mouse edition)
Donald Duck in Disneyland	1955	Little Golden Book (Mickey Mouse edition)
Donald Duck, Prize Driver	1956	Little Golden Book (Mickey Mouse edition)
Donald Duck's Safety Book	1954	Little Golden Book (Mickey Mouse edition)
Goofy, Movie Star	1956	Little Golden Book (Mickey Mouse edition)
The Hardy Boys	1956	One-shot comic magazine
The Hardy Boys Coloring Book	1957	Coloring book
The Hardy Boys in Mystery of Ghost Farm	1957	Comic
The Hardy Boys in Secret of the Old Mill	1957	Comic
Jiminy Cricket	1957	One-shot comic magazine
Jiminy Cricket	1958	Comic
Jiminy Cricket	1956	Little Golden Book (Mickey Mouse edition)
Jimmie Dodd Coloring Book	1956	Coloring book
Jimmie Dodd Magic Carpet Coloring Book	1957	Coloring book
Linda (Hughes)	1958	Doll portfolio
Little Golden Book, Mickey Mouse edition	1955	Little Golden Book
Little Man of Disneyland	1955	Little Golden Book (Mickey Mouse edition)
Mickey Mouse Album	1962	One-shot comic
Mickey Mouse and Pluto Pup	1953	24-page Mickey Mouse book

TABLE 6 *(continued)*

TITLE	DATE	ITEM
Mickey Mouse and the Missing Mouseketeers	1956	Little Golden Book (Mickey Mouse edition)
Mickey Mouse Club Coloring Book (two designs)	1956	Coloring book
Mickey Mouse Club Coloring Book (third design)	1957	Coloring book
Mickey Mouse Club Giant Funtime Coloring Book	1956	Coloring book
Mickey Mouse Club Scrap Book (first design)	1955	Scrapbook
Mickey Mouse Club Scrap Book (second design)	1957	Scrapbook
Mickey Mouse Coloring Book	1955	Coloring book
Mickey Mouse Dot-to-Dot Coloring Book	1957	Coloring book
Mickey Mouse Flies the Christmas Mail	1956	Little Golden Book (Mickey Mouse edition)
Mickey Mouse Stamp Book	1956	Stamp book
Mother Goose	1953	Little Golden Book (D-51 is Mickey Mouse edition. D-79 is reprint of D-51)
Mother Goose	1956	Little Golden Book (Mickey Mouse edition)
Mousekartoon Coloring Book	1956	Coloring book
Mouseketeers	1957	Cut-out book
Mouseketeers	1963	Cut-out book
Mouseketeers Try-out Time	1956	Tell-a-Tale Book
The Musical Highlights from the Mickey Mouse Club T.V. Show	1958	Recording
The Nature of Things	1956	One-shot comic magazine
Perri	1956	Little Golden Book (Mickey Mouse edition)
Peter and the Wolf	1956	Little Golden Book (Mickey Mouse edition)
Robin Hood	1955	Little Golden Book (Mickey Mouse edition)
Sleeping Beauty by Darlene Gillespie	1958	Recording
Songs for All the Holidays by the Mouseketeers	1958	Recording
Songs from the Mickey Mouse Club Serials	1958	Recording
Spin and Marty	1956	Book
Spin and Marty	1956	One-shot comic magazine
Spin and Marty	1957	One-shot comic magazine
Spin and Marty and Annette: Pirates of Shell Island	1957	Comic
Spin and Marty Coloring Book	1956	Coloring book
Spin and Marty: Trouble at the Triple R	1958	Book
Starlets	1961	Doll kit. Four stand-up dolls with kits
Twenty-Seven New Songs from the Mickey Mouse Club T.V. Show	1958	Recording
Walt Disney's Big Book	1958	Book by Whitman (from *Walt Disney's Magazine*)
Walt Disney's Mickey Mouse Club Annual	1956	Book by Simon & Schuster (from first four issues of *Walt Disney's Magazine*)
Walt Disney's Mickey Mouse Club Annual	1957	Book by Whitman (from the most recent issues of *Walt Disney's Magazine*)
Walt Disney's Mickey Mouse Club Box of 12 Books to Color	1955	Coloring book
Walt Disney's Mickey Mouse Club Magazine	1956	Volume 1, no. 1 (Winter)
	1956	Volume 1, no. 2 (Spring)
	1956	Volume 1, no. 3 (Summer)
	1956	Volume 1, no. 4 (Fall)
	1956	Volume 2, no. 1 (December)
	1957	Volume 2, no. 2 (February)
	1957	Volume 2, no. 3 (April)
Walt Disney's Mickey Mouse Club Magazine, changed to *Walt Disney's Magazine*	1957	Volume 2, no. 4 (June)
	1957	Volume 2, no. 5 (Sept.)
	1957	Volume 2, no. 6 (Dec.)
	1958	Volume 3, no. 1 (Jan.)
	1958	Volume 3, no. 2 (March)
	1958	Volume 3, no. 3 (May)
	1958	Volume 3, no. 4 (July)

Table 6 (*continued*)

Walt Disney's Magazine	1958	Volume 3, no. 5 (Sept.)
	1958	Volume 3, no. 6 (Nov.)
	1959	Volume 4, no. 1 (Jan.)
	1959	Volume 4, no. 2 (March)
	1959	Volume 4, no. 3 (May)
	1959	Volume 4, no. 4 (July)
	1959	Volume 4, no. 5 (Sept.)
	1959	Volume 4, no. 6 (Nov.)
Walt Disney's Song Fest	1958	Recording
We're the Mouseketeers	1957	Recording

These are the official emblems of the Mickey Mouse Club (*top*) and the Mouseketeers (*bottom*). Such emblems were often employed on character merchandise from the mid-1950s on. On both emblems the outside ring was done in bright red and the remainder of the emblem was black and white.

A picture of the members of television's Mickey Mouse Club. Pictured are Bobby Burgess, Margene Storey, Lonnie Burr, Eileen Diamond, Larry Larsen, Tommy Cole, Cheryl Holdridge, Darlene Gillespie, Charley Laney, Sharon Baird, Annette Funicello, Karen Pendleton, Cubby O'Brien, Sherry Allen, Dennis Day, Jay Jay Solari, Doreen Tracey, and chief Mouseketeer Jimmie Dodd (*center rear*). This photograph was taken in 1955, the year the program was first shown on television.

This 1958 photograph of some of the members of the Mickey Mouse Club illustrates how quickly the Mouseketeers grew.

This $2.00 "Mousegetar-Jr." was made by Mattel, Inc. By turning the crank one could hear the official mouseketeer song. The instrument measures 14" x 5" x 1½".

This is a "Mousegetar" made in Los Angeles, California, by Mattel, Inc. The 23" long, 8" wide, and 2½" deep instrument was red. It had a face of Mickey Mouse on the front. The "getar" was packaged in a carrying case with a Mickey Mouse Club song instruction book. The instrument retailed for $4.00.

299

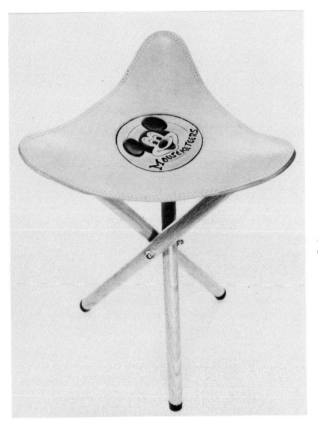

Mickey Mouse Club western saddle stool made by the Chambers Belt Company of Phoenix, Arizona. It was produced in two sizes: 11″ and 15″.

An advertisement for a Mickey Mouse Club dinner set by Molded Plastics, Inc., of Cleveland, Ohio.

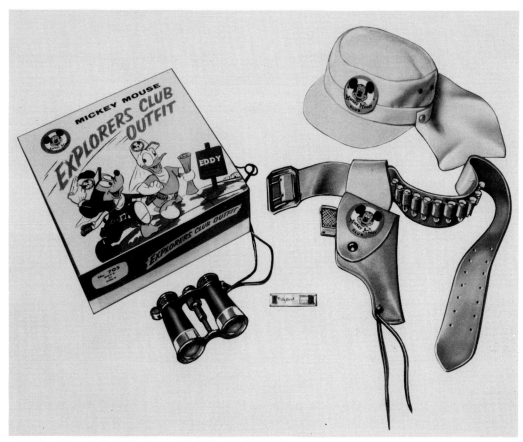

A Mickey Mouse Club "Explorers Club Outfit." Such items were sold mostly at Disneyland.

A Mouseketeer's "Western Outfit" by the L. M. Eddy Manufacturing Company, Inc., of Framingham, Massachusetts. The set came with a hat, tie, badge, belt, two guns, and two holsters.

An advertisement for Mickey Mouse Club coaster wagons and scooter. These items were manufactured by the Radio Steel & Manufacturing Company of Chicago, Illinois.

Mickey Mouse Club "Band Leader Outfit" by the L. M. Eddy Manufacturing Company, Inc.

Mickey Mouse Club "Mouseketeer Ears." These were made by the Empire Plastic Corporation of Tarboro, North Carolina.

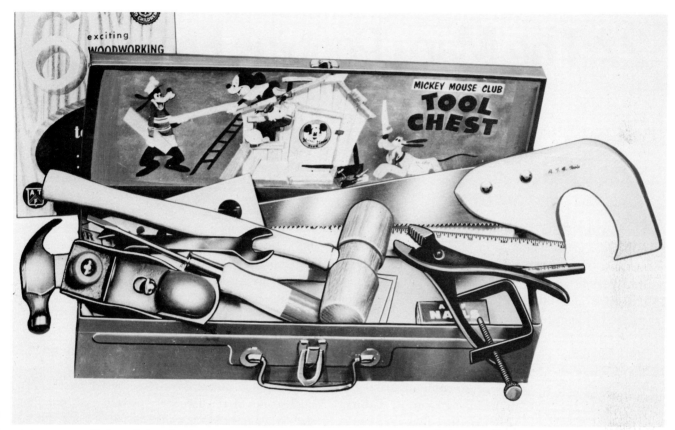

Mickey Mouse Club tool chest by the American Toy & Furniture Company, Inc., of Chicago, Illinois. Box measures 14¼" x 5" x 2½".

27. The Mary Poppins Era

Most of the Disney films since the mid-1950s have not had a great influence on the collecting of Disneyana. There have been, however, some films of this period which have inspired character merchandise and other things that today are considered collectible.

Sleeping Beauty, released on January 29, 1959, stimulated the character merchandising efforts of the Character Merchandising Division. The film was produced at a cost of $6 million, making it the most expensive animated cartoon of all time. Although the distribution of this film was not a great financial success, from the collectors' viewpoint, *Sleeping Beauty* was a successful motion picture.

In 1959, incidentally, Ub Iwerks made another major contribution to the art of animation in general and to Walt Disney Productions in particular. In that year he completed work on a process by which animators' drawings could be transferred directly to celluloids with the aid of a modified Xerox camera. This innovation eliminated the time-consuming and expensive step of inking.

The first feature-length film to utilize Iwerks's new process was *101 Dalmatians*, which was released on January 25, 1961, after three years work by approximately three hundred animators and $4 million had been expended. Coincidentally, this film was the next film after *Sleeping Beauty* that inspired an appreciable amount of collectible items.

It was not until February 22, 1964, that another film with merchandising potential came along. Unfortunately the film, *The Sword in the Stone*, did not live up to expectations. While it grossed a rather healthy $4.5 million, it did not sell very much in the way of what are today considered collectibles.

The biggest Disney hit and one of the greatest films in the history of the motion picture industry was *Mary Poppins*. This film, based on the classical works of the famous Australian author Pamela Travers, was prereleased by Walt Disney Productions on August 29, 1964. Both critically and financially, this film proved to be the best film the Disneys ever produced. It earned six awards from the Academy of Motion Picture Arts and Sciences, and grossed world-wide the fantastic sum of $45 million on its first release.

The film was also one of the most successful from a collecting standpoint. While it has historically been the completely animated films that have inspired the most character merchandise and other collectibles, *Mary Poppins* proved to be a conspicuous exception in that the film featured both live action and animation. Forty-six manufacturers were licensed to produce numerous Mary Poppins merchandise. The following table lists these manufacturers and the articles they produced.

TABLE 7

Licensed Manufacturers of Mary Poppins Merchandise

MANUFACTURER	LOCATION	PRODUCT(S)
Admiral Plastics Corp.	Brooklyn, N.Y.	Plastic cups, mugs, bowls
Alyssa Originals	New York, N.Y.	Dresses, sizes 0 to 14
American Telicard Corp.	Phoenix, Ariz.	Audiovisual greeting card
Arden Jewelry Manufacturing Co.	Providence, R.I.	Lockets, pendants, pins, pearls
Aristocrat Leather Products, Inc.	New York, N.Y.	Wallets, handbags, vinyl plastic stationery accesories
Banner Curtain Co.	New York, N.Y.	Cotton curtains, drapes, bedspreads
Benay-Albee Novelty Co.	Maspeth, N.Y.	Novelty hats
Childcraft Coat Co., Inc.	New York, N.Y.	Coats, coat and hat sets
Colgate-Palmolive Co.	New York, N.Y.	"Soaky" liquid bath soap
Ben Cooper, Inc.	Brooklyn, N.Y.	Masquerade costumes, masks
Deluxe Game Corp.	Wilkes Barre, Pa.	Toy chests
Dennison Manufacturing Co.	Framingham, Mass.	Decorative party prints
Dexter Manufacturing Co.	Providence, R.I.	Charm bracelets, necklaces
Disneyland Record Co.	Burbank, Calif.	Records, albums, record readers, story tellers
Dolly Toy Co.	Tipp City, Ohio	Die-cut wall plaques
Donald F. Duncan, Inc.	Evanston, Ill.	Kites
Empire Plastics, Inc.	Tarboro, N.C.	Plastic play items
E-Z Mills, Inc.	New York, N.Y.	Knitted cotton underwear, sleepwear, layettes
Geisha Robe Co.	New York, N.Y.	Robes, nightwear
A. C. Gilbert Co.	New Haven, Conn.	Placemats
Gund Manufacturing Co.	New York, N.Y.	Stuffed toys, hand puppets, marionettes
Hassenfeld Bros., Inc.	Pawtucket, R.I.	Coloring activities, pencil boxes, numbered coloring sets
F. Hollander & Son, Inc.	New York, N.Y.	Children's umbrellas
Horsman Doll Co.	New York, N.Y.	Dolls
Ideal Toy Corp.	Hollis, N.Y.	Inflatable toy figures, playhouse
Jaymar Specialty Co.	Brooklyn, N.Y.	Jigsaw puzzles
Lestoil Products	Holyoke, Mass.	Scuffy Shoe Polish
Lido Corp.	Bronx, N.Y.	Dancing magnetic dolls
Louis Marx & Co., Inc.	New York, N.Y.	Twistables, wind-up and friction mechanical, metal, and molded plastic toys, china tea set
Oak Rubber Co.	Ravenna, Ohio	Balloons, play balls
Parker Brothers, Inc.	Salem, Mass.	Games
Ross Products, Inc.	New York, N.Y.	Party candles
Sawyer's, Inc.	Portland, Ore.	3-D film cards, viewers, cartoon theater
Shirtees, Inc.	New York, N.Y.	Children's knitted polo shirts, infants' creepers
Silvestri Art Manufacturing Co.	Chicago, Ill.	Disney character displays
Standard Plastic Products, Inc.	South Plainfield, N.J.	Children's luggage, doll cases, cosmetic cases
Stetson Corp.	New York, N.Y.	Melmac dinnerware
Transogram Co., Inc.	New York, N.Y.	Action games
Valtex Fabrics, Inc.	New York, N.Y.	Val-dolls
Victor Cohen, Inc.	New York, N.Y.	Hats
Watkins-Strathmore Co.	Racine, Wis.	Magic slate items, activity sets, puzzles
Wells Lamont Corp.	Chicago, Ill.	Children's gloves and gauntlets, knitted mittens
Western Tablet & Stationery Corp.	St. Joseph, Mo.	Writing tablets, art paper, scribble pads, stationery

In addition, three publishers produced eighteen books and related items featuring Mary Poppins. The specific items are as follows.

TABLE 8

Mary Poppins Publications in 1964

PUBLISHER	ITEM	RETAIL PRICE	INITIAL PRINTING
Golden Press	Big Golden book	$1.00	50,000
Golden Press	Two Little Golden books	$ .29 ea.	500,000
Golden Press	Cut-Out coloring book	$ .29	200,000
Golden Press	Doll book	$ .29	250,000
Golden Press	Panorama book	$1.00	100,000
Golden Press	Look-inside book		100,000
Golden Press	Story book with photographs	$2.00	50,000
Gold Key	Comic magazines (2)	$ .25 $ .12	1,000,000
Whitman Publishing Co.	Giant Tell-a-Tale book	$1.00	100,000
Whitman Publishing Co.	Boy/girl fiction	$1.00	250,000
Whitman Publishing Co.	Top-top tale	$ .29	250,000
Whitman Publishing Co.	Frame tray puzzles	$ .29	400,000
Whitman Publishing Co.	Magic slates	$ .29	200,000
Whitman Publishing Co.	Coloring book	$ .29	300,000
Whitman Publishing Co.	Sticker Fun book	$ .59	300,000
Whitman Publishing Co.	Magic Doll box	$1.00	100,000
Whitman Publishing Co.	Doll portfolio	$ .59	300,000
Whitman Publishing Co.	Paintless paint and dot-to-dot book	$ .59	100,000

In keeping with the philosophy of the Character Merchandising Division, arrangements were made with four national advertisers for tie-in advertising campaigns in connection with *Mary Poppins*. These campaigns in themselves produced a number of Walt Disney collectibles.

Capitalizing on the hit tune from *Mary Poppins*, "A Spoonful of Sugar," the National Sugar Company initiated an intensive merchandising campaign offering a silver spoon for 50¢ and proof of purchase of their product. In addition to a direct mailing to 10,000 sugar brokers, food brokers, and grocery executives, $200,000 was spent on television advertising. One-half-page advertisements, in color, were run in 21 Sunday Comics sections and 10 million bags or boxes of sugar carried the news of the promotion. To complete the campaign, numerous point-of-purchase displays featuring 100,000 coupon pads were placed in supermarkets across the nation, and 5 full-page advertisements were placed in 5 different food or supermarket trade publications. While, of course, the spoon is the prime collectible involved in this promotion, the advertisements are considered desirable by collectors.

The National Biscuit Company (Nabisco) joined by offering a plastic device which showed either Mary Poppins or Bert, the chimney sweep, popping out of a roof-top chimney. These premiums were promoted on over 4 million Nabisco packages, through point-of-purchase displays, in trade advertising, and through $250,000 worth of television advertising. Again, the collectible of most interest is the plastic premium, but the packages and other advertising are interesting.

Because of the chimney sweep theme of *Mary Poppins*, the G. N. Coughlan Company promoted their Chimney Sweep Liquid and Chimney Sweep Fireplace Powder with a Mary Poppins doll premium offer. The offer was promoted in national magazines at a cost of seventy-five thousand dollars, with six-hundred-line newspaper advertisements through numerous point-of-purchase displays, with full-page and cover advertisements in trade magazines, and by a special mailing to eight thousand jobbers, hardware retailers, and department stores.

McCall's also joined with tie-in advertising by offering a seventeen-inch Mary Poppins doll pat-

28. Photo-Chronology Eight

A 1934 advertisement for a Mickey Mouse playhouse by the O. B. Andrews Company of Chattanooga, Tennessee. The playhouse came in 3 sizes and were made of fiberboard.

A 1934 advertisement for Mickey Mouse athletic goods by the Draper-Maynard Company of Plymouth, New Hampshire.

A 1935 advertisement for Mickey Mouse rugs. These rugs were produced by the Alexander Smith & Sons Carpet Company, New York.

Mickey Mouse pocket knives by the Imperial Knife Company of Providence, Rhode Island. These 1936 knives are desirable collector's items today, and for some unexplained reason none of the four styles pictured is plentiful. It has been speculated that in the 1930s few parents would let their children have a knife, so few were actually marketed.

Mickey Mouse giveaways sold in 1936 by Kay Kamen, Ltd., of New York. While all of the items are of interest to collectors today, the pin-back buttons (*lower right*) are of special interest.

Mirrors featuring Mickey and Minnie Mouse made in 1936 by Theo. Diamond, Inc., of New York.

A Mickey Mouse candy machine sold in 1938 by Hamilton Enterprises, Inc., of Kansas City, Missouri.

In 1938 these Mickey Mouse flower seeds were produced by the famous Germain Seed & Plant Company of Los Angeles, California. There were two sets of three packages each. Set 1: Mickey Mouse zinnias, Donald Duck cosmos, and Pluto marigolds. Set 2: Princess Snow White sweet peas, Wicked Queen zinnias, and Seven Dwarf varieties named for each of the dwarfs.

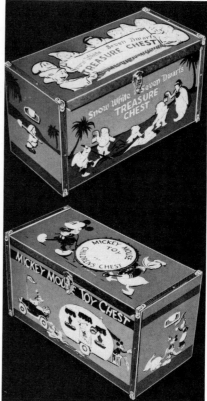

A 1939 toy chest assortment by Odora Company, Inc., of New York. The chests are made of wood and have metal corners, a lock, and handles.

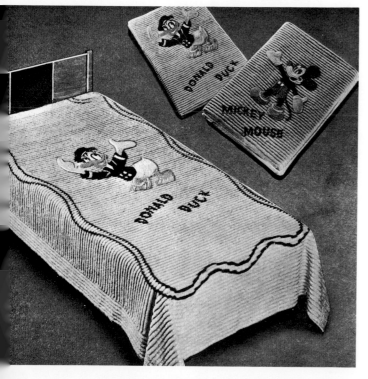

Bedspreads advertised in 1947 by Calorama, Inc., of Los Angeles, California. The spreads came in three sizes (crib, youth, and twin). These chenille spreads came with Mickey Mouse, Donald Duck, or Pluto on them.

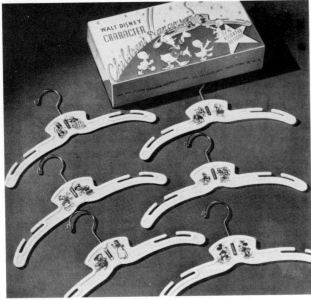

Children's plastic clothes hangers featuring Disney characters. These hangers were made in 1947 by the All-Styles Hanger Company, Inc., of New York.

A globe featuring Disney characters made by Rand McNally and Company.

A weather forecaster by The Weatherman of Chicago, Illinois. These sold originally for $1.00 in the late 1940s.

Christmas ornaments sold in 1949 by the North American Glass Corporation of New York. The balls, featuring Disney characters, came in three sizes: 2¼" ball, 2 for 15¢; 2 5/8" ball, 10¢ each; and 2 7/8" ball, 15¢ each.

Easter egg dyes (1947) by Paas Dye Company of Newark, New Jersey.

Umbrellas by Louis Weiss of New York. These character umbrellas were marketed in 1947 and sold for $1.98. The line consisted of six different handles: Donald Duck, Mickey Mouse, Dopey, Pinocchio, Thumper the Rabbit, and Pluto.

Bookplates and bookmarks (1947) by the Antioch Bookplate Company of Yellow Springs, Ohio. The bookplates came packaged to sell at 25¢, 50¢, and $1.00. The plastic bookmarks retailed for 10¢ each.

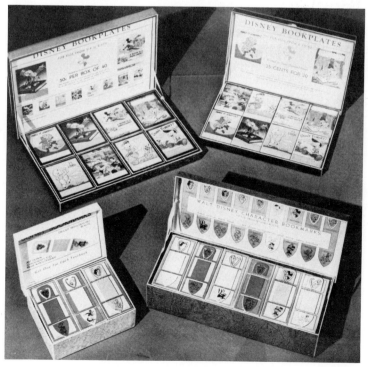

29. The Theme Parks and Their Influence on Collecting

Back in the early 1930s, Walt began dreaming and planning Disneyland—an amusement park for the entire family. (Actually, Walt preferred the term "theme park" to "amusement park," because Disneyland was divided into sections with each one featuring a theme, such as Main Street, Tomorrowland, Frontierland, and so forth.) When the park was opened on July 17, 1955, it represented a $17 million investment. By 1973 over $141 million had been invested successfully in Disneyland. Because of Walt's reputation for quality entertainment, the park was a success from the very beginning. On the first day over 28,000 people visited the facilities, and in only seven weeks the park welcomed its one millionth visitor. When the park opened with twenty-two major attractions, Walt was already planning additions. He felt that in order for Disneyland to continue to be successful he must make changes as needed:

> And the way I see it, Disneyland will never be finished. It's something we can keep developing and adding to. A motion picture is different. Once it's wrapped up and sent out for processing, we're through with it. If there are things that could be improved, we can't do anything about them any more. I've always wanted to work on something alive, something that keeps growing. We've got that in Disneyland. Even the trees will grow and be more beautiful every year.

In keeping with his philosophy, by 1957 a number of new attractions had been added, including the "Viewliner," a conventional train. By 1959 a monorail train was added along with a submarine attraction, "Matterhorn Mountain," the "Autopias," and a motorboat cruise. In 1960, "Nature's Wonderland," a new version of "America the Beautiful," and the "Art of Animation" were added. In 1963 "Walt Disney's Enchanted Tiki Room" was unveiled. This exhibit utilized a new medium called "Audio-Animatronics," which coordinated movement and sound in the birds, flowers, and Tiki gods in the display. "Great Moments with Mr. Lincoln," a more sophisticated application of the audio-animatronics used in the Tiki Room attraction, was added in 1965. Nineteen sixty-six saw the addition of "New Orleans Square," "It's a Small World," and "Primeval World." By the end of the year, Disneyland registered its 57 millionth visitor.

More audio-animatronics were added in 1967 with "Pirates of the Caribbean." In the same year a new Tomorrowland was opened; it included the "People-Mover," "Carousel of Progress," "Adventure thru Inner Space," "Flight to the Moon," "Rocket Jets," "Tomorrowland Terrace," and a 360° version of "America the Beautiful." Four new monorail trains and the "Haunted Mansion" were added in 1969. In 1971 Disneyland recorded its 100 millionth visitor. And in 1972, the seventeenth birthday of the park, the "Main Street Electrical Parade" was initiated, and the new land of Bear Country was opened with the feature "Country Bear Jamboree." "The Walt Disney Story," which opened in 1973, featured a display of Mickey Mouse collectibles from the 1930s from the collection of the Disney Archives.

Like almost all of the Disney activities throughout the years, Disneyland has special significance to collectors of Disney memorabilia. The park's theme sections and their numerous exhibits have inspired great quantities of merchandise. The park, in fact, has been a major continuing marketplace for potential collectibles. Collectors of the more recent generations have within their ranks those who specialize in gathering Disneyland collectibles. Even today, the many shops within the park sell Disney items that are sure to become the valued collectibles of tomorrow.

In 1964 the Disneys began to plan a second complex. The new one was to be called "Walt Disney World." A chief difference between the two Disney activities would be space. By October of 1965, Disney representatives had accumulated 27,443 acres (almost 43 square miles) in the central part of Florida for just over $5 million. The plan for Walt Disney World included much more than just another theme park. The new complex was to have a number of features, and a theme park—part of Vacation Kingdom—was only one component. Besides the Vacation Kingdom (2,500 acres) with its hotels, campsites, wide variety of land and water recreation facilities, and the theme park similar to Disneyland, the plan called for an airport of the future; a showcase industrial park; the vacation community of "Lake Buena Vista";

and an ultramodern "Experimental Prototype Community of Tomorrow."

On October 1, 1971, the first part of Walt Disney World, Vacation Kingdom, was opened to the public. It had taken 1,584 days of clearing and construction plus $400 million to ready this first section of the Disneys' biggest dream. Some of the features of the Vacation Kingdom were the 500-room Polynesian Village hotel; two 18-hole championship golf courses called the Palm Course and the Magnolia Course; the 200-acre Seven Seas Lagoon; the over 1,000-room Contemporary Resort; the 450-acre Bay Lake; Treasure Island; Tri-Circle-D Ranch; the 600-acre Fort Wilderness campground; and, most important of all to collectors, the Magic Kingdom theme park. The Magic Kingdom, with its six themed "lands," in its relatively short existence has been responsible for hundreds of pieces of merchandise that have great collecting potential.

Much of the character merchandise produced in 1973 was devoted to the fiftieth anniversary of what has evolved into Walt Disney Productions. The bulk of this merchandise can be credited to the newly formed Walt Disney Distributing Company, which is headquartered at Walt Disney World. This newly formed company is for the first time designing, manufacturing, and distributing Disney character merchandise. The result of this new approach will surely be higher quality merchandise and more accurate depictions of the Disney characters on the merchandise. Collectors of the future are certain to appreciate the products of the new company.

While as yet the two theme parks have not completely captured the imagination of collectors of Disneyana, it is almost inevitable that it will happen. At any rate, thousands of dollars worth of character merchandise are being sold each month. While these sales are not primarily to collectors, as in the past a percentage of the merchandise will be saved and eventually, when the collector interest is sufficient, it will appear on the market again. The next time, however, such merchandise will be sold at antique stores, flea markets, and the like as collectors' items.

A Disneyland Ferris Wheel made by J. Chein and Company of Newark, New Jersey. This metal toy features a mechanical bell that rings as the wheel goes around, and six gondolas that swing. This $1.98 toy is interesting because there are no ferris wheels at Disneyland.

A Disneyland "Melody Player" with changeable music reels. The music box is hand-operated.

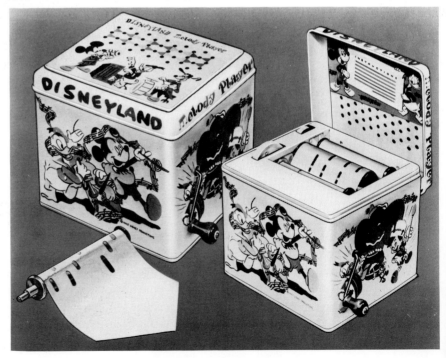

3 NEW TOYS

FROM WALT DISNEY'S *Disneyland* by STROMBECKER

COPYRIGHT
WALT DISNEY PRODUCTIONS

ACTION — COLOR — Play value — that's what we give you for SALES APPEAL in this new WALT DISNEY'S CASEY JR. LOCOMOTIVE. Bright colors make this appealing to the child. The drive rods are actuated by the wheels causing the boiler to swing back and forth, giving interesting and amusing motion.

Wheels are made of hardwood mounted on steel axles. Entire toy is finished with harmless lacquer finish. Packed in a set-up box with colors to match locomotive. Box size 5½" x 3½" x 7½". Packed 1 dozen. Shipping weight 10 lbs. Priced to sell at $2.00.

STROMBECKER Walt Disney's Casey Jr. Locomotive No. 424.

HERE'S another smash sales hit for sure fire retailing. The famous Casey Jr. Train in miniature, a floor train for the small child that's too young for a mechanical wind-up or electric train.

Locomotive and 3 cars, length 14". Packed in die-cut acetate window box 3¾" x 1½" x 14¼". Packed 1 dozen. Shipping weight 8 lbs. Priced to retail at $1.50.

STROMBECKER Walt Disney's Casey Jr. Train No. 425.

KIDS love Mickey Mouse. Here he is as a bus driver for his friends Pluto, Donald Duck and Dumbo. All made of good sturdy wood and realistic for many hours of hard play. Mickey and his buddies slide off the bus and can be played with separately and also placed back securely in any order the child desires. This is a quality toy to make your customers come back for more.
Bus is 10 3/16" long, boxed in die-cut acetate window box 3" x 5" x 10 1/16". Packed 1 dozen. Shipping weight 12 lbs. Priced to sell at $1.50.

**STROMBECKER
Walt Disney's Mickey Mouse Bus No. 423.**

An advertisement for three Disneyland toys made by the Strombeck-Becker Manufacturing Company of New York.

Mickey Mouse (6½″) and Minnie Mouse (6¼″) figurines of 1973 from the newly formed Walt Disney Distributing Company, which is headquartered at Walt Disney World in Florida.

plush

WALT DISNEY DISTRIBUTING CO.

P. O. BOX 40, BUENA VISTA, FLORIDA 32830

A selection of "plush" stuffed dolls featuring Disney characters.

30. Different Disneyana

The life of Walt Disney ended on December 15, 1966, at St. Joseph's Hospital in Burbank, California. During the creation of the feature-length animated film *The Jungle Book*, it was discovered that Walt was suffering from advanced cancer of the lungs. Six weeks after one lung was removed, the sixty-five-year-old genius of the motion picture industry was gone. The world was saddened and wondered what would happen to the many Disney enterprises.

Because Walt had evolved into the creative coordinating genius of Walt Disney Productions, the changes were slight. The many creative men working for the Disneys were able to carry on in the tradition Walt had established. From a business standpoint there were even fewer concerns, because Roy had always supervised that portion of the firm's activities. In fact Roy had been a vice-president and director of Walt Disney Productions since 1929, president since 1945, and in 1964, two years before Walt's unexpected death, he had assumed the additional responsibilities of chairman of the board and chief executive officer. Roy held all of those responsibilities until 1968, when he retired as president. He continued as chairman of the board and chief executive officer of the company until he died at the age of seventy-eight on December 20, 1971.

When both Walt and Roy Disney died, there was really little need for concern for the future of the Disney industry, because each of the two brothers had capable men working for them who could and did assume the necessary leadership. It is probably safe to go even further and assume that both of the Disneys had discussed the future leadership of the business long before either passed away.

In 1972 the two men who were chosen to take over the corporate empire with assets of more than $577 million, expected gross revenues in excess of $325 million, and a net worth of $433 million, were E. Cardon Walker and Donn Tatum. Walker had started with the Disneys in 1938 as a mailboy; and Tatum, an attorney and former chief of western operations for ABC television, had begun as production business manager in 1956. Functionally, the two men operate as a team, just as Walt and Roy did. Walker is president, chief operating officer in charge of the creative aspects of the business; and Tatum is board chairman, chief executive officer in charge of the financial aspects of the business.

In the five years between Walt's and Roy's death, Roy, Walker, and Tatum worked together closely in what has been described as an executive troika. One of the decisions they made along with the Disney family was to establish the Walt Disney Archives. The initial motive was to preserve Walt's papers, awards, and memorabilia. The archives were established on June 22, 1970, and the man selected to direct this activity was David R. Smith. Smith, formerly a reference librarian at the University of California, not only gathered, organized, and catalogued Walt's personal papers, business files, awards, and personal memorabilia, but also set up facilities for the scholarly study of the studio's motion picture products, character merchandise, artwork, publications, awards, photographs, and other business records.

Collectors today and in the future will most certainly benefit from Walt Disney Productions' interest in its history. The continual collecting, by the archivist, of the historical and current artifacts of the studio will ensure the preservation of the historic memorabilia of this great American business. Historians, collectors, and others with a legitimate interest in the history of Walt Disney Productions will have an organized source of information. In this respect Walt Disney Productions is far ahead of numerous other important American corporations that have not yet seen the value in professionally preserving their history.

Collectors will find it interesting that the Walt Disney Archives currently contain the most complete collection of Disney character merchandise in the world, along with contracts, correspondence, and other business records to back it up. Unfortunately, the pre-1950 portion of the collection is far from complete, because the old items were just not saved. Private collectors have gathered early character merchandise since the 1930s; thus, in their collections exist some of the rarest and most valuable examples of Disneyana.

Not all collectors of Disneyana, however, focus on items of the past. To be sure, most do; but there is a small group of collectors who search for and gather the contemporary and unusual items. For example, an ardent Mickey Mouse fan recently paid $2,000 for an ink wash of the famous mouse by the noted contemporary artist Claes Oldenburg. A number of collectors recently paid sculptor Ernest Trova $350 each for a limited edition of a silver sculpture honoring

Mickey Mouse's fortieth birthday. Trova also successfully marketed a limited number of signed Mickey Mouse lithographs for $150 each.

Of a more commercial nature are the firms producing limited editions of Disney-oriented sculptures and medals. One firm recently produced and sold sterling silver sculptures of Mickey Mouse with Pluto (1971) and Donald Duck (1972). The pieces were replicas of originals by the noted American sculptor Philip Kraczkowski. Each edition was limited to 500, and each one sold for several hundred dollars. In 1973, the Kirk silversmiths of Baltimore, Maryland, began to issue, one a month, silver and pewter medals featuring Disney characters. These ready-made collectors' items sold for $17.50 (silver) and $7.50 (pewter) each. The silver medals were a limited production of 2,500 and the pewter ones, 10,000.

In addition to the different items discussed above and others of a similar nature, collectors should be aware that there is a remote chance that they may find unusual items from Walt's and Roy's past. An example of anything Walt did in 1914 at the Kansas City Art Institute would be of great interest. Walt's work on the school newspaper at McKinley High School in Chicago or examples of his work while attending the Chicago Academy of Fine Arts would be valued pieces of Disneyana. Any examples of the art work Walt made while serving in the ambulance corps during the World War I era would be prized collectors' items. Items from the period during which Walt worked in Kansas City would be choice collectibles. In fact, anything related to the personal history of the Disneys deserves to be gathered and saved by those interested in Disneyana. The small ceramic potties Walt gave away as personal gifts to friends having babies are of interest, even though few have ever reached the collectors' market. Autographs of the two great men are a real possibility, as autograph collectors have long realized.

Only a few people ever have the opportunity to leave a mark on society as did Walt and Roy Disney. The honor of preserving the relics of their lives rightfully goes to those who were influenced by and who appreciated their work the most—the collectors of Disneyana.

A display, in the Walt Disney Archives, of early Disney memorabilia.

This is a photograph of a 14" x 14" ink wash of Mickey Mouse that was made in 1966 by the famous American artist Claes Oldenburg. The ink wash sold for $2,000.00 at a 1972 auction conducted by Sotheby, Parke-Bernet Galleries of Los Angeles.

A silver sculpture by the famous contemporary sculptor
Ernest Trova of St. Louis, Missouri. Trova is perhaps best
known as a producer of graphic and multiple editions. The
theme of "The Falling Man" is the symbol most associated
with Trova. In addition, he is one of the country's leading
collectors of Disneyana. The silver sculpture pictured was
done to commemorate the fortieth birthday of Mickey
Mouse (1928–1968). No more than 50 of these were made,
and they sold originally for $350.00 each.

Signed lithograph by Ernest Trova. These were produced by
the artist in a limited quantity and sold originally for
$150.00 each in 1969.

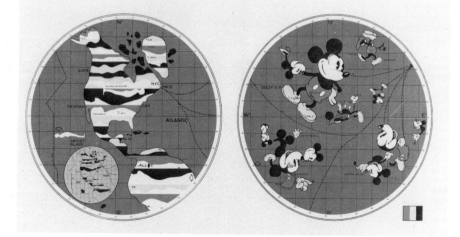

The obverse of a ceramic pottie that Walt Disney had made in lots of 500. He gave these potties to friends who had just had babies. Since those who received such a personalized gift have kept them, few are available to collectors. Occasionally, however, an example does reach the marketplace, and a few lucky collectors have had the opportunity to add one to their collection of Disneyana.

The reverse of the ceramic pottie that Walt Disney gave as a personal gift.

Appendix A:
Walt Disney Newspaper Comic Chronology

Twelve Disney newspaper comics, originating between 1930 and 1950, are listed below. The dates of origin are provided so that collectors may determine the oldest obtainable comic in each series. In addition, inclusive dates provide the collector with the exact number of comics in an entire set. Since a number of collectors gather comics by particular writers or artists, the chronological listing includes the writer, the artist ("penciled"), and the inker (one who completes the drawings).

I. MICKEY MOUSE daily black and white strip (Started January 13, 1930)

	Written	Penciled	Inked
Jan. 13, 1930–Feb. 8, 1930	Walt Disney	Ub Iwerks	Win Smith
Feb. 10, 1930–May 3, 1930	Walt Disney	Win Smith	Win Smith
May 5, 1930–May 17, 1930	Walt Disney	Floyd Gottfredson	Floyd Gottfredson
May 19, 1930–late 1932	Floyd Gottfredson	Floyd Gottfredson	Hardy Gramatky
			Earl Duvall
			Ted Thwaites
			Al Taliaferro
Late 1932–early 1933	Webb Smith	Floyd Gottfredson	Ted Thwaites
Early 1933–late 1933	Ted Osborne	Floyd Gottfredson	Ted Thwaites
Late 1933–mid-1934	Merrill de Maris	Floyd Gottfredson	Ted Thwaites
Mid-1934–mid-1937	Ted Osborne	Floyd Gottfredson	Ted Thwaites
Mid-1937–early 1942	Merrill de Maris	Floyd Gottfredson	Ted Thwaites
			Bill Wright
Early 1942–June 1943	Dick Shaw	Floyd Gottfredson	Dick Moores
June 1943–Feb. 10, 1962	Bill Walsh	Floyd Gottfredson	Floyd Gottfredson
Mar. 1, 1962–Nov. 22, 1968 (ending with releases for Dec. 23–28, 1968)	Roy Williams	Floyd Gottfredson	Floyd Gottfredson
Jan. 25, 1968 to date (starting with releases for Dec. 30, 1968–Jan. 4, 1969)	Del Connell	Floyd Gottfredson	Floyd Gottfredson

II. MICKEY MOUSE Sunday color page (Started January 10, 1932)

	Written	Penciled	Inked
Jan. 10, 1932	Earl Duvall	Earl Duvall	Earl Duvall
Jan. 17, 1932–late 1932	Floyd Gottfredson	Floyd Gottfredson	Al Taliaferro
			Ted Thwaites
Late 1932–early 1933	Webb Smith	Floyd Gottfredson	Ted Thwaites
Early 1933–late 1933	Ted Osborne	Floyd Gottfredson	Ted Thwaites
Late 1933–mid-1934	Merrill de Maris	Floyd Gottfredson	Ted Thwaites
Mid-1934–mid-1937	Ted Osborne	Floyd Gottfredson	Ted Thwaites
Mid-1937–mid-1938	Merrill de Maris	Floyd Gottfredson	Ted Thwaites
Mid-1938–early 1942	Merrill de Maris	Manuel Gonzales	Ted Thwaites
			Bill Wright
Early 1942–mid-1942	Hubie Karp	Manuel Gonzales	Bill Wright
Mid-1942–Oct. 1944	Hubie Karp	Bill Wright	Bill Wright
Oct. 1944–early 1946	Bill Walsh	Bill Wright	Bill Wright
Early 1946–Mar. 9, 1963	Bill Walsh	Manuel Gonzales	Manuel Gonzales
Mar. 11, 1963–Nov. 22, 1968	Roy Williams	Manuel Gonzales	Manuel Gonzales
Nov. 25, 1968 to date	Del Connell	Manuel Gonzales	Manuel Gonzales

III. SILLY SYMPHONIES Sunday color page (Started January 10, 1932)

1. "Bucky Bug" (Jan. 10, 1932–Mar. 4, 1934) Start to early 1933	Earl Duvall	Earl Duvall (to Apr. 1932)	Earl Duvall (to Apr. 1932)
Early 1933–late 1933	Ted Osborne	Al Taliaferro	Al Taliaferro
Late 1933–Mar. 4, 1934	Merrill de Maris	Al Taliaferro	Al Taliaferro
2. "Birds of a Feather" Mar. 11, 1934–June 17, 1934	Ted Osborne	Al Taliaferro	Al Taliaferro
3. "Peculiar Penguins" July 1, 1934–Sept. 9, 1934	Ted Osborne	Al Taliaferro	Al Taliaferro
4. "The Little Red Hen" Sept. 16, 1934–Dec. 16, 1934	Ted Osborne	Al Taliaferro	Al Taliaferro
5. "The Boarding School Mystery" Dec. 23, 1934–Feb. 17, 1935	Ted Osborne	Al Taliaferro	Al Taliaferro
6. "The Robber Kitten" Feb. 24, 1935–Apr. 21, 1935	Ted Osborne	Al Taliaferro	Al Taliaferro
7. "Cookieland" Apr. 28, 1935–July 21, 1935	Ted Osborne	Al Taliaferro	Al Taliaferro
8. "Three Little Kittens" July 28, 1935–Oct. 20, 1935	Ted Osborne	Al Taliaferro	Al Taliaferro
9. "The Life and Adventures of Elmer Elephant" Oct. 27, 1935–Jan. 12, 1936	Ted Osborne	Al Taliaferro	Al Taliaferro
10. "Three Little Pigs" Jan. 19, 1936–Aug. 23, 1936	Ted Osborne	Al Taliaferro	Al Taliaferro
11. "Donald Duck" Aug. 30, 1936–Dec. 5, 1937	Ted Osborne	Al Taliaferro	Al Taliaferro
12. "The Practical Pig" May 1, 1938–Aug. 7, 1938	Merrill de Maris	Al Taliaferro	Al Taliaferro
13. "Mother Pluto" Aug. 14, 1938–Oct. 16, 1938	Merrill de Maris	Al Taliaferro	Al Taliaferro
14. "Farmyard Symphony" Oct. 23, 1938–Nov. 27, 1938	Merrill de Maris	Al Taliaferro	Al Taliaferro
15. "Timid Elmer" Dec. 4, 1938–Feb. 12, 1939	Merrill de Maris	Al Taliaferro	Al Taliaferro
16. "Pluto the Pup" Feb. 19, 1939–Mar. 19, 1939	Merrill de Maris	Al Taliaferro	Al Taliaferro
17. "The Ugly Duckling" Mar. 26, 1939–Apr. 16, 1939	Merrill de Maris	Al Taliaferro	Al Taliaferro
18. "Pluto the Pup" (resumed) Apr. 23, 1939–Dec. 17, 1939	Hubie Karp	Bob Grant	Bob Grant
19. "Pluto the Pup" (resumed again) Apr. 14, 1940–Nov. 3, 1940	Hubie Karp	Bob Grant	Bob Grant
20. "Little Hiawatha" Nov. 10, 1940–July 12, 1942	Hubie Karp	Bob Grant	Bob Grant

IV. Early SUNDAY COLOR COMICS (Started December 12, 1937)

1. "Snow White and the Seven Dwarfs" Dec. 12, 1937–Apr. 24, 1938	Merrill de Maris	Hank Porter Bob Grant assisting	Hank Porter Bob Grant assisting
2. "Pinocchio" Dec. 24, 1939–Apr. 7, 1940	Merrill de Maris	Hank Porter Bob Grant assisting	Hank Porter Bob Grant assisting
3. "Bambi" July 19, 1942–Oct. 4, 1942	Merrill de Maris	Bob Grant	Karl Karpe
4. "Jose Carioca" (based on *Saludos Amigos*) Oct. 11, 1942–Oct. 1, 1944	Hubie Karp	Bob Grant Paul Murry	Karl Karpe Dick Moores
5. "Panchito" (based on *Three Caballeros*) (based on *Three Caballeros*)	Bill Walsh	Paul Murry	Dick Moores
6. "Cinderella" Mar. 5, 1950–June 18, 1950	Frank Reilly	Dick Moores	Manuel Gonzales
7. "Alice in Wonderland" Sept. 2, 1951–Dec. 16, 1951	Frank Reilly	Dick Moores	Manuel Gonzales

V. DONALD DUCK daily black and white strip (Started February 7, 1938)

Feb. 7, 1938 to early 1965 (ending with releases for March 15–20, 1965)	Bob Karp	Al Taliaferro	Al Taliaferro
Early 1965–Feb. 3, 1969	Bob Karp	Al Taliaferro	Manuel Gonzales Al Hubbard Kay Wright Ellis Eringer Bill Weaver Frank Grundeen
Feb. 3, 1969 to date (starting with releases for January 20–25, 1969)	Bob Karp	Frank Grundeen	Frank Grundeen

VI. DONALD DUCK Sunday color page (Started December 10, 1939)

Dec. 10, 1939 to early 1965 (ending with release for Apr. 25, 1965)	Bob Karp	Al Taliaferro	Al Taliaferro
Early 1965–Feb. 3, 1969	Bob Karp	Al Taliaferro	Manuel Gonzales Al Hubbard Kay Wright Ellis Eringer Bill Weaver Frank Grundeen
Feb. 3, 1969 to date (starting with release for Feb. 23, 1969)	Bob Karp	Frank Grundeen	Frank Grundeen

VII. UNCLE REMUS Sunday color page (Started October 14, 1945)

Start–Aug. 1946	Bill Walsh	Paul Murry (to early 1946)	Dick Moores (to early 1946)
Aug. 5, 1946–Mar. 16, 1956	George Stallings	Dick Moores	Dick Moores
Mar. 16, 1956–Sept. 1959	George Stallings	Riley Thomson, Jr.	Riley Thomson, Jr.
Sept. 1959–June 30, 1962 (ending with release for Sept. 2, 1962)	George Stallings	Bill Wright	Bill Wright
July 16, 1962–Aug. 12, 1963	George Stallings	John Ushler (releases for Sept. 9–Sept. 16, 1962: Chuck Fuson)	John Ushler (releases for Sept. 9–Sept. 16, 1962: Chuck Fuson)
Aug. 12, 1963–Dec. 31, 1972 (concluded)	Jack Boyd	John Ushler (releases for Nov. 17–Dec. 28, 1968: Mike Arens)	John Ushler (releases for Nov. 17–Dec. 29, 1968: Mike Arens)

VIII. MERRY MENAGERIE daily black and white panel (Started January 13, 1947; Concluded March 17, 1962)

Jan. 13, 1947–Mar. 17, 1962	Bob Karp	Bob Grant (except for periods of illness in 1960 and 1961 when Ben de Nunez, Don Lusk, and Chuck Fuson substituted)	Bob Grant (except for periods of illness in 1960 and 1961 when Ben de Nunez, Don Lusk, and Chuck Fuson substituted)

Appendix B:

Disney Periodicals (Domestic)

The following is a listing of all known periodicals published prior to 1950 by Walt Disney Productions in the United States.

Publication	Started	Concluded	Remarks
Annual Report	1940		Report year irregular
The Bulletin	January 6, 1939	April 4, 1941	Weekly and biweekly studio employee newsletter
Vol. 1, no. 1 to Vol. 3, no. 25			
Dispatch from Disney	1943	1943	One issue only published: for employees in the armed services
Vol. 1, no. 1			
Dumbo Weekly	1941	1941	Published weekly and distributed by Diamond D-X Service Stations. The looseleaf binder supplied with the issues is entitled "The New Adventures of Walt Disney's Dumbo"
No. 1 to No. 8			
The Mickey Mouse Globe Trotter Weekly	1937	1937	8½" x 5". Used in a national bakery campaign.
Vol. 1, no. 1 to Vol. 12, no. 12 [sic]			
Mickey Mouse Magazine	January 1933	September 1933	Issued monthly by various theaters and department stores
Vol. 1, nos. 1–9			
Mickey Mouse Magazine	November 1933	October 1935	Issued monthly by various dairies
Vol. 1, no. 1 to Vol. 2, no. 12			
Mickey Mouse Magazine	Summer 1935	September 1940	A monthly publication
Mickey Mouse Melodeon	November 1932	February 1933	House organ of the Disney studio
Vol. 1, nos. 1–4			
Mickey Mouse on the Home Front	September 1943		15" x 11⅜". Used mainly by aircraft companies during World War II. Was not successful. Probably not published after 1943
Official Bulletin of the Mickey Mouse Club			
Vol. 1, nos. 1–26	April 15, 1930	December 15, 1931	Semimonthly: 26 issues
Vol. 2, nos. 1–21	January 15, 1932	December 15, 1932	Semimonthly: 21 issues. This magazine may have been published for a short period in 1933
Travel Tykes Weekly	January 1939	September 1939	20 copies were released between January and September 1939
No. 1 to No. 20			

Appendix C:

Disney Comic Books

The following is a listing of Disney comic books published between 1938 and 1970. The extensiveness and diversity of the subject made it necessary to divide the books into five categories. Within each category the title and number, publisher, publication date, and remarks are all provided. Section 1 is a listing of books alphabetically by major character(s), who were introduced before 1970. In Section 2 "Giant Size Comic Books" are listed alphabetically by title. Section 3 is devoted to comic books distributed as premiums ("giveaways"); these are also listed alphabetically by titles. Since giveaways are almost always imprinted with the name of the sponsoring firm, this section is further divided by the twenty participating businesses. The fourth major category of comic books is presented as "One-Shot Comic Books." Each of these one-of-a-kind publications is listed alphabetically by title. Section 5 is appropriately titled, "Miscellaneous." In this final section comic books that did not fit into the four other categories are listed alphabetically by title.

1.

Listed by Character

Title & Number	Publication Date	Remarks
The Beagle Boys		Quarterly, beginning with No. 3
(Gold Key)		
No. 1 to No. 19	1964 to date	
Bongo and Lumpjaw		Two one-shots
(Dell Color Comics)		
No. 706	1956	
No. 886	1958	
Chip 'n Dale		Three one-shots
(Dell Color Comics)		
No. 517	1953	
No. 581	1954	
No. 636	1955	
No. 4 to No. 30	Dec./Feb. 1956 to June/Aug. 1962	Quarterly
(Gold Key)		Reprints
No. 1 to 24	1967 to date	
Comic Album		Two one-shots
(Dell Color Comics)		
No. 1: "Donald Duck"	Mar./May 1958	
No. 3: "Donald Duck"	Sept./Nov. 1958	

Title & Number	Publication Date	Remarks
Daisy Duck's Diary		Eight one-shots
(Dell Color Comics)		
No. 600	1954	
No. 659	1955	
No. 743	1956	
No. 858	1957	
No. 948	1958	
No. 1055	1959	Drawn: Carl Barks
No. 1150	1960	Drawn: Carl Barks
No. 1247	1961	
Donald Duck		
(Whitman/K.K. Publications)		
No number	1938	Black and white
(Dell Black and White Comics)		
No. 16	1940	
No. 20	1941	Donald Duck comic paint book
(Dell Color Comics)		
No. 4	Feb. 1940	
(Dell Four-Color Comics)		
No. 9: "Pirate Gold"	1942	Written and drawn: Carl Barks
No. 29: "Mummy's Ring"	1943	Written and drawn: Carl Barks
No. 62: "Frozen Gold"	1944	Written and drawn: Carl Barks
(Dell Color Comics)		
No. 108: "Terror in the River"	1946	Written and drawn: Carl Barks
No. 147: "Volcano Valley"	1947	Written and drawn: Carl Barks
No. 159: "The Ghost of the Grotto"	1947	Written and drawn: Carl Barks
No. 178: "Christmas on Bear Mountain"	1947	Written and drawn: Carl Barks
No. 189: "The Old Castle's Secret"	1948	Written and drawn: Carl Barks
No. 199: "Sheriff of Bullet Valley"	1948	Written and drawn: Carl Barks
No. 203: "The Golden Christmas Tree"	1948	Written and drawn: Carl Barks
No. 223: "Lost in the Andes"	1949	Written and drawn: Carl Barks (The famous "Square egg" story)
No. 238: "Voodoo Hoodoo"	1949	Written and drawn: Carl Barks
No. 256: "Luck of the North"	1949	Written and drawn: Carl Barks
No. 263: "Land of the Totem Poles"	1950	Written and drawn: Carl Barks
No. 275: "Ancient Persia"	1950	Written and drawn: Carl Barks
No. 282: "The Pixilated Parrot"	1950	Written and drawn: Carl Barks
No. 291: "The Magic Hourglass"	1950	Written and drawn: Carl Barks
No. 300: "Bigtop Bedlam"	1950	Written and drawn: Carl Barks
No. 308: "Dangerous Disguise"	1950	Written and drawn: Carl Barks
No. 318: "No Such Varmint"	1951	Written and drawn: Carl Barks
No. 328: "Old California"	1951	Written and drawn: Carl Barks
No. 339: "The Magic Fountain"	1951	
No. 348: "The Crocodile Collector"	1951	Cover only: Carl Barks
No. 356: "Rags to Riches"	1951	Cover only: Carl Barks
No. 367: "A Christmas for Shacktown"	1951	Written and drawn: Carl Barks
No. 379: "Southern Hospitality"	1952	
No. 394: "Malayalaya"	1952	Cover only: Carl Barks
No. 408: "The Golden Helmet'	1952	Written and drawn: Carl Barks
No. 422: "The Gilded Man"	Sept./Oct. 1952	Written and drawn: Carl Barks Starting with No. 26, books were issued bimonthly, except No. 83 (June/Aug. 1962) and No. 84 (Sept./Nov. 1962) were issued quarterly
No. 26: "Donald Duck"	Nov./Dec. 1952	Written and drawn: Carl Barks
No. 27: "Donald Duck"	1953	Cover: Carl Barks
No. 28: "Donald Duck"		Cover: Carl Barks
No. 29: "Donald Duck"		Cover: Carl Barks
No. 30: "Donald Duck"		Cover: Carl Barks

Title & Number	Publication Date	Remarks
No. 31: "Donald Duck"		
No. 32: "Donald Duck"		
No. 33: "Donald Duck"	1954	
No. 34: "Donald Duck"		
No. 35: "Donald Duck"		Cover: Carl Barks
No. 36: "Donald Duck"		
No. 37: "Donald Duck"		
No. 38: "Donald Duck"		
No. 39: "Donald Duck"	1955	
No. 40: "Donald Duck"		
No. 41: "Donald Duck"		
No. 42: "Donald Duck"		
No. 43: "Donald Duck"		
No. 44: "Donald Duck"		Cover: Carl Barks
No. 45: "Donald Duck"	1956	
No. 46: "Donald Duck"		Written and drawn: Carl Barks
No. 47: "Donald Duck"		Written and drawn: Carl Barks
No. 48: "Donald Duck"		
No. 49: "Donald Duck"		
No. 50: "Donald Duck"		
No. 51: "Donald Duck"	1957	Written and drawn: Carl Barks
No. 52: "Donald Duck"		Written and drawn: Carl Barks
No. 53: "Donald Duck"		
No. 54: "Donald Duck"		Written and drawn: Carl Barks
No. 55: "Donald Duck"		Cover: Carl Barks
No. 56: "Donald Duck"		
No. 57: "Donald Duck"	1958	Cover: Carl Barks
No. 58: "Donald Duck"		
No. 59: "Donald Duck"		
No. 60: "Donald Duck"		Written and drawn: Carl Barks
No. 61: "Donald Duck"		
No. 62: "Donald Duck"		
No. 63: "Donald Duck"	1959	
No. 64: "Donald Duck"		
No. 65: "Donald Duck"		Cover: Carl Barks
No. 66: "Donald Duck"		
No. 67: "Donald Duck"		
No. 68: "Donald Duck"		Written and drawn: Carl Barks
No. 69: "Donald Duck"	1960	
No. 70: "Donald Duck"		Cover: Carl Barks
No. 71: "Donald Duck"		Cover: Carl Barks
No. 72: "Donald Duck"		
No. 73: "Donald Duck"		Cover: Carl Barks
No. 74: "Donald Duck"		
No. 75: "Donald Duck'	1961	
No. 76: "Donald Duck"		
No. 77: "Donald Duck"		
No. 78: "Donald Duck"		Cover: Carl Barks
No. 79: "Donald Duck"		Cover: Carl Barks
No. 80: "Donald Duck"		Cover: Carl Barks
No. 81: "Donald Duck"	1962	Cover: Carl Barks
No. 82: "Donald Duck"		
No. 83: "Donald Duck"	June/Aug. 1962	Cover: Carl Barks
No. 84: "Donald Duck"		
(Gold Key)		
No. 85: "Donald Duck"	Sept./Nov. 1962	
No. 86: "Donald Duck"	1963	
No. 87: "Donald Duck"		
No. 88: "Donald Duck"		
No. 89: "Donald Duck"		
No. 90: "Donald Duck"		
No. 91: "Donald Duck"		

Title & Number	Publication Date	Remarks
No. 92: "Donald Duck"	1964	
No. 93: "Donald Duck"		
No. 94: "Donald Duck"		
No. 95: "Donald Duck"		
No. 96: "Donald Duck"		Titled *Comic Album*
No. 97: "Donald Duck"		
No. 98: "Donald Duck"		Written and drawn: Carl Barks
No. 99: "Donald Duck"	1965	Titled *Christmas Album*
No. 100: "Donald Duck"		
No. 101: "Donald Duck"		
No. 102: "Donald Duck"		
No. 103: "Donald Duck"		
No. 104: "Donald Duck"		
No. 105: "Donald Duck"	1966	
No. 106: "Donald Duck"		
No. 107: "Donald Duck"		
No. 108: "Donald Duck"		
No. 109: "Donald Duck"		
No. 110: "Donald Duck"		
No. 111: "Donald Duck"	1967	
No. 112: "Donald Duck"		
No. 113: "Donald Duck"		
No. 114: "Donald Duck"		
No. 115: "Donald Duck"		
No. 116: "Donald Duck"		
No. 117: "Donald Duck"	1968	Written: Carl Barks
No. 118: "Donald Duck"		
No. 119: "Donald Duck"		
No. 120: "Donald Duck"		
No. 121: "Donald Duck"		
No. 122: "Donald Duck"		
No. 123: "Donald Duck"	1969	
No. 124: "Donald Duck"		
No. 125: "Donald Duck"		
No. 126: "Donald Duck"		
No. 127: "Donald Duck"		
No. 128: "Donald Duck"		
No. 129: "Donald Duck"	1970	
No. 130: "Donald Duck"		
No. 131: "Donald Duck"		
No. 132: "Donald Duck"		
No. 133: "Donald Duck"		
No. 134: "Donald Duck"		Written and drawn: Carl Barks
No. 135: "Donald Duck"	1971	Written and drawn: Carl Barks
No. 136: "Donald Duck"		
No. 137: "Donald Duck"		
No. 138: "Donald Duck"		
No. 139: "Donald Duck"		
No. 140: "Donald Duck"		
No. 141: "Donald Duck"	1972	
No. 142: "Donald Duck"		
No. 143: "Donald Duck"		
No. 144: "Donald Duck"		
No. 145: "Donald Duck"		
No. 146: "Donald Duck"		
No. 147: "Donald Duck"	1973	
No. 148: "Donald Duck"		
No. 149: "Donald Duck"		
No. 150: "Donald Duck"		
No. 151: "Donald Duck"		
No. 152: "Donald Duck"		
No. 153: "Donald Duck"		
No. 154: "Donald Duck"	to date	

Title & Number	Publication Date	Remarks
Duck Album		Seventeen one-shots
(Dell Color Comics)		
No. 353: "Duck Album"	1951	Cover: Carl Barks
No. 450: "Duck Album"	1953	Cover: Carl Barks
No. 492: "Duck Album"		
No. 531: "Duck Album"		
No. 560: "Duck Album"	1954	
No. 586: "Duck Album"		
No. 611: "Duck Album"		
No. 649: "Duck Album"		
No. 686: "Duck Album"		
No. 726: "Duck Album"		
No. 782: "Duck Album'		
No. 840: "Duck Album"		
No. 995: "Donald Duck Album"	1959	
No. 1099: "Donald Duck Album"	1960	Cover: Carl Barks
No. 1140: "Donald Duck Album"		Cover: Carl Barks
No. 1182: "Donald Duck Album"		
No. 1239: "Donald Duck Album"	1963	Cover: Carl Barks
(Gold Key)		
No. 01204–207: "Donald Duck Album"	1962	
No. 1	Aug. 1963	
No. 2	Oct. 1963	
Dumbo Comic Paint Book		
(Dell Black and White Comic)		
No. 19	1941	
Goofy	1953–62	
(Dell Color Comics)		
No. 468: "Goofy"		
No. 562: "Goofy"		
No. 627: "Goofy"		
No. 658: "Goofy"		
No. 702: "The Goofy Success Story"		
No. 747: "Goofy"		
No. 802: "Goofy"		
No. 857: "The Goofy Adventure Story"		
No. 899: "Goofy"		
No. 952: "Goofy"		
No. 987: "Goofy"		
No. 1053: "Goofy"		
No. 1094: "Goofy"		
No. 1149: "Goofy"		
No. 1201: "Goofy"		
No. 12308–211: "Goofy"		
Grandma Duck's Farm Friends	1956–62	Seven one-shots
(Dell Color Comics)		
No. 763		
No. 873		
No. 965		
No. 1010		
No. 1073		
No. 1161		Drawn: Carl Barks
No. 1279		Drawn: Carl Barks
Gyro Gearloose	1959–62	Five one-shots
(Dell Color Comics)		
No. 1047		Written and drawn: Carl Barks
No. 1095		Written and drawn: Carl Barks
No. 1184		Written and drawn: Carl Barks
No. 1267		Written and drawn: Carl Barks
No. 01329–207	July 1962	Cover: Carl Barks
The Hardy Boys	1956–58	Four one-shots
(Dell Color Comics)		
No. 760		
No. 830		
No. 887		
No. 964		

Title & Number	Publication Date	Remarks
(Gold Key)		
No. 1	1959	
No. 2	1959	
No. 3	1959	
No. 4	1959	
No. 5	1959	
Huey, Dewey and Louie: Junior Woodchucks		
(Gold Key)		
No. 1 to No. 23	1966 to date	
		Four one-shots
Jiminy Cricket		
(Dell Color Comics)		
No. 701	1956	
No. 795	1957	
No. 897	1958	
No. 989	1959	
		Three one-shots
Li'l Bad Wolf		
(Dell Color Comics)		
No. 403	1952	
No. 473	1953	
No. 564	1954	
		Four one-shots
Little Hiawatha		
(Dell Color Comics)		
No. 439	1952	
No. 787		
No. 901		
No. 988		
Ludwig Von Drake		
(Dell Color Comics)		
No. 1	Nov./Dec. 1961	Bimonthly
No. 2	Jan./Feb. 1962	Bimonthly
No. 3	Mar./Apr. 1962	Bimonthly
No. 4	June/Aug. 1962	Quarterly
		Twenty-one one-shots
Mickey Mouse		
(Dell Four-Color Comics)		
No. 16: "Mickey Mouse vs. the Phantom Blot"	1941	First Mickey Mouse comic book
No. 27: "7 Colored Terror"	1943	
No. 79: "Mickey Mouse"	1945	Written and drawn: Carl Barks
(Dell Color Comics)		
No. 116: "Mickey Mouse and the House of Many Mysteries"	1946	
No. 141: "Mickey Mouse"	1947	
No. 157: "Mickey Mouse"	1947	
No. 170: "Mickey Mouse on Spooks Island"		
No. 181: "Mickey Mouse"	1947	
No. 194: "Mickey Mouse in the World under the Sea"	1948	
No. 214: "Mickey Mouse and His Sky Adventure"	1949	
No. 231: "Mickey Mouse"	1949	
No. 248: "Mickey Mouse"	1949	
No. 261: "Mickey Mouse"	1949	
No. 268: "Mickey Mouse"	1950	
No. 279: "Mickey Mouse"	1950	
No. 286: "Mickey Mouse"	1950	
No. 296: "Mickey Mouse"	1950	
No. 304: "Mickey Mouse"	1950	
No. 313: "Mickey Mouse"	1950	
No. 325: "Mickey Mouse"	1951	
No. 334: "Mickey Mouse"	1951	

Title & Number	Publication Date	Remarks
(Dell Color Comics)	Aug./Sept. 1951 to Oct./Nov. 1952	Bimonthly: Eight issues
No. 343: "Mickey Mouse"		
No. 352: "Mickey Mouse"		
No. 362: "Mickey Mouse"		
No. 371: "Mickey Mouse"		
No. 387: "Mickey Mouse"		
No. 401: "Mickey Mouse"		
No. 411: "Mickey Mouse"		
No. 427: "Mickey Mouse"		
(Dell Color Comics)	Dec./Jan. 1953 to Apr./May 1962	Bimonthly: Fifty-five issues
No. 28: "Mickey Mouse"	1953	
No. 29: "Mickey Mouse"		
No. 30: "Mickey Mouse"		
No. 31: "Mickey Mouse"		
No. 32: "Mickey Mouse"		
No. 33: "Mickey Mouse"	1954	
No. 34: "Mickey Mouse"		
No. 35: "Mickey Mouse"		
No. 36: "Mickey Mouse"		
No. 37: "Mickey Mouse"		
No. 38: "Mickey Mouse"		
No. 39: "Mickey Mouse"	1955	
No. 40: "Mickey Mouse"		
No. 41: "Mickey Mouse"		
No. 42: "Mickey Mouse"		
No. 43: "Mickey Mouse"		
No. 44: "Mickey Mouse"		
No. 45: "Mickey Mouse"	1956	
No. 46: "Mickey Mouse"		
No. 47: "Mickey Mouse"		
No. 48: "Mickey Mouse"		
No. 49: "Mickey Mouse"		
No. 50: "Mickey Mouse"		
No. 51: "Mickey Mouse"	1957	
No. 52: "Mickey Mouse"		
No. 53: "Mickey Mouse"		
No. 54: "Mickey Mouse"		
No. 55: "Mickey Mouse"		
No. 56: "Mickey Mouse"		
No. 57: "Mickey Mouse"	1958	
No. 58: "Mickey Mouse"		
No. 59: "Mickey Mouse"		
No. 60: "Mickey Mouse"		
No. 61: "Mickey Mouse"		
No. 62: "Mickey Mouse"		
No. 63: "Mickey Mouse"	1959	
No. 64: "Mickey Mouse"		
No. 65: "Mickey Mouse"		
No. 66: "Mickey Mouse"		
No. 67: "Mickey Mouse"		
No. 68: "Mickey Mouse"		
No. 69: "Mickey Mouse"	1960	
No. 70: "Mickey Mouse"		
No. 71: "Mickey Mouse"		
No. 72: "Mickey Mouse"		
No. 73: "Mickey Mouse"		
No. 74: "Mickey Mouse"		
No. 75: "Mickey Mouse"	1961	
No. 76: "Mickey Mouse"		
No. 77: "Mickey Mouse"		
No. 78: "Mickey Mouse"		
No. 79: "Mickey Mouse"		
No. 80: "Mickey Mouse"		
No. 81: "Mickey Mouse"	1962	
No. 82: "Mickey Mouse"		
No. 83: "Mickey Mouse"		

Title & Number	Publication Date	Remarks
(Dell Color Comics)	July/Sept. 1962 to May 1963	Quarterly
No. 84: "Mickey Mouse"		
No. 85: "Mickey Mouse"		
No. 86: "Mickey Mouse"	1963	
No. 87: "Mickey Mouse"		
(Gold Key)	July 1963 to Aug. 1967	Bimonthly
No. 88: "Mickey Mouse"		
No. 89: "Mickey Mouse"		
No. 90: "Mickey Mouse"		
No. 91: "Mickey Mouse"		
No. 92: "Mickey Mouse"	1964	
No. 93: "Mickey Mouse"		
No. 94: "Mickey Mouse Comic Album"		
No. 95: "Mickey Mouse"		
No. 96: "Mickey Mouse"		
No. 97: "Mickey Mouse"		
No. 98: "Mickey Mouse"		
No. 99: "Mickey Mouse"	1965	
No. 100: "Mickey Mouse"		
No. 101: "Mickey Mouse"		
No. 102: "Mickey House"		
No. 103: "Mickey Mouse"		
No. 104: "Mickey Mouse"		
No. 105: "Mickey Mouse"	1966	
No. 106: "Mickey Mouse"		
No. 107: "Mickey Mouse"		
No. 108: "Mickey Mouse"		
No. 109: "Mickey Mouse"		
No. 110: "Mickey Mouse"		
No. 111: "Mickey Mouse"	1967	
No. 112: "Mickey Mouse"		
No. 113: "Mickey Mouse"		
No. 114: "Mickey Mouse"		
No. 115: "Mickey Mouse"	Nov. 1967 to Feb. 1971	Quarterly
No. 116: "Mickey Mouse"	1968	
No. 117: "Mickey Mouse"		
No. 118: "Mickey Mouse"		
No. 119: "Mickey Mouse"		
No. 120: "Mickey Mouse"	1969	
No. 121: "Mickey Mouse"		
No. 122: "Mickey Mouse"		
No. 123: "Mickey Mouse"		
No. 124: "Mickey Mouse"	1970	
No. 125: "Mickey Mouse"		
No. 126: "Mickey Mouse"		
No. 127: "Mickey Mouse"		
No. 128: "Mickey Mouse"	1971	
No. 129: "Mickey Mouse"	Apr. 1971 to present	Bimonthly
No. 130: "Mickey Mouse"		
No. 131: "Mickey Mouse"		
No. 132: "Mickey Mouse"		
No. 133: "Mickey Mouse"		
No. 134: "Mickey Mouse"	1972	
No. 135: "Mickey Mouse"		
No. 136: "Mickey Mouse"		
No. 137: "Mickey Mouse"		
No. 138: "Mickey Mouse"		
No. 139: "Mickey Mouse"		
No. 140: "Mickey Mouse"	1973	
No. 141: "Mickey Mouse"		
No. 142: "Mickey Mouse"		
No. 143: "Mickey Mouse"		
No. 144: "Mickey Mouse"		
No. 145: "Mickey Mouse"		
No. 146: "Mickey Mouse"	To date	

Title & Number	Publication Date	Remarks
Mickey Mouse Album		Three one-shots
(Dell Color Comics)		
No. 1057	1959	
No. 1151	1960	
No. 1246	1961	
(Gold Key)		Two one-shots
No. 12512–210	1962	
No. 10082–309	1963	
Moby Duck	Oct. 1967 to Oct. 1970	Eleven issues. Quarterly beginning with No. 2
(Gold Key)		
No. 1: "Moby Duck"		
No. 2: "Moby Duck"		
No. 3: "Moby Duck"		
No. 4: "Moby Duck"		
No. 5: "Moby Duck"		
No. 6: "Moby Duck"		
No. 7: "Moby Duck"		
No. 8: "Moby Duck"		
No. 9: "Moby Duck"		
No. 10: "Moby Duck"		
No. 11: "Moby Duck"		
No. 12: "Moby Duck"	Jan. 1974	
The Phantom Blot	1964 to 1966	
(Gold Key)		
No. 1: "The Phantom Blot"		
No. 2: "The Phantom Blot"		
No. 3: "The Phantom Blot"		
No. 4: "The Phantom Blot"		
No. 5: "The Phantom Blot"		
No. 6: "The Phantom Blot"		
No. 7: "The Phantom Blot"		
Pluto		
(Dell Large Feature Comic)		
No. 7	1942	Black and white
(Dell Color Comics)	1952–61	
No. 429: "Pluto"		
No. 509: "Pluto"		
No. 595: "Pluto"		
No. 654: "Pluto"		
No. 736: "Pluto"		
No. 853: "Pluto"		
No. 941: "Pluto"		
No. 1039: "Pluto"		
No. 1143: "Pluto"		
No. 1248: "Pluto"		
Scamp	1956–57	Four one-shots
(Dell Color Comics)		
No. 703: "Scamp"		
No. 777: "Scamp"		
No. 806: "Scamp"		
No. 833: "Scamp"		
No. 1: "Scamp"	1956	Quarterly
No. 2: "Scamp"		Quarterly
No. 3: "Scamp"		Quarterly
No. 4: "Scamp"		Quarterly
No. 5: "Scamp"	Mar./May 1958	Quarterly
No. 6: "Scamp"		Quarterly
No. 7: "Scamp"		Quarterly
No. 8: "Scamp"		Quarterly
No. 9: "Scamp"		Quarterly

Title & Number	Publication Date	Remarks
No. 10: "Scamp"	1959	Quarterly
No. 11: "Scamp"		Quarterly
No. 12: "Scamp"		Quarterly
No. 13: "Scamp"		Quarterly
No. 14: "Scamp"		Quarterly
No. 15: "Scamp"		Quarterly
No. 16: "Scamp"	Dec./Feb. 1961	Quarterly
No. 1204: "Scamp"	1961	
(Gold Key)		
No. 1: "Scamp"	1967	Reprint
No. 2: "Scamp"	1969	Reprint
No. 3: "Scamp"		
No. 4: "Scamp"		
No. 5: "Scamp"		
No. 6: "Scamp"		
No. 7: "Scamp"		
No. 8: "Scamp"		
No. 9: "Scamp"		
No. 10: "Scamp"		
No. 11: "Scamp"		
No. 12: "Scamp"		
No. 13: "Scamp"		
No. 14: "Scamp"	to date	
Spin and Marty	1956–57	Four one-shots
(Dell Color Comics)		
No. 714: "Spin and Marty"		
No. 767: "Spin and Marty"		
No. 808: "Spin and Marty"		
No. 826: "Spin and Marty and Annette"		
No. 5: "Spin and Marty"	Mar./May 1958	Quarterly
No. 6: "Spin and Marty"	June/Aug. 1958	Quarterly
No. 7: "Spin and Marty"	Sept./Nov. 1958	Quarterly
No. 8: "Spin and Marty"	Dec./Feb. 1959	Quarterly
No. 9: "Spin and Marty"	Mar./May 1959	Quarterly
No. 1026: "Spin and Marty"	1959	One-shot
No. 1082: "Spin and Marty"	1960	One-shot
Super Goof	1965 to date	
(Gold Key)		
No. 1: "Super Goof"		
No. 2: "Super Goof"		
No. 3: "Super Goof"		
No. 4: "Super Goof"		
No. 5: "Super Goof"		
No. 6: "Super Goof"		
No. 7: "Super Goof"		
No. 8: "Super Goof"		
No. 9: "Super Goof"		
No. 10: "Super Goof"		
No. 11: "Super Goof"		
No. 12: "Super Goof"		
No. 13: "Super Goof"		
No. 14: "Super Goof"		
No. 15: "Super Goof"		
No. 16: "Super Goof"		
No. 17: "Super Goof"		
No. 18: "Super Goof"		
No. 19: "Super Goof"		
No. 20: "Super Goof"		
No. 21: "Super Goof"		
No. 22: "Super Goof"		
No. 23: "Super Goof"		
No. 24: "Super Goof"		
No. 25: "Super Goof"		
No. 26: "Super Goof"		
No. 27: "Super Goof"		
No. 28: "Super Goof"	to date	

Title & Number	Publication Date	Remarks	
Thumper		Two one-shots	
(Dell Four-Color Comics)			
No. 19: "Thumper and the 7 Dwarfs"			
(Dell Color Comics)			
No. 243: "Thumper"	1949		
Tinker Bell		Two one-shots	
(Dell Color Comics)			
No. 896: "Tinker Bell"	1958		
No. 982: "Tinker Bell"	1959		
Uncle $crooge			
(Dell Color Comics)			
No. 386: "Only a Poor Old Man"	1952	Written and drawn:	Carl Barks
No. 456: "Back to the Klondike"		Written and drawn:	Carl Barks
No. 495: "Uncle $crooge"		Written and drawn:	Carl Barks
(Dell)			
No. 4: "Uncle $crooge"	Dec./Feb. 1954	Quarterly	
No. 5: "Uncle $crooge"		Written and drawn:	Carl Barks
No. 6: "Uncle $crooge"		Written and drawn:	Carl Barks
No. 7: "Uncle $crooge"		Written and drawn:	Carl Barks
No. 8: "Uncle $crooge"	1955	Written and drawn:	Carl Barks
No. 9: "Uncle $crooge"		Written and drawn:	Carl Barks
No. 10: "Uncle $crooge"		Written and drawn:	Carl Barks
No. 11: "Uncle $crooge"		Written and drawn:	Carl Barks
No. 12: "Uncle $crooge"	1956	Written and drawn:	Carl Barks
No. 13: "Uncle $crooge"		Written and drawn:	Carl Barks
No. 14: "Uncle $crooge"		Written and drawn:	Carl Barks
No. 15: "Uncle $crooge"		Written and drawn:	Carl Barks
No. 16: "Uncle $crooge"	1957	Written and drawn:	Carl Barks
No. 17: "Uncle $crooge"		Written and drawn:	Carl Barks
No. 18: "Uncle $crooge"		Written and drawn:	Carl Barks
No. 19: "Uncle $crooge"		Written and drawn:	Carl Barks
No. 20: "Uncle $crooge"	1958	Written and drawn:	Carl Barks
No. 21: "Uncle $crooge"		Written and drawn:	Carl Barks
No. 22: "Uncle $crooge"		Written and drawn:	Carl Barks
No. 23: "Uncle $crooge"		Written and drawn:	Carl Barks
No. 24: "Uncle Scrooge"	1959	Written and drawn:	Carl Barks
No. 25: "Uncle $crooge"		Written and drawn:	Carl Barks
No. 26: "Uncle $crooge"		Written and drawn:	Carl Barks
No. 27: "Uncle $crooge"		Written and drawn:	Carl Barks
No. 28: "Uncle $crooge"	1960	Written and drawn:	Carl Barks
No. 29: "Uncle $crooge"		Written and drawn:	Carl Barks
No. 30: "Uncle $crooge"		Written and drawn:	Carl Barks
No. 31: "Uncle $crooge"		Written and drawn:	Carl Barks
No. 32: "Uncle $crooge"	1961	Written and drawn:	Carl Barks
No. 33: "Uncle $crooge"		Written and drawn:	Carl Barks
No. 34: "Uncle $crooge"		Written and drawn:	Carl Barks
No. 35: "Uncle $crooge"		Written and drawn:	Carl Barks
No. 36: "Uncle $crooge"	1962	Written and drawn:	Carl Barks
No. 37: "Uncle $crooge"		Written and drawn:	Carl Barks
No. 38: "Uncle $crooge"		Written and drawn:	Carl Barks
No. 39: "Uncle $crooge"	Sept./Nov. 1962	Written and drawn:	Carl Barks
No. 40: "Uncle $crooge"	Jan. 1963. Bimonthly	Written and drawn:	Carl Barks
No. 41: "Uncle $crooge"		Written and drawn:	Carl Barks
No. 42: "Uncle $crooge"		Written and drawn:	Carl Barks
No. 43: "Uncle $crooge"		Written and drawn:	Carl Barks
No. 44: "Uncle $crooge"		Written and drawn:	Carl Barks
No. 45: "Uncle $crooge"		Written and drawn:	Carl Barks
No. 46: "Uncle $crooge"		Written and drawn:	Carl Barks
No. 47: "Uncle $crooge"	1964	Written and drawn:	Carl Barks
No. 48: "Uncle $crooge"		Written and drawn:	Carl Barks
No. 49: "Uncle $crooge"		Written and drawn:	Carl Barks
No. 50: "Uncle $crooge"		Written and drawn:	Carl Barks
No. 51: "Uncle $crooge"		Written and drawn:	Carl Barks
No. 52: "Uncle $crooge"		Written and drawn:	Carl Barks
No. 53: "Uncle $crooge"		Written and drawn:	Carl Barks
No. 54: "Uncle $crooge"		Written and drawn:	Carl Barks

Title & Number	Publication Date	Remarks
No. 55: "Uncle $crooge"	1965	Written and drawn: Carl Barks
No. 56: "Uncle $crooge"		Written and drawn: Carl Barks
No. 57: "Uncle $crooge"		Written and drawn: Carl Barks
No. 58: "Uncle $crooge"		Written and drawn: Carl Barks
No. 59: "Uncle $crooge"		Written and drawn: Carl Barks
No. 60: "Uncle $crooge"		Written and drawn: Carl Barks
No. 61: "Uncle $crooge"		Written and drawn: Carl Barks
No. 62: "Uncle $crooge"	1966	Written and drawn: Carl Barks
No. 63: "Uncle $crooge"		Written and drawn: Carl Barks
No. 64: "Uncle $crooge"		Written and drawn: Carl Barks
No. 65: "Uncle $crooge"		Written and drawn: Carl Barks
No. 66: "Uncle $crooge"		Written and drawn: Carl Barks
No. 67: "Uncle $crooge"	1967	Written and drawn: Carl Barks
No. 68: "Uncle $crooge"		Written and drawn: Carl Barks
No. 69: "Uncle $crooge"		Written and drawn: Carl Barks
No. 70: "Uncle $crooge"		Written and drawn: Carl Barks
No. 71: "Uncle $crooge"		Written: Carl Barks
No. 72: "Uncle $crooge"		Written and drawn: Carl Barks
No. 73: "Uncle $crooge"	1968	Written and drawn: Carl Barks
No. 74: "Uncle $crooge"		
No. 75: "Uncle $crooge"		
No. 76: "Uncle $crooge"		
No. 77: "Uncle $crooge"		
No. 78: "Uncle $crooge"		
No. 79: "Uncle $crooge"	1969	
No. 80: "Uncle $crooge"		
No. 81: "Uncle $crooge"		
No. 82: "Uncle $crooge"		Carl Barks reprint
No. 83: "Uncle $crooge"		
No. 84: "Uncle $crooge"		Carl Barks reprint
No. 85: "Uncle $crooge"	1970	
No. 86: "Uncle $crooge"		Carl Barks reprint
No. 87: "Uncle $crooge"		Carl Barks reprint
No. 88: "Uncle $crooge"		Carl Barks reprint
No. 89: "Uncle $crooge"		Carl Barks reprint
No. 90: "Uncle $crooge"		Carl Barks reprint
No. 91: "Uncle $crooge"	1971	Carl Barks reprint
No. 92: "Uncle $crooge"		Carl Barks reprint
No. 93: "Uncle $crooge"		Carl Barks reprint
No. 94: "Uncle $crooge"		Carl Barks reprint
No. 95: "Uncle $crooge"		Carl Barks reprint
No. 96: "Uncle $crooge"		Carl Barks reprint
No. 97: "Uncle $crooge"	1972	Carl Barks reprint
No. 98: "Uncle $crooge"		Carl Barks reprint
No. 99: "Uncle $crooge"		Carl Barks reprint
No. 100: "Uncle $crooge"		Carl Barks reprint
No. 101: "Uncle $crooge"		Carl Barks reprint
No. 102: "Uncle $crooge"		Carl Barks reprint
No. 103: "Uncle $crooge"	1973	Carl Barks reprint
No. 104: "Uncle $crooge"		Carl Barks reprint
No. 105: "Uncle $crooge"		Carl Barks reprint
No. 106: "Uncle $crooge"		Carl Barks reprint
No. 107: "Uncle $crooge"		Carl Barks reprint
No. 108: "Uncle $crooge"		Carl Barks reprint
No. 109: "Uncle $crooge"	to date	Carl Barks reprint

Zorro

(Dell Color Comics)		Five one-shots
No. 882: "Zorro"	1957	Written and drawn: Alex Toth
No. 920: "Zorro"		Written and drawn: Alex Toth
No. 933: "Zorro"		Written and drawn: Alex Toth
No. 960: "Zorro"		Written and drawn: Alex Toth
No. 976: "Zorro"	1959	Drawn: Alex Toth
No. 1003: "Zorro"	June/Aug. 1959	
No. 1037: "Zorro"	Sept./Nov. 1959	Drawn: Alex Toth

Title & Number	Publication Date	Remarks
(Dell)		Quarterly
No. 8: "Zorro"	Dec./Feb. 1960	
No. 9: "Zorro"	Mar./May 1960	
No. 10: "Zorro"	June/Aug. 1960	
No. 11: "Zorro"	Sept./Nov. 1960	
No. 12: "Zorro"	Dec./Feb. 1961	
No. 13: "Zorro"	Mar./May 1961	
No. 14: "Zorro"	June/Aug. 1961	
No. 15: "Zorro"	Sept./Nov. 1961	
(Gold Key)		All nine issues are reprints and were is-
No. 1: "Zorro"	1965	sued quarterly
No. 2: "Zorro"		
No. 3: "Zorro"		
No. 4: "Zorro"		
No. 5: "Zorro"		
No. 6: "Zorro"		
No. 7: "Zorro"		
No. 8: "Zorro"		
No. 9: "Zorro"	Mar. 1968	

2.

Giant Size Comic Books

Title & Number	Publication Date	Remarks
The Best of Donald Duck and Uncle $crooge		
(Dell)		
No. 1	1964	Reprints of *Donald Duck* No. 189 and No. 408
No. 2	1967	Reprint of *Donald Duck* No. 256
The Best of Uncle $crooge and Donald Duck		
(Dell)		
No. 1	1966	Reprints of *Donald Duck* No. 159 and No. 456, and Uncle $crooge No. 6
Christmas in Disneyland		
(Dell)		
No. 1	1957	Written and drawn: Carl Barks
Christmas Parade		
(Dell)		
No. 1	1949	Written and drawn: Carl Barks
No. 2	1950	Written and drawn: Carl Barks
No. 3	1951	
No. 4	1952	
No. 5	1953	
No. 6	1954	
No. 7	1955	
No. 8	1956	Written and drawn: Carl Barks
No. 9	1958	Written and drawn: Carl Barks
No. 26	1959	Drawn: Carl Barks
(Gold Key)		
No. 1	1962	Drawn: Carl Barks
No. 5	1966	1949 reprint: By Carl Barks
No. 6	1967	1950 reprint: By Carl Barks
No. 7	1969	
No. 8	1970	
Daisy Duck and Uncle $crooge		
Picnic Time		
(Dell)		
No. 33	1960	

Title & Number	Publication Date	Remarks

Daisy Duck and Uncle $crooge
  Show Boat
  (Dell)
    No. 55
	Sept. 1961	

Davy Crockett, King of the Wild Frontier
  (Dell Four-Color Comics)
    No. 1
	1955	Annual: 100 pages

Disneyland Birthday Party
  (Dell)
    No. 1
	1958	Written and drawn: Carl Barks

Disneyland U.S.A.
  (Dell)
    No. 30
	1960	

Donald Duck Beach Party
  (Dell)
    No. 1
    No. 2
    No. 3
    No. 4
    No. 5
    No. 6
	1954
	1955
	1956
	1957
	1958
	1959
		1949 reprint: By Carl Barks
		
		Titled *Donald Duck's Beach Party*

Donald Duck in Disneyland
  (Dell)
    No. 1
	1953	

Donald Duck Fun Book
  (Dell)
    No. 1
    No. 2
	1953
	1954	

Donald Duck Merry Xmas
  (Dell)
    No. 53
	1961	

Donald and Mickey in Disneyland
  (Dell)
    No. 1
	1958	

Huey, Dewey and Louie Back to School
  (Dell)
    No. 1
    No. 22
    No. 35
    No. 49
	1958
	1959
	1960
	1961	

The Jungle Book
  (Gold Key)
    No. 1
	1967	Also published by Whitman in large size

Lady and the Tramp
  (Dell)
    No. 1
	1955	

Man in Space
  (Dell)
    No. 27
	1959	

Mary Poppins
  (Gold Key)
    No. 1
	1964	

Merry Christmas
  (Dell)
    No. 39
	1960	

Mickey and Donald in Vacationland
  (Dell)
    No. 47
	1961	

342

Title & Number	Publication Date	Remarks
Mickey Mouse Almanac		
(Dell)		
No. 1	1957	
Mickey Mouse Birthday Party		
(Dell)		
No. 1	1953	
Mickey Mouse Club Parade		
(Dell)		
No. 1	1955	
Mickey Mouse in Fantasyland		
(Dell)		
No. 1	1957	
Mickey Mouse in Frontierland		
(Dell)		
No. 1	1956	
Mickey Mouse Summer Fun		
(Dell)		
No. 1	1958	
No. 2	1959	Drawn: Carl Barks
Mickey Mouse Surprise Party		
(Dell)		
No. 1	1968	
Peter Pan Treasure Chest		
(Dell)		
No. 1	1952	
Picnic Party		Continuation of *Vacation Parade*
(Dell)		
No. 6	1955	
No. 7	1956	
No. 8	1957	Writen and drawn: Carl Barks
Shaggy Dog and the Absent-Minded Professor		
(Gold Key)		
No. 30032–708	1967	
Silly Symphonies		
(Dell)		
No. 1	1952	
No. 2	1953	
No. 3	1954	
No. 4	1954	
No. 5	1955	
No. 6	1955	
No. 7	1957	
No. 8	1958	
No. 9	1959	
Sleeping Beauty		
(Dell)		
No. 1	1959	
(Gold Key)		
No. 1	1970	
Summer Fun		
(See *Mickey Mouse Summer Fun*)		
The Sword in the Stone		
(Gold Key)		
No. 1	1963	
Uncle Donald and His Nephew's Dude Ranch		
(Dell)		
No. 52	1961	

Title & Number	Publication Date	Remarks
Uncle Donald and His Nephew's Family Fun (Dell) No. 38	1960	
Uncle $crooge and Donald Duck (Gold Key) No. 1	1965	Reprint of *Uncle $crooge* No. 386 and No. 29. Drawn: Carl Barks
Uncle $crooge Goes to Disneyland (Dell) No. 1	1957	
Vacation in Disneyland (Dell) No. 1	1958	
(Gold Key) No. 1	1965	
Vacation Parade (Dell) No. 1	1950	Written and drawn: Carl Barks
No. 2	1951	
No. 3	1952	
No. 4	1953	
No. 5	1954	

3.

Giveaways

PART A: AMERICAN DAIRY ASSOCIATION

Title & Number	Publication Date	Remarks
Br'er Rabbit in Ice Cream for the Party	1955	16 pages
Cinderella in Fairest of the Fair	1955	16 pages
Lady and the Tramp in Butter Late than Never	1955	16 pages
Snow White and the Seven Dwarfs in the Milky Way	1955	16 pages

PART B: BENDIX

A New Adventure of Snow White and the Seven Dwarfs (Walt Disney Productions)	1952	32 pages

PART C: CHEERIOS PREMIUMS

(Walt Disney Productions)

Pocket size. 16 titles in series. All published in 1947

Set W:
Bucky Bug and the Cannibal King
Donald Duck and the Pirates   1947
Mickey Mouse and the Haunted House
Pluto Joins the FBI

Set X:
Br'er Rabbit Outwits Br'er Fox
Donald Duck, Counter Spy
Goofy Lost in the Desert
Mickey Mouse at the Rodeo

Set Y:
Br'er Rabbit's Secret
Donald Duck's Atom Bomb   Written and drawn: Carl Barks
Dumbo and the Circus Mystery
Mickey Mouse Meets the Wizard

344

Set Z:
Donald Duck Pilots a Jet Plane
Mickey Mouse's Secret Room
Pluto Turns Sleuth Hound
The Seven Dwarfs and the Enchanted Mountain

PART D: CHEERIOS 3-D GIVEAWAYS

(Walt Disney Productions)   Pocket size. 24 titles in series. All published in 1954

Set 1:
Donald Duck: Apache Gold
Donald Duck with Huey, Dewey, and Louie
Donald Duck and Uncle $crooge: The Firefighters   1954
Donald Duck's Nephews: The Fabulous Inventors
Mickey Mouse: Flight to Nowhere
Mickey Mouse and Goofy: Pirate Plunder
Mickey Mouse: Moaning Mountain
Mickey Mouse: Secret of the Ming Vase

Set 2:
Donald Duck: Circus Adventures
Donald Duck in the Magic Cows
Donald Duck: Mystery Ship
Donald Duck: Treasure of Timbuktu
Mickey Mouse: Arctic Explorers
Mickey Mouse and Goofy: Kid Kokonut
Mickey Mouse: Phantom Sheriff
Mickey Mouse and Pluto: Operation China

Set 3:
Donald Duck in the Foreign Legion
Donald Duck in Robot Reporter
Donald Duck and Uncle $crooge: Timber Trouble
Donald Duck and Witch Hazel
Mickey Mouse: Airwalking Wonder
Mickey Mouse in Darkest Africa
Mickey Mouse: Rajah's Rescue
Mickey Mouse: Slumbering Sleuth

PART E: FIRESTONE ANNUAL CHRISTMAS GIVEAWAY

Donald and Mickey	1944	20 pages. Reprint of *Walt Disney Comics and Stories* No. 35
Donald and Mickey	1945	8 pages. Written and drawn: Carl Barks
Donald and Mickey	1946	8 pages. Written and drawn: Carl Barks
Donald and Mickey	1947	8 pages. Written and drawn: Carl Barks
Donald and Mickey	1948	8 pages. Written and drawn: Carl Barks
Donald and Mickey	1949	8 pages. Written and drawn: Carl Barks
Firestone Presents Comics by Walt Disney	1943	20 pages

PART F: FRITOS GIVEAWAY

Donald Duck: Plotting Picnicker	1962	16 pages
Ludwig Von Drake: Fish Stampede	1962	16 pages
Mickey Mouse and Goofy: Bicep Bungle	1962	16 pages

PART G: ICY FROST TWINS ICE CREAM BARS

Donald Duck's Surprise Party	1948	16 pages

PART H: KEEP AMERICA BEAUTIFUL, INC.

Donald Duck in the Litterbug	1963	16 pages

Br'er Rabbit in a Kite Tail	1955	16 pages; half-size
(Walt Disney Productions)		
Donald Duck Tells about Kites	1954	Drawn: Carl Barks
Pinocchio Learns about Kites	1954	8 pages

PART J: RICHFIELD OIL COMPANY

Adventure in Disneyland	1955	16 pages
(Walt Disney Productions)		

PART K: SEARS, ROEBUCK & COMPANY

Walt Disney's Comics and Stories	1943	36 pages

PART L: WHEATIES

(Walt Disney Productions)   Pocket size. 32 titles in series

Set A:
Donald Duck and the Giant Ape	1950
Donald Duck and the Haunted Jewels	1950
Goofy: Tightrope Acrobat	1950
Grandma Duck: Homespun Detective	1950
Li'l Bad Wolf: Forest Ranger	1950
Mickey Mouse and the Disappearing Island	1950
Mickey Mouse: Roving Reporter	1950
Pluto and the Bogus Money	1950

Set B:
Donald Duck and the Buccaneers	1950
Donald Duck: Klondike Kid	1950
Donald Duck: Trail Blazer	1950
Goofy and the Gangsters	1950
Li'l Bad Wolf in the Hollow Tree Hideout	1950
Mickey Mouse and the Mystery Sea Monster	1950
Mickey Mouse and the Pharaoh's Curse	1950
Pluto: Canine Cowpoke	1950

Set C:
Donald Duck and the Inca Idol	1951
Donald Duck in the Lost Lakes	1951
Goofy: Big Game Hunter	1951
Gus and Jaq Save the Ship	1951
Li'l Bad Wolf: Fire Fighter	1951
Mickey Mouse and the Magic Mountain	1951
Mickey Mouse and the Stagecoach Bandits	1951
Minnie Mouse: Girl Explorer	1951

Set D:
Br'er Rabbit's Sunken Treasure	1951
Donald Duck in Indian Country	1951
Donald Duck: Mighty Mystic	1951
Li'l Bad Wolf and the Secret of the Woods	1951
Mickey Mouse and the Abandoned Mine	1951
Mickey Mouse and the Medicine Man	1951
Minnie Mouse: Girl Explorer	1951
Pluto and the Mysterious Package	1951

PART M: HORLICK'S MALTED MILK

Bambi		32 pages. Also given away by various toy
(K. K. Publications)	1941	stores

PART N: CANADA DRY

The Swamp Fox
No. 1: "Tory Masquerade"	1960	16 pages
No. 2: "Rindau Rampage"	1960	16 pages
No. 3: "Turnabout Tactics"	1960	16 pages

PART O: AMERICAN MOTORS, HUDSON DIVISION

Davy Crockett in the Raid at Piney Creek	1955	16 pages

PART P: ADMIRAL

New Adventures of Peter Pan	1953	32 pages

PART Q: ROBIN HOOD FLOUR

New Adventures of Robin Hood
No. 1: "Ghosts Of Waylea Castle"	1952	32 pages
No. 2: "The Miller's Ransom"	1952	32 pages

PART R: SALES PROMOTIONS, INC.

Santa and Pollyanna Play the Glad Game	1960	16 pages

PART S: MARCH OF COMICS

(K. K. Publications)
No. 4: "Donald Duck"	1947	Written and drawn: Carl Barks
No. 8: "Mickey Mouse"	1947	
No. 20: "Donald Duck"	1948	Written and drawn: Carl Barks
No. 27: "Mickey Mouse"	1948	
No. 41: "Donald Duck"	1949	Written and drawn: Carl Barks
No. 45: "Mickey Mouse"	1949	
No. 56: "Donald Duck"	1950	
No. 60: "Mickey Mouse"	1950	
No. 69: "Donald Duck"	1951	
No. 74: "Mickey Mouse"	1951	
No. 258: "The Sword in the Stone"	1963	
No. 263: "Donald Duck"	1964	

PART T: MISCELLANEOUS

Donald Duck (K. K. Publications)	1944	Christmas giveaway. 16 pages
Snow White and the Seven Dwarfs in *Mystery of the Missing Magic*	1958	16 pages. Market premium

4.

One-shot Comic Books

(Dell Color Comics)
The Absent-Minded Professor No. 1199	1961	
The African Lion No. 665	1955	
Alice in Wonderland No. 331	1951	
Alice in Wonderland No. 10144–503	1965	Reprint
Andy Burnett No. 865	1957	

Annette		
No. 905	1958	
Annette's Life Story		
No. 1100	1960	
Babes in Toyland		
No. 1282	1961	
Baloo and Little Britches		
No. 10217–803	1967	
Bambi		
No. 12	1942	
Bambi		
No. 186	1948	Reprinted with new covers as *Bambi*, No. 3, 1956
Bambi		
No. 10087–309	1963	Reprint of No. 186
Bambi		
No. 10087–607	1966	Reprint
Bambi's Children		
No. 30	1943	
Bear Country		
No. 758	1956	
Beaver Valley		
No. 625	1955	
Ben and Me		
No. 539	1954	
The Best of Donald Duck		
No. 10166–511	1965	No. 1 Reprint of *Donald Duck* No. 223
Big Red		
No. 10026–211	1962	
Big Red		
No. 10026–503	1964	Reprint
Blackbeard's Ghost		
No. 10222–806	1968	
Bon Voyage		
No. 12068–212	1962	
Br'er Rabbit Does It Again		
No. 208	1948	
Bullwhip Griffin		
No. 10181–706	1967	
Captain Hook and Peter Pan		
No. 446	1952	
Cinderella		
No. 272	1950	
Cinderella		
No. 786	1957	Partial reprint of No. 272
Cinderella		
No. 10152–508	1965	Reprint
Clint and Mac		
No. 889	1958	
Comanche		
No. 1350	1962	Reprint of No. 966
Corky and White Shadow		
No. 707	1956	Mickey Mouse Club
Covered Wagons, Ho		
No. 814	1957	
Darby O'Gill and the Little People		
No. 1024	1959	
Davy Crockett		
No. 10106–911	1969	
Davy Crockett at the Alamo		
No. 639	1955	
Davy Crockett in the Great Keelboat Race		
No. 664	1955	
Davy Crockett: Indian Fighter		
No. 631	1955	
Davy Crockett: King of the Wild Frontier		
No. 10106–312	1963	Reprint

Davy Crockett and the River Pirates		
No. 671	1955	
Donald Duck Beach Party		
No. 10158–509	1965	Reprint of *Donald Duck Beach Party* No. 1
Donald in Mathmagic Land		
No. 1051	1959	
Donald in Mathmagic Land		
No. 1198	1961	Reprint of No. 1051
Donald and the Wheel		
No. 1190	1961	Cover: Carl Barks
Dumbo		
No. 17	1941	
Dumbo		
No. 668	1955	
Dumbo		
No. 10090–310	1963	Reprint
Dumbo in Sky Voyage		
No. 234	1949	
Emil and the Detectives		
No. 10120–502	1964	
Escapade in Florence		
No. 10043–301	1962	
The Fighting Prince of Donegal		
No. 10193–701	1966	
The First Americans		
No. 843	1957	
Gallegher, Boy Reporter		
No. 10149–505	1965	
The Great Cat Family		
No. 750	1956	
Great Locomotive Chase		
No. 712	1956	
Greyfriars Bobby		
No. 1189	1961	
The Gnome-mobile		
No. 10207–710	1967	
Hans Brinker		
No. 1273	1962	
The Happiest Millionaire		
No. 10221–804	1968	
The Horse without a Head		
No. 10109–401	1963	
The Horsemasters		
No. 1260	1961	
In Search of the Castaways		
No. 10048–303	1962	
Jungle Cat		
No. 1136	1960	
Kidnapped		
No. 1101	1960	
Kidnapped		
No. 10080–306	1963	Reprint of No. 1101
King Louie and Mowgli (Little Britches)		
No. 10223–805	1968	
Lady and the Tramp		
No. 629	1955	
Lady and the Tramp		
No. 10042–301	1962	Reprint of No. 629
Lady and the Tramp Album		
No. 634	1955	
The Legend of Lobo		
No. 10059–303	1962	
The Legend of Young Dick Turpin		
No. 10176–605	1966	
Light in the Forest		
No. 891	1958	

The Littlest Outlaw		
No. 609	1954	
The Love Bug		
No. 10237–906	1969	
Lt. Robin Crusoe, U.S.N.		
No. 10191–610	1966	
Man in Flight		
No. 836	1957	
Man in Space		
No. 716	1956	
Man in Space-Satellites		
No. 954	1958	
Mars and Beyond		
No. 866	1957	
Mary Poppins		
No. 10136–501	1964	
Merlin Jones as the Monkey's Uncle		
No. 10115–510	1965	
Mickey Mouse Club		
No. 10099–401	1963	
Mickey Mouse in Magic Land		
No. 819	1957	
The Miracle of the White Stallions		
No. 10065–306	1963	
The Misadventures of Merlin Jones		
No. 10115–405	1964	
Moon Pilot		
No. 1313	1962	
The Moon-Spinners		
No. 10124–410	1964	
The Nature of Things		
No. 727	1956	
The Nature of Things		
No. 842	1957	
Nikki, Wild Dog of the North		
No. 1226	1961	
Nikki, Wild Dog of the North		
No. 10141–412	1964	
Old Ironsides with Johnny Tremain		
No. 874	1957	
Old Yeller		
No. 869	1957	
Old Yeller		
No. 10168–601	1965	Reprint
101 Dalmatians		
No. 1183	1961	
101 Dalmatians		
No. 10247–002	1969	
The Parent Trap		
No. 1210	1961	
Paul Revere's Ride with Johnny Tremain		
No. 822	1957	
Perri		
No. 847	1957	
Peter Pan		
No. 442	1952	
Peter Pan		
No. 926	1958	Reprint of No. 442
Peter Pan		
No. 10086–309	1963	Reprint
Peter Pan		
No. 10086–909	1969	
Pinocchio		
No. 92	1945	Written and drawn: Walt Kelly
Pinocchio		
No. 252	1949	Written and drawn: Walt Kelly
Pinocchio		
No. 545	1954	Written and drawn: Walt Kelly
		Partial reprint of No. 92

Pinocchio		
No. 1203	1961	
Pinocchio		
No. 10089–310	1963	Reprint
Pollyanna		
No. 1129	1960	
The Prince and the Pauper		
No. 01654–207	1962	
The Reluctant Dragon		
No. 13	1941	
Robin Hood		
No. 413	1952	
Robin Hood		
No. 669	1955	Reprint of No. 413
Robin Hood		
No. 10163–506	1965	Reprint
Rob Roy		
No. 544	1954	
Secrets of Life		
No. 749	1956	
Seven Dwarfs		
No. 227	1949	
Shaggy Dog		
No. 985	1959	
Sleeping Beauty and the Prince		
No. 973	1959	
Sleeping Beauty's Fairy Godmother		
No. 984	1959	
Snow White and the Seven Dwarfs		
No. 49	1944	
Snow White and the Seven Dwarfs		
No. 382	1952	Partial reprint of No. 49
Snow White and the Seven Dwarfs		
No. 10091–310	1963	Reprint
Snow White and the Seven Dwarfs		
No. 10091–709	1967	Reprint
Son of Flubber		
No. 10057–304	1963	
Song of the South, Featuring Br'er Rabbit		
No. 693	1956	Partial reprint of No. 129
Stormy		
No. 537	1954	
Summer Magic		
No. 10076–309	1963	
The Swamp Fox		
No. 1179	1961	
Swiss Family Robinson		
No. 1156	1960	
Swiss Family Robinson		
No. 10236–904	1969	
Sword and the Rose		
No. 505	1953	
Ten Who Dared		
No. 1178	1960	
Texas John Slaughter		
No. 1181	1961	
That Darn Cat		
No. 10171–602	1965	
This Is Your Life, Donald Duck		
No. 1109	1960	
The Three Caballeros		
No. 71	1945	Written and drawn: Walt Kelly
The Three Little Pigs		
No. 10114–405	1964	
The Three Little Pigs		
No. 10114–809	1968	Reprint
The Three Little Pigs and the Wonderful Magic Lamp		
No. 218	1949	

A Tiger Walks		
No. 10117–406	1964	
Toby Tyler		
No. 1092	1960	
Toby Tyler		
No. 10142–502	1964	Reprint
Tonka		
No. 966	1958	
Treasure Island		
No. 624	1955	
Treasure Island		
No. 01845–211	1962	Reprint of No. 624
Treasure Island		
No. 10200–703	1966	Reprint
The Truth about Mother Goose		
No. 862	1957	
20,000 Leagues under the Sea		
No. 614	1954	
20,000 Leagues under the Sea		
No. 10095–312	1963	Reprint
Unbirthday Party with Alice in Wonderland		
No. 341	1951	
Uncle Remus and His Tales of Br'er Rabbit		
No. 129	1946	
Uncle $crooge and Money		
No. 10167–703	1966	
Vacation in Disneyland		
No. 1025	1959	Drawn: Carl Barks
Wart and the Wizard		
No. 10102–402	1963	
Water Birds and the Olympic Elk		
No. 700	1956	
Westward Ho the Wagons		
No. 738	1956	
When Knighthood Was in Flower		
No. 682	1956	Reprint of No. 505
White Wilderness		
No. 943	1958	
Wringle Wrangle		
No. 821	1957	

5.

Miscellaneous

Title & Number	Publication Date	Remarks
Christmas Parade		Three one-shots
(Dell Color Comics)		
No. 2	1963	
No. 3	1964	
No. 4	1965	
Dell Junior Treasury		
(Dell Color Comics)		
No. 1: Alice in Wonderland	June 1955	Only Disney title in series
Golden Picture Stories Books		
No. ST-3	1961	
No. ST-4	1961	

Walt Disney Presents
(Dell)
No. 997   1959
No. 2   Dec./Feb. 1960   Quarterly
No. 3   Mar./May 1960   Quarterly
No. 4   June/Aug. 1960   Quarterly
No. 5   Sept./Nov. 1960   Quarterly
No. 6   Dec./Feb. 1961   Quarterly

Walt Disney's Comics and Stories
(Dell)
No. 1 to No. 399   Oct. 1940 to date

Continuation of *Mickey Mouse Magazine*
(monthly)

Issues Nos. 1–30 contain Donald Duck newspaper reprints
Issue No. 31 is the first Donald Duck by Carl Barks
Issue Nos. 32–36, 38–40, 41–112, 114, 117, 124–283, 286, 288, 289, 291, 292, 294, 297, and 312 were all done by Carl Barks.
Issue Nos. 298–308, 328, 335, 342 contain Barks reprints.
Issue Nos. 290, 295–96, 298, 301, 303–4, 306–7, 309–10, 313–16, 319, 321–22, 324, 326, 328, 329, 331–32, 334, 341–42, 350–51, have Barks covers.

Walt Disney's Comics Digest
(Gold Key)
No. 1 to No. 44   1968 to date

Walt Disney's Showcase
(Gold Key)
No. 1 to No. 19   Oct. 1970

Wonderful World of Adventure
(Gold Key)
No. 1   Apr. 1963   Mooncussers/Captain Nemo
No. 2   July 1963   Johnny Shiloh/Captain Nemo
No. 3   Oct. 1963   Savage Sam/Captain Nemo

Appendix D:

Disney Books

The following is an extensive list of books produced through 1950 by Walt Disney Productions and its predecessor companies. (It should be noted that many books published in the United States were marketed in the other English-speaking countries. The reverse is also true.) All entries are presented alphabetically by book title. The publisher and date of publication are given.

Title	Publisher	Date	Remarks
ABC Mickey Mouse Alphabet Book	Racine: Whitman	1936	30 pages. No. 936. "A Mickey Mouse Alphabet Book from A to Z" on cover
ABC's of Hand Tools: Their Correct Usage and Care	Detroit: General Motors Corp.	1945	Later edition, 1967, 47 pp. Also 1971 reprint
The Adventures of Mickey Mouse	Philadelphia: McKay	1931	Book 1: 32 pp.
The Adventures of Mickey Mouse	Philadelphia: McKay	1932	Book 2: 32 pp.
The Adventures of Mr. Toad	New York: Simon and Schuster	1949	25 pp. Big Golden Book. From the original story The Wind in the Willows by Kenneth Grahame. Adapted by John Hench
Animals from Snow White and the Seven Dwarfs	Racine: Whitman	1938	11 pp. No. 922
The Art of Walt Disney	New York: Macmillan	1942	290 pp. By Robert D. Feild
Ave Maria: An Interpretation from Fantasia	New York: Random House	1940	36 pp. Inspired by the music of Franz Schubert. Lyrics by Rachel Field
Baby Weems	New York: Doubleday	1941	62 pp. By Joe Grant and Dick Huemer, from the motion picture The Reluctant Dragon. Introduction by Robert Benchley
Bambi	New York: Simon and Schuster	1941	52 pp. Adapted from the novel by Felix Salten
Bambi	New York: Grosset and Dunlap	1942	32 pp.
Bambi	Boston: Heath	1944	101 pp. Retold by Idella Purnell
Bambi	New York: Simon and Schuster	1948	42 pp. (with later reprints of 28 pp. and 24 pp.). Little Golden Book No. D7. Revised reprint, Golden Press, 1960, Little Golden Book No. D90. A later printing revises the cover, removing a large tree. Illustrated and adapted by Bob Grant
Bambi	New York: Simon and Schuster	1949	28 pp. Fuzzy Golden Book No. 443. There is also a version without flocking
Bambi Picture Book	Racine: Whitman	1942	14 pp. No. 930
Bambi Plays Follow the Leader	New York: Simon and Schuster	1950	18 pp. Tiny Golden Book by Jane Werner. Illustrated by Campbell Grant. On cover: Bambi
Bambi Story Book	Racine: Whitman	1942	96 pp. No. 725
Bambi, the Prince of the Forest	Racine: Whitman	1942	424 pp. Better Little Book No. 1469
Bambi's Children	Racine: Whitman	1943	424 pp. Better Little Book No. 1497
The Big Bad Wolf and Little Red Riding Hood	New York: Blue Ribbon Books	1934	60 pp.
The Blue Fairy	Racine: Whitman	1940	24 pp. No. 1059. A story paint book from box of six Pinocchio books for reading, coloring, and playing.
Bongo	New York: Simon and Schuster	1947	26 pp. Big Golden Book. Based on an adaptation of the original story by Sinclair Lewis. Illustrated by Edgar Starr

Title	Publisher	Date	Remarks
Bongo	Racine: Whitman	1948	32 pp. Story Hour Series No. 803. Also issued in paperback
Bongo	New York: Simon and Schuster	1948	42 pp. Little Golden Library No. D9. Revised reprint: 24 pp. 1957. Little Golden Book No. D62. Illustrations adapted by Campbell Grant
Bongo Stars Again	New York: Simon and Schuster	1950	18 pp. Tiny Golden Book. By Jane Werner. Illustrated by Campbell Grant
Bootle Beetle's Adventures	New York: Simon and Schuster	1950	18 pp. Tiny Golden Book. By Jane Werner. Illustrated by Campbell Grant
Brave Little Tailor	Racine: Whitman	1938	24 pp. No. 972
Brave Little Tailor	Racine: Whitman	1939	64 pp. No. 1058
Brave Little Tailor	Racine: Whitman	1939	12 pp. Penny Book No. 1145
Br'er Rabbit	Racine: Whitman	1947	282 pp. Better Little Book No. 1426
Br'er Rabbit	Racine: Whitman	1949	192 pp. New Better Little Book No. 704
Br'er Rabbit Plays a Trick	New York: Simon and Schuster	1950	18 pp. Tiny Golden Book. By Jane Werner. Illustrated by Campbell Grant
Br'er Rabbit Rides the Fox	New York: Grosset and Dunlap	1946	32 pp. Told by Marion Palmer based on the original stories by Joel Chandler Harris
Cinderella	Racine: Whitman	1950	24 pp. Cozy-Corner Book No. 2416. Also No. 2037, with different end papers and on cheaper paper. Adapted by Julius Svendsen
Cinderella	New York: Simon and Schuster	1950	26 pp. Big Golden Book No. 425. (There are two versions of No. 425—one is slightly smaller and without the gold plate and tipped in pumpkin.) Reprinted in 1955, Walt Disney Library and 1962, 28 pp. Big Golden Book No. 10425
Cinderella	New York: Golden Press	1950	28 pp. Little Golden Book No. D13. Revised printings as Little Golden Book No. D59 and D114, 24 pp., the latter in 1964. Illustrations adapted by Campbell Grant
Cinderella and the Magic Wand	Racine: Whitman	1950	188 pp. New Better Little Book No. 711
Cinderella Puppet Show	New York: Simon and Schuster	1949	Unpaged. Golden Toy Book
Cinderella's Ball Gown	New York: Simon and Schuster	1950	18 pp. Tiny Golden Book. By Jane Werner. Illustrated by Campbell Grant
Cinderella's Friends	New York: Simon and Schuster	1950	28 pp. Little Golden Book No. D17. Revised reprints, 24 pp. in 1956 as Little Golden Book No. D58 and in 1964 as Little Golden Book No. D115. Told by Jane Werner. Illustrations adapted by Al Dempster
Circus	New York: Simon and Schuster	1944	28 pp. Big Golden Book
Clock Cleaners	Racine: Whitman	1938	12 pp. Walt Disney Picture Book No. 947. Linen-like
The Cold-Blooded Penguin	New York: Simon and Schuster	1944	24 pp. Walt Disney's Little Library. Adapted from *The Three Caballeros* by Robert Edmunds
Come Play with Donald Duck	New York: Grosset and Dunlap	1948	32 pp. Walt Disney Picture-Story Books. Adapted by Ernest Terrazas
Come Play with Mickey Mouse	New York: Grosset and Dunlap	1948	32 pp. Walt Disney Picture-Story Books. Adapted by Manuel Gonzales
Come Play with Pluto Pup	New York: Grosset and Dunlap	1948	32 pp. Walt Disney Picture-Story Books. Adapted by Julius Svendsen
Come Play with the Seven Dwarfs	New York: Grosset and Dunlap	1948	32 pp. Walt Disney Picture-Story Books. Adapted by Julius Svendsen
The Country Cousin	Philadelphia: McKay	1937	20 pp.
Dance of the Hours, from Fantasia	New York: Harper	1940	36 pp.
Danny, the Little Black Lamb	Racine: Whitman	1949	32 pp. Story Hour Series No. 807. Also issued in paperback
Donald Duck	Racine: Whitman	1935	14 pp. No. 978. First Donald Duck Book
Donald Duck	New York: Grosset and Dunlap	1936	33 pp.
Donald Duck and the Boys	Racine: Whitman	1948	96 pp. No. 845
Donald Duck in Bringing up the Boys	Racine: Whitman	1948	32 pp. Story Hour Series No. 800. Also issued in paperback
Donald Duck and the Ducklings	New York: Dell	1938	191 pp. Fast-Action
Donald Duck Gets Fed Up	Racine: Whitman	1940	424 pp. Better Little Book No. 1462

Title	Publisher	Date	Remarks
Donald Duck and Ghost Morgan's Treasure	Racine: Whitman	1946	348 pp. Better Little Book No. 1411
Donald Duck in the Great Kite Maker	Racine: Whitman	1949	20 pp. Tiny Tales No. 1030. Also in 1959, Tiny Tales No. 2952
Donald Duck and the Green Serpent	Racine: Whitman	1947	284 pp. Better Little Book No. 1432
Donald Duck Has His Ups and Downs	Racine: Whitman	1937	16 pp. No. 1077
Donald Duck Has His Ups and Downs	Racine: Whitman	1937	24 pp. Picture Story Book No. 883
Donald Duck Headed for Trouble	Racine: Whitman	1942	424 pp. Better Little Book No. 1430
Donald Duck in the High Andes	New York: Grosset and Dunlap	1943	32 pp. From the Walt Disney feature production *Saludos Amigos*
Donald Duck and His Cat Troubles	Racine: Whitman	1948	95 pp. No. 845
Donald Duck and His Friends	Racine: Whitman	1937	45 pp. Donald Duck Story Book No. 5050
Donald Duck and His Friends	Boston: Heath	1939	102 pp. By Jean Ayer
Donald Duck and His Nephews	Boston: Heath	1940	66 pp. By Florence Brumbaugh
Donald Duck Hunting for Trouble	Racine: Whitman	1938	424 pp. Better Little Book No. 1478
Donald Duck Is Here Again	Racine: Whitman	1944	346 pp. Better Little Book No. 1484
Donald Duck Lays Down the Law	Racine: Whitman	1948	286 pp. Better Little Book No. 1449
Donald Duck and the Mystery of the Double X	Racine: Whitman	1949	176 pp. New Better Little Book No. 705
Donald Duck Off the Beam	Racine: Whitman	1943	424 pp. Better Little Book No. 1438
Donald Duck Out of Luck	New York: Dell	1940	192 pp. Fast-Action
Donald Duck Says Such Luck	Racine: Whitman	1941	424 pp. Better Little Book No. 1424
Donald Duck Sees South America	Boston: Heath	1945	137 pp. By Marion Palmer
Donald Duck Sees Stars	Racine: Whitman	1941	424 pp. Better Little Book No. 1422
Donald Duck Takes It on the Chin	New York: Dell	1941	192 pp. Fast-Action
Donald Duck Up in the Air	Racine: Whitman	1945	346 pp. Better Little Book No. 1486
Donald Duck in Volcano Valley	Racine: Whitman	1949	286 pp. Better Little Book No. 1457
Donald Duck's Adventure	New York: Simon and Schuster	1950	28 pp. Little Golden Book No. D14. Also a Mickey Mouse Club Book and a 24-page edition with a new cover, green lettering instead of red. By Annie North Bedford. Illustrations adapted by Campbell Grant
Donald Duck's Cousin Gus	Racine: Whitman	1939	12 pp. Penny Book No. 1145
Donald Duck's Toy Train	New York: Simon and Schuster	1950	28 pp. Little Golden Book No. D18. By Jane Werner. Illustrations adapted by Dick Kelsey and Bill Justice from the motion picture *Out Of Scale*. Also a 24-page edition
Donald Duck's Wild Goose Chase	New York: Simon and Schuster	1950	18 pp. Tiny Golden Book. By Jane Werner. Illustrated by Campbell Grant
Donald Forgets to Duck	Racine: Whitman	1939	424 pp. Better Little Book No. 1434
Donald and Mickey, Cub Scouts	Racine: Whitman	1950	24 pp. Cozy-Corner Book No. 2031
Donald's Better Self	Racine: Whitman	1939	12 pp. Penny Book No. 1145
Donald's Lucky Day	Racine: Whitman	1939	20 pp. No. 897
Donald's Lucky Day	Racine: Whitman	1939	12 pp. Penny Book No. 1145
Donald's Penguin	New York: Garden City	1940	24 pp.
Dopey: He Don't Talk None	Racine: Whitman	1938	11 pp. No. 955
Dopey and the Wicked Witch	New York: Simon and Schuster	1950	18 pp. Tiny Golden Book. By Jane Werner. Illustrated by Campbell Grant
Dumbo	New York: Simon and Schuster	1947	42 pp. Little Golden Book No. D3. Also published in 24- and 28-page editions, with several revised covers
Dumbo of the Circus	New York: Garden City	1941	52 pp
Dumbo of the Circus	New York: K.K. Publications	1941	48 pp.
Dumbo of the Circus	Boston: Heath	1948	90 pp. By Dorothy Walter Baruch. Illustrations adapted by Melvin Shaw
Dumbo of the Circus: Only His Ears Grew	Racine: Whitman	1941	424 pp. Better Little Book No. 1400
Dumbo, the Flying Elephant	New York: Dell	1941	192 pp. Fast-Action
Dumbo, the Flying Elephant	Racine: Whitman	1941	32 pp. By Helen Aberson and Harold Pearl
Dumbo: The Story of the Flying Elephant	Racine: Whitman	1942	24 pp. No. 710
Dumbo: The Story of the Little Elephant with the Big Ears	Burbank: Walt Disney Productions	1941	12 pp.
Dumbo's Magic Feather	New York: Simon and Schuster	1950	18 pp. Tiny Golden Book. By Jane Werner. Illustrated by Campbell Grant
Edgar Bergen's Charlie McCarthy Meets Walt Disney's Snow White	Racine: Whitman	1938	23 pp. No. 986
Elmer Elephant	Philadelphia: McKay	1936	46 pp.
Elmer Elephant	Racine: Whitman	1938	12 pp. No. 948. Linenlike

Title	Publisher	Date	Remarks
The Famous Movie Story of Walt Disney's Snow White and the Seven Dwarfs	New York: K. K. Publications	1938	15 pp.
Famous Seven Dwarfs	Racine: Whitman	1938	20 pp. No. 944
Famous Seven Dwarfs	Racine: Whitman	1938	12 pp. No. 933. Linenlike
Fantasia	New York: Simon and Schuster	1940	158 pp. By Deems Taylor with foreword by Leopold Stokowski
Fantasia in Technicolor and Fantasound	New York: Walt Disney Productions	1940	28 pp. Illustrated program
The Farmyard Symphony	Racine: Whitman	1939	64 pp. No. 1058
Farmyard Symphony	Racine: Whitman	1939	12 pp. Penny Book No. 1145
Ferdinand the Bull	Racine: Whitman	1938	12 pp. Linenlike No. 903
Ferdinand the Bull	Racine: Whitman	1938	31 pp. No. 842
Ferdinand the Bull	New York: Dell	1938	16 pp.
Figaro and Cleo	New York: Random House	1940	27 pp. Based on the motion picture Pinocchio
Figaro and Cleo: A Story Paint Book	Racine: Whitman	1940	24 pp. No. 1059. From box of 6 Pinocchio Books for Reading, Coloring, Playing
Forest Friends from Snow White	New York: Grosset and Dunlap	1938	28 pp.
Forty Big Pages of Mickey Mouse	Racine: Whitman	1936	40 pp. No. 945
Funny Stories about Donald and Mickey	Racine: Whitman	1945	128 pp. No. 714
Geppetto: A Story Paint Book	Racine: Whitman	1940	24 pp. No. 1059. From box of 6 Pinocchio Books for Reading, Coloring, Playing
The Golden Touch	Racine: Whitman	1937	212 pp.
Goofy and Wilbur	Racine: Whitman	1939	12 pp. Penny Book No. 1145
The Gremlins	New York: Random House	1943	52 pp. A Royal Air Force story, by Flight Lieutenant Roald Dahl
He Drew as He Pleased: A Sketchbook	New York: Simon and Schuster	1948	188 pp. By Albert Hurter
Here They Are	Boston: Heath	1940	56 pp. By Ardra Wavle
Hiawatha	Philadelphia: McKay	1937	20 pp.
Hiawatha	Racine: Whitman	1938	12 pp. Walt Disney Picture Book No. 924. Linenlike
Honest John and Giddy	New York: Random House	1940	27 pp. Based on Pinocchio
J. Worthington Foulfellow and Gideon: A Story Paint Book	Racine: Whitman	1940	24 pp. No. 1059. From box of 6 Pinocchio books for Reading, Coloring, Playing
Jiminy Cricket	New York: Random House	1940	27 pp.
Jiminy Cricket: A Story Paint Book	Racine: Whitman	1940	24 pp. No. 1059. From box of 6 Pinocchio books for Reading, Coloring, Playing
Johnny Appleseed	New York: Simon and Shuster	1949	42 pp. Little Golden Book No. D11. Illustrations adapted by Ted Parmalee from the motion picture Melody Time
Johnny Appleseed	Racine: Whitman	1949	32 pp. Story Hour Series No. 808. Also issued in paperback
The Life of Donald Duck	New York: Random House	1941	72 pp.
Little Pig's Picnic and Other Stories	Boston: Heath	1939	102 pp. By Margaret Wise Brown
Little Red Riding Hood and the Big Bad Wolf	Philadelphia: McKay	1934	32 pp.
Magnificent Mr. Toad	New York: Grosset and Dunlap	1949	32 pp. Walt Disney Picture Story Book. From the motion picture Ichabod and Mr. Toad based on The Wind in the Willows by Kenneth Grahame. Illustrations adapted by John Hench
Mickey and the Beanstalk	New York: Grosset and Dunlap	1947	32 pp. Pictures by Campbell Grant. Based on the motion picture Fun And Fancy Free
Mickey and the Beanstalk	Racine: Whitman	1948	32 pp. Story Hour Series No. 804. Also in paperback
Mickey and Minnie at the Carnival	Racine: Whitman	1934	38 pp. "Mickey Mouse at the Carnival" on the cover. Wee Little Book Set No. 512
Mickey Mouse	Philadelphia: McKay	1931	48 pp. Book No. 1
Mickey Mouse	Philadelphia: McKay	1932	48 pp. Book No. 2
Mickey Mouse	Philadelphia: McKay	1933	48 pp. Book No. 3
Mickey Mouse	Racine: Whitman	1933	316 pp. Big Little Book No. 717
Mickey Mouse	Racine: Whitman	1933	30 pp. No. 948
Mickey Mouse	Philadelphia: McKay	1934	48 pp. Book No. 4

Title	Publisher	Date	Remarks
Mickey Mouse	Racine: Whitman	1936	29 pp. Stand-out Book No. 841
Mickey Mouse	Racine: Whitman	1937	12 pp. Linenlike No. 973
A Mickey Mouse A B C Story	Racine: Whitman	1936	31 pp. No. 921
A Mickey Mouse Alphabet ABC	Racine: Whitman	1938	16 pp. No. 889
Mickey Mouse and the Bat Bandit	Racine: Whitman	1935	426 pp. Big Little Book No. 1153
Mickey Mouse, Bellboy Detective	Racine: Whitman	1945	346 pp. Better Little Book No. 1483
Mickey Mouse in Blaggard Castle	Racine: Whitman	1934	314 pp. Big Little Book No. 726
Mickey Mouse the Boat Builder	New York: Grosset and Dunlap	1938	28 pp. Story Time Book
Mickey Mouse and Bobo the Elephant	Racine: Whitman	1935	424 pp. Big Little Book No. 1160
Mickey Mouse Book	New York: Bibo and Lang	1930	15 pp. Story and game by Bobette Bibo. On title page: "Hello Everybody"
Mickey Mouse and the Boy Thursday	Racine: Whitman	1948	96 pp. No. 845
Mickey Mouse on the Caveman Island	Racine: Whitman	1944	346 pp. Better Little Book No. 1499
Mickey Mouse Crusoe	Racine: Whitman	1936	70 pp. No. 711
Mickey Mouse and the Desert Palace	Racine: Whitman	1948	286 pp. Better Little Book No. 1451
Mickey Mouse the Detective	Racine: Whitman	1934	294 pp. Big Little Book No. 1139
Mickey Mouse, Donald Duck, and All Their Pals	Racine: Whitman	1937	40 pp. No. 887
Mickey Mouse and Donald Duck Gag Book	Racine: Whitman	1937	48 pp. No. 886
Mickey Mouse and the Dude Ranch Bandit	Racine: Whitman	1943	424 pp. Better Little Book No. 1471
The Mickey Mouse Fire Brigade	Racine: Whitman	1936	66 pp. No. 2029
Mickey Mouse in the Foreign Legion	Racine: Whitman	1940	424 pp. Better Little Book No. 1428
Mickey Mouse in Giantland	Philadelphia: McKay	1934	45 pp.
Mickey Mouse; Goofy and Mickey's Nephews	New York: Dell	1938	191 pp. Fast-Action
Mickey Mouse, Goofy and the Night Prowlers	Racine: Whitman	1949	18 pp. Tiny Tales No. 1030. Also in 1959 Tiny Tales No. 2952
Mickey Mouse Has a Busy Day	Racine: Whitman	1937	24 pp. No. 883
Mickey Mouse Has a Busy Day`	Racine: Whitman	1937	16 pp. No. 1077
Mickey Mouse Has a Party	Racine: Whitman	1938	48 pp. No. 798. A School Reader
Mickey Mouse on the Haunted Island	Racine: Whitman	1950	188 pp. New Better Little Book No. 708
Mickey Mouse and His Friends	Racine: Whitman	1936	12 pp. Linenlike No. 904
Mickey Mouse and His Friends	New York: Nelson	1937	102 pp. By Walt Disney and Jean Ayer
Mickey Mouse and His Friends Wait for the County Fair	Racine: Whitman	1937	24 pp. Picture Story Book No. 883
Mickey Mouse and His Friends Wait for the County Fair	Racine: Whitman	1937	16 pp. No. 1077
Mickey Mouse and His Horse Tanglefoot	Philadelphia: McKay	1936	60 pp.
Mickey Mouse in King Arthur's Court	New York: Blue Ribbon Books	1933	48 pp.
Mickey Mouse and the Lazy Daisy Mystery	Racine: Whitman	1947	286 pp. Better Little Book No. 1433
Mickey Mouse and the 'Lectro Box	Racine: Whitman	1946	346 pp. Better Little Book No. 1413
Mickey Mouse and the Magic Carpet	New York: Kay Kamen	1935	144 pp.
Mickey Mouse and the Magic Lamp	Racine: Whitman	1942	424 pp. Better Little Book No. 1429
Mickey Mouse the Mail Pilot	Racine: Whitman	1933	296 pp. Big Little Book No. 731
Mickey Mouse the Mail Pilot	Racine: Whitman	1933	286 pp. Premium for American Oil Company
Mickey Mouse and Minnie March to Macy's	New York: R.H. Macy	1935	142 pp.
Mickey Mouse the Miracle Maker	Racine: Whitman	1948	96 pp. No. 845
Mickey Mouse and Mother Goose	Racine: Whitman	1937	136 pp. No. 4011
Mickey Mouse Movie Stories	Philadelphia: McKay	1931	190 pp.
Mickey Mouse Movie Stories	Philadelphia: McKay	1934	196 pp. Book No. 2
Mickey Mouse in Numberland	Racine: Whitman	1938	96 pp. No. 745. "A Very Easy Arithmetic Work Book"
Mickey Mouse in Pigmyland	Racine: Whitman	1936	70 pp. No. 711
Mickey Mouse and the Pirate Submarine	Racine: Whitman	1939	424 pp. Big Little Book No. 1463
Mickey Mouse and Pluto	Racine: Whitman	1936	66 pp. No. 2028
Mickey Mouse and Pluto	New York: Dell	1942	192 pp. Fast-Action No. 16
Mickey Mouse and Pluto the Racer	Racine: Whitman	1936	424 pp. Big Little Book No. 1128

Title	Publisher	Date	Remarks
Mickey Mouse Presents Walt Disney's Silly Symphonies	Racine: Whitman	1934	234 pp. Big Little Book No. 756
Mickey Mouse in the Race for Riches	Racine: Whitman	1938	424 pp. Better Little Book No. 1476
Mickey Mouse Recipe Scrap Book	Los Angeles: Walt Disney Enterprises	1936	52 pp.
Mickey Mouse Runs His Own Newspaper	Racine: Whitman	1937	424 pp. Big Little Book No. 1409. Also abridged edition of 292 pp.
Mickey Mouse and the Sacred Jewel	Racine: Whitman	1936	424 pp. Big Little Book No. 1187
Mickey Mouse Sails for Treasure Island	Racine: Whitman	1933	314 pp. Big Little Book No. 750
Mickey Mouse Sails for Treasure Island	Racine: Whitman	1935	192 pp. Premium for Kolynos Dental Cream
Mickey Mouse and the Seven Ghosts	Racine: Whitman	1940	424 pp. Better Little Book No. 1475
Mickey Mouse the Sheriff of Nugget Gulch	New York: Dell	1938	192 pp. Fast-Action
Mickey Mouse on Sky Island	Racine: Whitman	1941	424 pp. Better Little Book No. 1417
Mickey Mouse and the Stolen Jewels	Racine: Whitman	1949	286 pp. Better Little Book No. 1464
Mickey Mouse Stories	Philadelphia: McKay	1934	62 pp. Book No. 2. (For Book No. 1 see *Mickey Mouse Story Book*.) Also a paperback
Mickey Mouse Story Book	Philadelphia: McKay	1931	62 pp. Also in paperback
Mickey Mouse and Tanglefoot	Racine: Whitman	1934	40 pp. Wee Little Books, Set No. 512
Mickey Mouse in the Treasure Hunt	Racine: Whitman	1941	424 pp. Better Little Book No. 1401
Mickey Mouse Waddle Book	New York: Blue Ribbon Books	1934	33 pp.
Mickey Mouse Will Not Quit	Racine: Whitman	1934	38 pp. Wee Little Books, Set No. 512
Mickey Mouse Wins the Race	Racine: Whitman	1934	38 pp. Wee Little Books, Set No. 512
Mickey Mouse in the World of Tomorrow	Racine: Whitman	1948	286 pp. Better Little Book No. 1444
Mickey Mouse in Ye Olden Days, with "Pop-up Picture"	New York: Blue Ribbon Books	1934	60 pp.
Mickey Mouse's Misfortune	Racine: Whitman	1934	38 pp. Wee Little Books, Set No. 512
Mickey Mouse's Picnic	New York: Simon and Schuster	1950	28 pp. Little Golden Book No. D15. Story by Jane Werner. Also 24-page versions
Mickey Mouse's Summer Vacation	Racine: Whitman	1948	32 pp. Story Hour Series No. 801. Also in paperback
Mickey Mouse's Uphill Fight	Racine: Whitman	1934	38 pp. Wee Little Books, Set No. 512
Mickey Never Fails	Boston: Heath	1939	102 pp. By Robin Palmer
Mickey Sees the U.S.A.	Boston: Heath	1944	138 pp. By Caroline D. Emerson
Mickey's Dog Pluto	Racine: Whitman	1943	187 pp. Tall Comics All-Picture Book No. 532
Mickey's Gold Rush	Racine: Whitman	1939	12 pp. Penny Book No. 1145
Mickey's Magic Hat and the Cookie Carnival	Racine: Whitman	1937	24 pp. No. 883
Mickey's Magic Hat; Cookie Carnival	Racine: Whitman	1937	16 pp. No. 1077
Mickey's New Car	New York: Simon and Schuster	1950	18 pp. Tiny Golden Book. By Jane Werner. Illustrated by Campbell Grant
Minnie Mouse and the Antique Chair	Racine: Whitman	1948	95 pp. No. 845
Mother Goose	New York: Simon and Schuster	1949	28 pp. Big Golden Book. Reprinted in 1970 as No. 10878, with a new cover. Adapted by Al Dempster
Mother Pluto	Racine: Whitman	1939	64 pp. No. 1058
Mystery in Disneyville	New York: Simon and Schuster	1949	126 pp. Golden Story Book No. 7. Illustrations adapted by Richard Moores and Manuel Gonzales
Nursery Stories from Walt Disney's Silly Symphony	Racine: Whitman	1937	212 pp.
The Nutcracker Suite from Walt Disney's Fantasia	Boston: Little, Brown	1940	72 pp. Story and illustrations inspired by the music of Peter Ilich Tchaikovsky. Special arrangements freely transcribed for piano by Frederick Stark
Once upon a Wintertime	New York: Simon and Schuster	1950	42 pp. Little Golden Book No. D12. Adapted by Tom Oreb from the motion picture *Melody Time*
Pablo the Penguin Takes a Trip	New York: Simon and Schuster	1950	18 pp. Tiny Golden Book. By Jane Werner. Illustrated by Campbell Grant

Title	Publisher	Date	Remarks
Pastoral from Walt Disney's Fantasia	New York: Harper	1940	36 pp.
Peculiar Penguins	Philadelphia: McKay	1934	45 pp.
Pedro: The Story of a Little Airplane	New York: Grosset and Dunlap	1943	32 pp.
Peter and the Wolf	New York: Simon and Schuster	1947	42 pp. Little Golden Book No. D5. Also printed in 1956, 24 pp. as Little Golden Book No. D56. A fairy tale adapted from Serge Prokofieff's musical theme. Pictures by Richard Kelsey. Based on the animated cartoon sequence in *Make Mine Music*
Pinocchio	New York: Dell	1939	16 pp.
Pinocchio	Racine: Whitman	1940	16 pp. No. 846
Pinocchio	Racine: Whitman	1940	12 pp. No. 6881
Pinocchio	Racine: Whitman	1940	12 pp. Linenlike No. 1039
Pinocchio	Racine: Whitman	1940	12 pp. No. 1061
Pinocchio	Boston: Heath	1940	90 pp. By Dorothy Walter Baruch
Pinocchio	New York: Simon and Schuster	1948	42 pp. Little Golden Book No. D8. Also printed in 1962, 24 pages, as Little Golden Book No. D100. Based on the story by Collodi. Adapted by Campbell Grant
Pinocchio and Jiminy Cricket	Racine: Whitman	1940	425 pp. Better Little Book No. 1435
Pinocchio Picture Book	New York: Grosset and Dunlap	1940	12 pp.
Pinocchio Picture Book	Racine: Whitman	1940	12 pp. No. 849
Pinocchio: A Story Paint Book	Racine: Whitman	1940	24 pp. No. 1059. From Box of 6 Pinocchio Books for Reading, Coloring, Playing
Pinocchio: The Story of a Puppet	New York: Dell	1940	192 pp. Fast-Action
Pinocchio's Christmas Party	New York: Cramer-Tobias-Meyer	1939	16 pp. Christmas giveaway
Pinocchio's Surprise	New York: Simon and Schuster	1950	18 pp. Tiny Golden Book. By Jane Werner. Illustrated by Campbell Grant
Pluto the Pup	Racine: Whitman	1937	12 pp. No. 894
Pluto the Pup	Racine: Whitman	1938	424 pp. Big Little Book No. 1467
Pluto and the Puppy	New York: Grosset and Dunlap	1937	36 pp.
Poor Pluto	Racine: Whitman	1948	96 pp. No. 845
The Pop-Up Mickey Mouse	New York: Blue Ribbon Books	1933	24 pp.
The Pop-Up Minnie Mouse	New York: Blue Ribbon Books	1933	29 pp.
The Pop-Up Silly Symphonies, Containing Babes in the Woods and King Neptune	New York: Blue Ribbon Books	1933	48 pp.
The Practical Pig	Racine: Whitman	1939	12 pp. Penny Book No. 1145
The Practical Pig	Racine: Whitman	1939	64 pp. No. 1058
The Practical Pig	New York: Garden City	1940	24 pp.
The Robber Kitten	Racine: Whitman	1935	40 pp.
The Robber Kitten	Philadelphia: McKay	1935	46 pp.
The Runaway Lamb at the County Fair	New York: Grosset and Dunlap	1949	31 pp. Walt Disney Picture Story Book. From the picture *So Dear to My Heart*, based on the original story by Sterling North. Illustrated by Julius Svendsen
Santa's Toy Shop	New York: Simon and Schuster	1950	28 pp. Little Golden Book No. D16. Illustrations adapted by Al Dempster. Also 24-page edition and revised cover
School Days in Disneyville	Boston: Heath	1939	102 pp. Told by Caroline D. Emerson
Silly Symphonies: Stories Featuring Donald Duck, Peter Pig, Benny Bird, and Bucky Bug	Racine: Whitman	1936	423 pp. Big Little Book No. 1111
Silly Symphony, Featuring Donald Duck and His Misadventures	Racine: Whitman	1937	424 pp. Big Little Book No. 1441
Silly Symphony Featuring Donald Duck	Racine: Whitman	1937	424 pp. Big Little Book No. 1169
Snow White and the Seven Dwarfs	New York: Harper	1937	79 pp. No. 1
Snow White and the Seven Dwarfs	New York: Grosset and Dunlap	1937	79 pp. Reprint of No. 1. Adapted from Grimm's *Fairy Tales*

Title	Publisher	Date	Remarks
Snow White and the Seven Dwarfs	Philadelphia: McKay	1937	41 pp.
Snow White and the Seven Dwarfs	New York: Grosset and Dunlap	1938	38 pp.
Snow White and the Seven Dwarfs	Racine: Whitman	1938	16 pp. Linenlike No. 925
Snow White and the Seven Dwarfs	Racine: Whitman	1938	94 pp. No. 714
Snow White and the Seven Dwarfs	Racine: Whitman	1938	11 pp. No. 927
Snow White and the Seven Dwarfs	Racine: Whitman	1938	63 pp. No. 777
Snow White and the Seven Dwarfs	New York: Simon and Schuster	1948	42 pp. Little Golden Book No. D4. Also published in 1957, 24 pages, as Little Golden Book No. D66. Adapted by Ken O'Brien and Al Dempster
So Dear to My Heart	New York Dell	1949	191 pp. Dell Book No. 291. By Sterling North
So Dear to My Heart	New York: Simon and Schuster	1950	125 pp. Golden Story Book No. 12. Story adapted by Helen Palmer. Illustrations adapted by Bill Peet. Based on the novel by Sterling North
Society Dog Show	Racine: Whitman	1939	12 pp. Penny Book No. 1145
The Sorcerer's Apprentice	New York: Grosset and Dunlap	1940	35 pp.
Stories from Walt Disney's Fantasia	New York: Random House	1940	72 pp.
A Story of Bashful	Racine: Whitman	1938	24 pp. Seven Dwarf Books No. 1044
The Story of Casey, Jr.	New York: Garden City	1941	28 pp.
Story of Clarabelle Cow	Racine: Whitman	1938	92 pp. No. 1066
Story of Dippy the Goof	Racine: Whitman	1938	92 pp. No. 1066
A Story of Doc	Racine: Whitman	1938	24 pp. Seven Dwarf Books No. 1044
Story of Donald Duck	Racine: Whitman	1938	92 pp. No. 1066
A Story of Dopey	Racine: Whitman	1938	24 pp. Seven Dwarf Books No. 1044
A Story of Grumpy	Racine: Whitman	1938	24 pp. Seven Dwarf Books No. 1044
A Story of Happy	Racine: Whitman	1938	24 pp. Seven Dwarf Books No. 1044
Story of Mickey Mouse	Racine: Whitman	1938	92 pp. No. 1066
The Story of Mickey Mouse and the Smugglers	Racine: Whitman	1935	316 pp. Big Big Book No. 4062. Also a revised edition with a new cover, Mickey and Minnie at the wheel of a boat
Story of Minnie Mouse	Racine: Whitman	1938	92 pp. No. 1066
Story of Pluto the Pup	Racine: Whitman	1938	92 pp. No. 1066
Story of the Reluctant Dragon	New York: Garden City	1941	72 pp. Introduced by Robert Benchley. From Kenneth Grahame's *Dream Days*
A Story of Sleepy	Racine: Whitman	1938	24 pp. Seven Dwarf Books No. 1044
A Story of Sneezy	Racine: Whitman	1938	24 pp. Seven Dwarf Books No. 1044
A Story of Snow White	Racine: Whitman	1938	24 pp. Seven Dwarf Books No. 1044
The Story of Snow White and the Seven Dwarfs	Racine: Whitman	1938	280 pp. Big Little Book No. 1460. On cover: Snow White and The Seven Dwarfs
The Story of Timothy's House	New York: Garden City	1941	28 pp.
Such a Life, Says Donald Duck	Racine: Whitman	1939	424 pp. Better Little Book No. 1404
Surprise Package	New York: Simon and Schuster	1944	90 pp. Giant Golden Book. Abbreviated edition, 1948, 76 pp. Stories adapted by H. Marion Palmer from originals by Hans Christian Andersen and others
The Three Caballeros	New York: Random House	1944	56 pp. By Marion Palmer
Three Little Pigs	New York: Blue Ribbon Books	1933	62 pp.
The Three Little Pigs	New York: Simon and Schuster	1948	42 pp. Little Golden Book No. D10. Also issued in 28- and 24-page editions, the latter in 1958 as Little Golden Book No. D78. Adapted by Milt Banta and Al Dempster
Three Little Pigs Fool a Wolf	New York: Simon and Schuster	1950	18 pp. Tiny Golden Book. By Jane Werner. Illustrated by Campbell Grant
Three Little Wolves	Racine: Whitman	1937	16 pp. Walt Disney Picture Book No. 895
The Three Orphan Kittens	Philadelphia: McKay	1935	46 pp.
The Three Orphan Kittens	Racine: Whitman	1935	40 pp.
The Three Orphan Kittens	Racine: Whitman	1949	32 pp. Story Hour Series No. 809. Also issued in paperback
Through the Picture Frame	New York: Simon and Schuster	1944	24 pp. Walt Disney's Little Library. Adapted by Robert Edmunds from the Hans Christian Andersen story "Ole Lukoie"
Thumper	New York: Grosset and Dunlap	1942	32 pp.
Thumper and the Seven Dwarfs	Racine: Whitman	1944	348 pp. Better Little Book No. 1409

Title	Publisher	Date	Remarks
Timid Elmer	Racine: Whitman	1939	64 pp. No. 1058
Toby Tortoise and the Hare	Racine: Whitman	1938	10 pp. Walt Disney Picture Book No. 928
The Tortoise and the Hare	Philadelphia: McKay	1935	48 pp.
The Tortoise and the Hare	Racine: Whitman	1935	40 pp.
Treasure Chest	New York: Simon and Schuster	1948	66 pp. Big Golden Book
The Ugly Duckling	Philadelphia: Lippincott	1939	40 pp. Adapted from Hans Christian Andersen
The Ugly Duckling	Racine: Whitman	1939	64 pp. No. 1058
The Ugly Duckling	Racine: Whitman	1939	12 pp. Penny Book No. 1145
Uncle Remus	New York: Simon and Schuster	1947	42 pp. Little Golden Book No. D6. Also published in 28- and 24-page editions, the latter in 1959 as Little Golden Book No. D85. Retold by Marion Palmer from the original stories by Joel Chandler Harris. Illustrated by Bob Grant
Uncle Remus Stories	New York: Simon and Schuster	1947	92 pp. Giant Golden Book. Abridged edition 1959, 57 pages as Giant Golden Book No. 554. Retold by Marion Palmer. Illustrated by Al Dempster and Bill Justice. Also Nos. 12554, 1962 and 15551, 1966
The Victory March; or the Mystery of the Treasure Chest	New York: Random House	1942	12 pp. By Walt Disney and Chester Williams
Walt Disney Annual	Racine: Whitman	1937	123 pp. No. 4001
The Walt Disney Parade	New York: Garden City	1940	176 pp.
Walt Disney Tells the Story of Pinocchio	Racine: Whitman	1939	144 pp. No. 556
Walt Disney's Version of Pinocchio	New York: Grosset and Dunlap	1939	48 pp.
Walt Disney's Version of Pinocchio	New York: Random House	1939	41 numbered leaves including 30 plates. 100 copies printed
Walt Disney's Version of Pinocchio	New York: Random House	1939	76 pp.
Walt Disney's Version of Pinocchio	Racine: Whitman	1939	48 pp.
Walt Disney's Version of Pinocchio	Racine: Whitman	1939	95 pp. No. 709. Also revised cover
Walt Disney's Version of Pinocchio	Racine: Whitman	1940	95 pp. No. 6880
Walt Disney's Version of Pinocchio	Racine: Whitman	1940	24 pp.
Water Babies' Circus and Other Stories	Boston: Heath	1940	78 pp. By Georgiana Browne
Who's Afraid of the Big Bad Wolf? Three Little Pigs	Philadelphia: McKay	1933	31 pp.
The Wise Little Hen	Philadelphia: McKay	1934	48 pp.
The Wise Little Hen	Racine: Whitman	1935	40 pp.
The Wise Little Hen	Racine: Whitman	1937	12 pp. Walt Disney Picture Book No. 888
The Wonderful Tar Baby	New York: Grosset and Dunlap	1946	32 pp. By Marion Palmer. Adapted from the original Uncle Remus story by Joel Chandler Harris

Appendix E:

Disney Sheet Music and Song Folios

The following is a listing of Disney music published through 1950. The listing is presented in two sections. Section 1 is an alphabetical presentation of sheet music by title. Section 2 is a list of song folios presented alphabetically by title.

1. Sheet Music

Song Title	Source	Date
"All the Cats Join In"	Make Mine Music	1945
"Angel-May-Care"	The Three Caballeros	1945
"Apple Song"	The Three Caballeros	1948
"Baby Mine"	Dumbo	1941
"Baia"	The Three Caballeros	1944
"Beanero"	Fun and Fancy Free	1947
"Bibbidi-Bobbidi-Boo"	Cinderella	1949
"Bluddle-Uddle-Um-Dum"	Snow White and the Seven Dwarfs	1938
"Blue Bayou"	Make Mine Music	1946
"Blue Shadows on the Trail"	Melody Time	1948
"Brazil" ("Aquarela do Brasil")	Saludos Amigos	1942
"Casey Junior"	Dumbo	1941
"Casey, the Pride of Them All"	Make Mine Music	1945
"Cinderella"	Cinderella	1948
"The County Fair"	So Dear to My Heart	1948
"Dance of the Bogey Man"	Lullaby Land	1933
"Der Fuehrer's Face"	Der Fuehrer's Face	1942
"A Dream Is a Wish Your Heart Makes"	Cinderella	1949
"The Dwarfs' Yodel Song" ("The Silly Song")	Snow White and the Seven Dwarfs	1938
"Everybody Has a Laughing Place"	Song of the South	1946
"Fee-Fi-Fo-Fum"	Fun and Fancy Free	1947
"Ferdinand the Bull"	Ferdinand the Bull	1938
"Figaro and Cleo"	Pinocchio	1939
"Fun and Fancy Free"	Fun and Fancy Free	1947
"Give a Little Whistle"	Pinocchio	1940
"Happy Go Lucky Fellow"	Fun and Fancy Free	1947
"The Headless Horseman"	The Adventures of Ichabod and Mr. Toad	1949
"Heigh-Ho"	Snow White and the Seven Dwarfs	1938
"Hi-Diddle-Dee-Dee"	Pinocchio	1940
"Honest John"	Pinocchio	1940
"Hop on Your Pogo Stick"	Victory Vehicles	1942
"How Do You Do?"	Song of the South	1946
"Ichabod"	The Adventures of Ichabod and Mr. Toad	1949
"I'm Wishing"	Snow White and the Seven Dwarfs	1937
"In a World of My Own"	Alice in Wonderland	1949
"It's Whatcha Do with Whatcha Got"	So Dear to My Heart	1948
"I've Got No Strings"	Pinocchio	1940
"Jesusita en Chihauhau" ("The Cactus Polka")	The Three Caballeros	1944
"Jiminy Cricket"	Pinocchio	1939
"Jing-A-Ling, Jing-A-Ling"	Beaver Valley	1950
"Johnny Fedora and Alice Blue Bonnet"	Make Mine Music	1946
"Katrina"	The Adventures of Ichabod and Mr. Toad	1949
"Lavender Blue" ("Dilly Dilly")	So Dear to My Heart	1948
"Lazy Countryside"	Fun and Fancy Free	1947
"Let's Sing a Gay Little Spring Song"	Bambi	1942
"Little April Shower"	Bambi	1942

Song Title	Source	Date
"Little Toot"	Melody Time	1948
"Little Wooden Head"	Pinocchio	1940
"Look Out for Mister Stork"	Dumbo	1941
"Looking for Romance" ("I Bring You a Song")	Bambi	1942
"The Lord Is Good to Me"	Melody Time	1948
"Love Is a Song"	Bambi	1942
"Make Mine Music"	Make Mine Music	1946
"Melody Time"	Melody Time	1948
"The Merrily Song"	The Adventures of Ichabod and Mr. Toad	1949
"Mexico"	The Three Caballeros	1945
"Mickey Mouse and Minnie's in Town"		1933
"Mickey Mouse's Birthday Party"		1936
"Minnie's Yoo Hoo"	Mickey's Follies	1930
"Monstro the Whale"	Pinocchio	1940
"My Favorite Dream"	Fun and Fancy Free	1947
"My, What a Happy Day"	Fun and Fancy Free	1947
"Oh Sing, Sweet Nightingale"	Cinderella	1949
"One Song"	Snow White and the Seven Dwarfs	1937
"Pink Elephants on Parade"	Dumbo	1941
"The Pioneer Song"	Melody Time	1948
"The Reluctant Dragon"	The Reluctant Dragon	1941
"Saludos Amigos"	Saludos Amigos	1942
"Say It with a Slap"	Fun and Fancy Free	1947
"Snow White"	Snow White and the Seven Dwarfs	1938
"So Dear to My Heart"	So Dear to My Heart	1949
"So This Is Love"	Cinderella	1949
"Some Day My Prince Will Come"	Snow White and the Seven Dwarfs	1937
"Song of the Eagle"	Victory Through Air Power	1943
"Song of the Roustabouts"	Dumbo	1941
"Song of the South"	Song of the South	1946
"Sooner or Later"	Song of the South	1946
"Stick-to-it-Ivity"	So Dear to My Heart	1948
"The Three Caballeros"	The Three Caballeros	1944
"Three Cheers for Anything"	Pinocchio	1940
"Thumper Song"	Bambi	1942
"Too Good to Be True"	Fun and Fancy Free	1947
"Trick or Treat"	Trick or Treat	1948
"Turn on the Old Music Box"	Pinocchio	1939
"Twitterpated"	Bambi	1942
"Two Silhouettes"	Make Mine Music	1945
"Uncle Remus Said"	Song of the South	1946
"Very Good Advice"	Alice In Wonderland	1949
"The Victory March"	Victory Through Air Power	1943
"The Wedding Party of Mickey Mouse"		1931
"What: No Mickey Mouse?" ("What Kind of a Party Is This?")		1932
"When I See an Elephant Fly"	Dumbo	1941
"When You Wish upon a Star"	Pinocchio	1940
"Whistle While You Work"	Snow White and the Seven Dwarfs	1937
"Who's Afraid of the Big Bad Wolf?"	Three Little Pigs	1933
"With a Smile and a Song"	Snow White and the Seven Dwarfs	1937
"Without You"	Make Mine Music	1945
"The Work Song"	Cinderella	1949
"The World Owes Me a Living"	Grasshopper and the Ants	1934
"The Yankee Doodle Spirit"	The New Spirit	1942
"You Belong to My Heart"	The Three Caballeros	1943
"You're Nothin' but a Nothin'"	The Flying Mouse	1934
"Zip-A-Dee-Doo-Dah"	Song of the South	1946

2. Song Folios

Song Title	Publisher	Date
Cinderella (Vocal Selections)	Walt Disney Music Company	1949
Folio of Songs from Walt Disney's Famous Pictures, Mickey Mouse and Silly Symphony, vol. 1	Irving Berlin, Inc.	1934
Folio of Songs from Walt Disney's Famous Pictures, Mickey Mouse and Silly Symphony, vol. 2	Irving Berlin, Inc.	1936
The Nutcracker Suite (Piano Arrangements)	Walt Disney Music Company	1940
Pinocchio: Souvenir Album	Bourne, Inc.	1945
Snow White (Children's Simplified)	Bourne, Inc.	1938
Snow White Fantasy	Bourne, Inc.	1945
Songs from Walt Disney Pictures	Southern Music Publishing Company, Inc.	1943
Souvenir Album of Songs from Pinocchio	Bourne, Inc.	1938
Souvenir Album of Songs from Snow White	Bourne, Inc.	1945
The Three Caballeros	Peer Music Company	1944

Appendix F:
Disney Animated Characters

The following is a listing of Disney animated characters created during the years of 1924 until 1950. They are listed alphabetically and, in addition, the year and where the character was introduced are presented. From this listing the collector can readily determine the first date Disney merchandise could have been manufactured for each character. It should be noted that many of the lesser-known characters have not been used on merchandise; therefore it would be impossible to obtain an example of merchandise for each name in the listing.

Character	When Introduced	Where Introduced
Abner	1936	Short: *Country Cousin*
Agnes	1942	Comic strip: *Mickey Mouse*
Alice Blue Bonnet	1946	Feature: *Make Mine Music*
Ambrose	1935	Short: *The Robber Kitten*
Apollo	1940	Feature: *Fantasia*
Aracuan Bird	1945	Feature: *The Three Caballeros*
Aunt Ena	1942	Feature: *Bambi*
Aunt Jemima	1935	Short: *Broken Toys*
Baby Weems	1941	Feature: *The Reluctant Dragon*
Bacchus	1940	Feature: *Fantasia*
Baltus Van Tassel	1949	Feature: *The Adventures of Ichabod and Mr. Toad*
Bambi	1942	Feature: *Bambi*
Bambi's Mother	1942	Feature: *Bambi*
Bashful	1937	Feature: *Snow White and the Seven Dwarfs*
Ben Ali Gator	1940	Feature: *Fantasia*
Ben Buzzard	1943	Short: *Flying Jalopy*
Bent-Tail	1949	Short: *Sheep Dog*
Bent-Tail Junior	1949	Short: *Sheep Dog*
Big Bad Wolf	1933	Short: *Three Little Pigs*
Big Toot	1948	Feature: *Melody Time*
Billie Beetle	1947	Short: *Bootle Beetle*
Blackie	1945	Short: *Legend of Coyote Rock*
Blue Fairy	1940	Feature: *Pinocchio*
Blynken	1938	Short: *Wynken, Blynken and Nod*
Bobo	1936	Short: *Mickey's Elephant*
Bongo	1947	Feature: *Fun and Fancy Free*
Bootle Beetle	1947	Short: *Bootle Beetle*
Bo-Peep	1931	Short: *Mother Goose Melodies*
Br'er Bear	1946	Feature: *Song of the South*
Br'er Fox	1946	Feature: *Song of the South*
Br'er Rabbit	1946	Feature: *Song of the South*
Brom Bones	1949	Feature: *The Adventures of Ichabod and Mr. Toad*
Bucky Bug	1932	Comic strip: *Bucky Bug*
Burrito	1945	Feature: *The Three Caballeros*
Butch	1940	Short: *Bone Trouble*
Capt. Churchmouse	1932	Comic strip: *Mickey Mouse*
Capt. Doberman	1933	Comic strip: *Mickey Mouse*
Capt. Katt	1936	Short: *Three Blind Mouseketeers*
Casey	1946	Feature: *Make Mine Music*
Casey, Jr.	1941	Feature: *The Reluctant Dragon*
Catty	1941	Feature: *Dumbo*
Chernabog	1940	Feature: *Fantasia*
Chicken Little	1943	Short: *Chicken Little*
Chief O'Hara	1939	Comic strip: *Mickey Mouse*

Character	When Introduced	Where Introduced
Chip	1943	Short: *Private Pluto*
(first known as Chip 'n Dale)	1947	Short: *Chip 'n Dale*
Christopher Columbus	1949	Feature: *So Dear to My Heart*
Clara Cluck	1934	Short: *Orphan's Benefit*
Clarabelle Cow	1929	Short: *The Plow Boy*
Clementine	1941	Feature: *The Reluctant Dragon*
Cleo	1940	Feature: *Pinocchio*
Cock Robin	1935	Short: *Who Killed Cock Robin?*
Cocky Locky	1943	Short: *Chicken Little*
Colonel	1933	Short: *The Steeplechase*
Cyril Proudbottom	1949	Feature: *The Adventures of Ichabod and Mr. Toad*
Daisy Duck	1937	Short: *Don Donald*
(first called Daisy)	1940	Short: *Mr. Duck Steps Out*
Dale	1943	Short: *Private Pluto*
(first known as Chip 'n Dale)	1947	Short: *Chip 'n Dale*
Dan Cupid	1935	Short: *Who Killed Cock Robin?*
Dan Patch	1949	Feature: *So Dear to My Heart*
Danny	1949	Feature: *So Dear to My Heart*
David	1949	Feature: *So Dear to My Heart*
Dewey	1938	Short: *Donald's Nephews*
Diana	1940	Feature: *Fantasia*
Dinah	1942	Short: *The Sleepwalker*
Dirty Bill	1935	Short: *The Robber Kitten*
Doc	1937	Feature: *Snow White and the Seven Dwarfs*
Dolores	1947	Short: *The Big Wash*
Donald Duck	1934	Short: *The Wise Little Hen*
Donna Duck	1937	Short: *Don Donald*
(forerunner of Daisy)		
Dopey	1937	Feature: *Snow White and the Seven Dwarfs*
Ducky Lucky	1943	Short: *Chicken Little*
Dumbo	1941	Feature: *Dumbo*
Eega Beeva	1948	Comic strip: *Mickey Mouse*
Einstein	1941	Feature: *The Reluctant Dragon*
Elephanchine	1940	Feature: *Fantasia*
Eli Squinch	1934	Comic strip: *Mickey Mouse*
Elmer Elephant	1936	Short: *Elmer Elephant*
Emotion	1943	Short: *Reason and Emotion*
Esther	1948	Short: *Mickey Down Under*
Ezra Beetle	1947	Short: *Bootle Beetle*
Faline	1942	Feature: *Bambi*
Father Neptune	1945	Feature: *The Three Caballeros*
Ferdinand the Bull	1938	Short: *Ferdinand the Bull*
Ferdy	1934	Short: *Mickey's Steamroller*
Fiddler Pig	1933	Short: *The Three Little Pigs*
Fidgity	1941	Feature: *Dumbo*
Fifer Pig	1933	Short: *The Three Little Pigs*
Fifinella	1943	Book: *The Gremlins*
Figaro	1940	Feature: *Pinocchio*
Flower	1942	Feature: *Bambi*
Fluffy	1935	Short: *Three Orphan Kittens*
Flutter Foot	1947	Short: *Mail Dog*
Flying Gauchito	1945	Feature: *The Three Caballeros*
Foxey Loxey	1943	Short: *Chicken Little*
Frankie	1947	Short: *Figaro and Frankie*
Friday	1934	Short: *Mickey's Man Friday*
Friend Owl	1942	Feature: *Bambi*
Geppetto	1940	Feature: *Pinocchio*
Germania	1943	Short: *Education for Death*
Gertie	1949	Feature: *The Adventures of Ichabod and Mr. Toad*
Giddy	1941	Feature: *Dumbo*
Gideon	1940	Feature: *Pinocchio*
Giggles	1941	Feature: *Dumbo*
Gladstone Gander	1948	Comic book: *Walt Disney's Comics and Stories No. 88*
The Gleam	1942	Comic strip: *Mickey Mouse*
Goldie	1935	Short: *The Golden Touch*
Goliath	1949	Feature: *So Dear to My Heart*
Goofy	1932	Short: *Mickey's Revue*

Character	When Introduced	Where Introduced
Goosey Poosey	1943	Short: *Chicken Little*
Goosie Gander	1933	Short: *Old King Cole*
Grace Martin	1946	Feature: *Make Mine Music*
Grandma	1934	Short: *The Big Bad Wolf*
Grasshopper	1934	Short: *Grasshopper and the Ants*
Gremlin	1943	Book: *The Gremlins*
Grumpy	1937	Feature: *Snow White and the Seven Dwarfs*
Gunpowder	1949	Feature: *The Adventures of Ichabod and Mr. Toad*
Gus Goose	1939	Short: *Donald's Cousin Gus*
Ham	1933	Short: *Father Noah's Ark*
Hans	1943	Short: *Education for Death*
Happy	1937	Feature: *Snow White and the Seven Dwarfs*
Headless Horseman	1949	Feature: *The Adventures of Ichabod and Mr. Toad*
Henny Penny	1943	Short: *Chicken Little*
Henry Coy	1946	Feature: *Make Mine Music*
Hitler	1943	Short: *Education for Death*
Honest John (J. Worthington Foulfellow)	1940	Feature: *Pinocchio*
Hop Low	1940	Feature: *Fantasia*
Horace Horsecollar	1929	Short: *The Plow Boy*
Hortense	1937	Short: *Donald's Ostrich*
Huey	1938	Short: *Donald's Nephews*
Humpty Dumpty	1931	Short: *Mother Goose Melodies*
Hyacinth Hippo	1940	Feature: *Fantasia*
Ichabod Crane	1949	Feature: *The Adventures of Ichabod and Mr. Toad*
Iris	1940	Feature: *Fantasia*
Isolde	1946	Feature: *Make Mine Music*
Ivan	1946	Feature: *Make Mine Music*
J. Thaddeus Toad	1949	Feature: *The Adventures of Ichabod and Mr. Toad*
J. Worthington Foulfellow. *See* Honest John		
Jack	1931	Short: *Mother Goose Melodies*
Jack Horner	1931	Short: *Mother Goose Melodies*
Jack Spratt	1933	Short: *Old King Cole*
Japheth	1933	Short: *Father Noah's Ark*
Jenny Wren	1935	Short: *Who Killed Cock Robin?*
Jill	1931	Short: *Mother Goose Melodies*
Jiminy Cricket	1940	Feature: *Pinocchio*
Joe	1941	Feature: *Dumbo*
Joey	1948	Short: *Daddy Duck*
John Doakes	1943	Short: *Reason and Emotion*
Johnnie	1946	Short: *Wet Paint*
Johnny Appleseed	1948	Feature: *Melody Time*
Johnny Fedora	1946	Feature: *Make Mine Music*
Johnny's Angel	1948	Feature: *Melody Time*
Jose Carioca	1945	Feature: *The Three Caballeros*
Joshua	1949	Feature: *So Dear to My Heart*
Julius	1924	Short: *The Cat in Alice Comedies*
June Bug	1932	Comic strip: *Bucky Bug*
Junior	1933	Short: *Night before Christmas*
Jupiter	1944	Short: *Trombone Trouble*
Katrina Van Tassel	1949	Feature: *The Adventures of Ichabod and Mr. Toad*
King Midas	1935	Short: *The Golden Touch*
King Neptune	1932	Short: *King Neptune*
Lampwick	1940	Feature: *Pinocchio*
Legs Sparrow	1935	Short: *Who Killed Cock Robin?*
Little Boy Blue	1931	Short: *Mother Goose Melodies*
Little Hiawatha	1937	Short: *Little Hiawatha*
Little Minnehaha	1940	Comic strip: *Little Hiawatha*
Little Toot	1948	Feature: *Melody Time*
Louie	1938	Short: *Donald's Nephews*
Lulubelle	1947	Feature: *Fun and Fancy Free*
Lumpjaw	1947	Feature: *Fun and Fancy Free*
MacBadger	1949	Feature: *The Adventures of Ichabod and Mr. Toad*
Mademoiselle Upanova	1940	Feature: *Fantasia*
Magic Mirror	1937	Feature: *Snow White and the Seven Dwarfs*
Mammy Two Shoes	1935	Short: *Three Orphan Kittens*
Marblehead	1946	Short: *Lighthouse Keeping*

Character	When Introduced	Where Introduced
Mary, Mary, Quite Contrary	1933	Short: *Old King Cole*
Matriarch	1941	Feature: *Dumbo*
Max Hare	1935	Short: *Tortoise and the Hare*
Mayor of Hamelin	1933	Short: *The Pied Piper*
Mickey Mouse	1928	Short: *Steamboat Willie*
Minnie Mouse	1928	Short: *Steamboat Willie*
Miss Muffet	1931	Short: *Mother Goose Melodies*
Mole	1949	Feature: *The Adventures of Ichabod and Mr. Toad*
Monstro	1940	Feature: *Pinocchio*
Montmorency Rodent	1941	Comic strip: *Mickey Mouse*
Monty	1936	Short: *Country Cousin*
Morpheus	1940	Feature: *Fantasia*
Mortimer Mouse	1936	Short: *Mickey's Rival*
Morty	1934	Short: *Mickey's Steamroller*
Mother Goose	1931	Short: *Mother Goose Melodies*
Mother Hubbard	1933	Short: *Old King Cole*
Mother Noah	1933	Short: *Father Noah's Ark*
Mr. Bluebird	1946	Feature: *Song of the South*
Mr. John Weems	1941	Feature: *The Reluctant Dragon*
Mr. Sandman	1933	Short: *Lullaby Land*
Mrs. Ham	1933	Short: *Father Noah's Ark*
Mrs. Japheth	1933	Short: *Father Noah's Ark*
Mrs. Jumbo	1941	Feature: *Dumbo*
Mrs. Shem	1933	Short: *Father Noah's Ark*
Mrs. Spratt	1933	Short: *Old King Cole*
Mrs. Weems	1941	Feature: *The Reluctant Dragon*
Noah	1933	Short: *Father Noah's Ark*
Nod	1938	Short: *Wynken, Blynken and Nod*
Old King Cole	1931	Short: *Mother Goose Melodies*
Old Woman in a Shoe	1933	Short: *Old King Cole*
Orville	1948	Short: *Pluto's Fledgling*
Oswald the Lucky Rabbit	1927	Short: *Trolley Troubles*
Otto	1933	Short: *Birds in the Spring*
Pablo	1945	Feature: *The Three Caballeros*
Pan	1930	Short: *Playful Pan*
Panchito	1945	Feature: *The Three Caballeros*
Pecos Bill	1948	Feature: *Melody Time*
Pedro	1943	Feature: *Saludos Amigos*
Pegleg Pete	1928	Short: *Steamboat Willie*
Persephone	1934	Short: *Goddess of Spring*
Peter	1946	Feature: *Make Mine Music*
Peter Penguin	1934	Short: *Peculiar Penguin*
Peter Pig	1934	Short: *Wise Little Hen*
Peter Piper	1933	Short: *Old King Cole*
Peter Pumpkin Eater	1933	Short: *Old King Cole*
Phantom Blot	1939	Comic strip: *Mickey Mouse*
Pied Piper	1933	Short: *The Pied Piper*
Pinocchio	1940	Feature: *Pinocchio*
Pluto	1930	Short: *The Chain Gang*
(first called Pluto)	1931	Short: *The Moose Hunt*
Pluto (Devil)	1934	Short: *Goddess of Spring*
Pluto, Jr.	1942	Short: *Pluto Junior*
Polly Penguin	1934	Short: *Peculiar Penguins*
Practical Pig	1933	Short: *Three Little Pigs*
Prince	1937	Feature: *Snow White and the Seven Dwarfs*
Princess Penelope	1946	Short: *Knight for a Day*
Prissy	1941	Feature: *Dumbo*
Queen Ant	1934	Short: *Grasshopper and the Ants*
Rat	1949	Feature: *The Adventures of Ichabod and Mr. Toad*
Reason	1943	Short: *Reason and Emotion*
Red Riding Hood	1934	Short: *The Big Bad Wolf*
Reluctant Dragon	1941	Feature: *The Reluctant Dragon*
Ronnie	1946	Short: *The Purloined Pup*
Ronno	1942	Feature: *Bambi*
Rover (forerunner of Pluto)	1930	Short: *The Picnic*
Salty	1947	Short: *Rescue Dog*
Santa Claus	1932	Short: *Santa's Workshop*

Character	When Introduced	Where Introduced
Sasha	1946	Feature: *Make Mine Music*
Satan	1929	Short: *Hell's Bells*
Shem	1933	Short: *Father Noah's Ark*
Simple Simon	1931	Short: *Mother Goose Melodies*
Sir Giles	1941	Feature: *The Reluctant Dragon*
Sleepy	1937	Feature: *Snow White and the Seven Dwarfs*
Sluefoot Sue	1948	Feature: *Melody Time*
Sneezy	1937	Feature: *Snow White and the Seven Dwarfs*
Snow White	1937	Feature: *Snow White and the Seven Dwarfs*
Sonia	1946	Feature: *Make Mine Music*
Spike	1948	Short: *Inferior Decorator*
Stromboli	1940	Feature: *Pinocchio*
Susie	1946	Short: *Wet Paint*
Sylvester Shyster	1930	Comic strip: *Mickey Mouse*
Tanglefoot	1933	Comic strip: *Mickey Mouse*
Tar Baby	1946	Feature: *Song of the South*
Tetti Tatti	1946	Feature: *Make Mine Music*
Three Blind Mice	1931	Short: *Mother Goose Melodies*
Three Blind Mouseketeers	1936	Short: *Three Blind Mouseketeers*
Three Little Wolves	1936	Short: *Three Little Wolves*
Thumper	1942	Feature: *Bambi*
Thursday	1940	Comic strip: *Mickey Mouse*
Tilda	1949	Feature: *The Adventures of Ichabod and Mr. Toad*
Tillie Tiger	1936	Short: *Elmer Elephant*
Timothy Mouse	1941	Feature: *Dumbo*
Toby Tortoise	1935	Short: *Tortoise and the Hare*
Tony	1933	Short: *The Pet Store*
Tuffy	1935	Short: *Three Orphan Kittens*
Turkey Lurkey	1943	Short: *Chicken Little*
Ugly Duckling	1931	Short: *The Ugly Duckling*
Vidi	1944	Short: *Pelican and the Snipe*
Vulcan	1944	Short: *Trombone Trouble*
Widget	1943	Book: *The Gremlins*
Widowmaker	1948	Feature: *Melody Time*
Wilbur	1939	Short: *Goofy and Wilbur*
Willie (giant)	1947	Feature: *Fun and Fancy Free*
Willie (whale)	1946	Feature: *Make Mine Music*
Winky	1949	Feature: *The Adventures of Ichabod and Mr. Toad*
Wise Little Hen	1934	Short: *Wise Little Hen*
Wolf	1946	Feature: *Make Mine Music*
Wynken	1938	Short: *Wynken, Blynken and Nod*
Yensid	1940	Feature: *Fantasia*
Zeus	1940	Feature: *Fantasia*

Appendix G:

Disney Artifacts Sold at Auction

Since values change almost daily, no attempt has been made, in this book, to indicate values other than in a general way. To give the collector an idea of possible values, this listing of items sold at auction in May of 1972 by the Sotheby Parke-Bernet Gallery in Los Angeles, California, is presented. The listing of the items and prices was obtained from records in the Anaheim Public Library.

Description of Items	Auction Price
LAMP BASE: Globular, painted beige, decal figures of Mickey Mouse, ca. 1935	$15.00
WRIST WATCH: Ingersoll, rectangular, Donald Duck indicates time with white-gloved hands, turquoise leather band, ca. 1946	$25.00
TOOTHBRUSH HOLDER: Figures of three little pigs molded in front, ca. 1934	$25.00
RADIO: Emerson, wooden case painted beige and green, metal figure of Mickey Mouse playing a cello applied to speaker, ca. 1935	$65.00
BOOKS: (1) *Mickey Mouse in Numberland,* Whitman Publishing Co., 1938; (2) *Mickey Mouse and His Friends,* Whitman Publishing Company, 1936	$30.00 (for both)
CHRISTMAS TREE LIGHTS: Bell shaped with Christmas decals, ca. 1935	$35.00
WRIST WATCH: New Haven Clock and Watch Co., Swiss Copyright, 1951, Mad Hatter beats in time to movement while Alice in Wonderland looks on	$25.00
POCKET WATCH AND WRIST WATCH: Pocket watch, Ingersoll, 1933, circular, Mickey Mouse indicates time with yellow-gloved hands; Wrist watch, Ingersoll, 1933, green and orange with black enamelled fob	$340.00 (for both)
BISQUE FIGURINES: Snow White, 5"; Dwarfs, 4"; ca. 1939	$50.00 (for set)
WRIST WATCH BANDS (2) AND BELT BUCKLE: Bands are flexible openwork metal with Mickey Mouse decoration at each end; buckle decorated with Mickey Mouse in classical pose, ca. 1935	$50.00 (for 3)
RUBBER FIGURE: In shape of Mickey Mouse, restored to original colors, h. 6", ca. 1935	$25.00
STUFFED DOLL: In shape of Mickey Mouse, h. 12", orange rubber shoes, red pants, yellow gloves and felt ears, ca. 1935	$50.00
POCKET WATCH: Inscribed "Ingersoll, 1935, W. D. Productions." Mickey Mouse indicates time with hands	$140.00
OLD MAID CARDS AND STAMP PAD: Cards depict Disney characters, stamp pad shows Mickey Mouse on cover	$20.00 (for both)
POSTERS: Spare the Rod, 1953; Sleepy Time Donald, 1947; Flying Jalopy, 1943; all Donald Duck	$50.00 (for 3)
POSTERS: Donald's Vacation, 1940; Plastic Inventor, 1944; Fall Out, Fall In, 1943; all Donald Duck	$35.00 (for 3)
POSTERS: Commando Duck, 1944; Trombone Trouble, 1944; Donald's Garden, 1942; all Donald Duck	$75.00 (for 3)
CERAMIC MUG: Inscribed "Pluto The Pup" and decorated with figures of Pluto and Mickey, ca. 1935	$15.00
POSTCARDS AND DECALS: A collection including Snow White and the Seven Dwarfs, Bashful, Mickey Mouse, Donald Duck, Pinocchio, Cinderella	$45.00 (for set of 10)
RING SET: 20 official Prince Philip rings and display holder	$45.00
THEATER PROGRAM: For the December 21, 1937, world premiere of *Snow White and the Seven Dwarfs*	$35.00
TOY GRAND PIANO: Wooden case with decal showing Mickey Mouse playing the piano while Minnie Mouse listens to him, ca. 1935	$45.00
SNOW SHOVEL: 26" long, decorated with picture showing Mickey Mouse and Pluto making a snowman	$125.00
CELLULOID: Picture of Lake Titicaca from film *Saludos Amigos,* with the stamp original WDP, and signed by Walt Disney. On the reverse side is a label from Courvoisier Galleries, dated 1942, 7½" x 7"	$150.00

WOODEN DOLL: In shape of Mickey Mouse with flexible arms and legs, ca. 1933 — $40.00

ELECTRIC CLOCK: In plastic shape of Pluto, hands on the clock are in the shape of dog bones, Allied Manufacturing Co., ca. 1946 — $90.00

WRIST WATCH: Ingersol, 1946, rectangular, Mickey Mouse indicates the time with yellow-gloved hands — $95.00

WRIST WATCHES: (1) Bambi, (2) Dopey, and (3) Bongo Bear — $130.00

WRIST WATCH: Ingersoll, ca. 1935, circular dial, wristband decorated with small metal Mickeys — $45.00

ALARM CLOCK: Ingersoll, ca. 1935. Mickey Mouse's red-gloved hands indicate the time while Mickey's head beats to the movement — $150.00

PLANT WATERING CAN: Picture on side of Mickey Mouse watering his garden, ca. 1935 — $70.00

MICKEY MOUSE CLUB BUTTON: White circular button picturing Mickey Mouse with a very pointed nose and inscribed "Mickey Mouse Club" — $10.00

TOY: Three small Mickey Mouse dolls crossing a plastic bridge, spanning a carved wooden stream. The dolls are dressed traditionally except that they are wearing purple shoes, ca. 1933 — $30.00

CELLULOIDS (2): (1) Picturing Pluto playing at the sea, label from Courvoisier Galleries, dated 1939; (2) "Goblins" from *Sleeping Beauty,* 1959 — $60.00 (for both)

TOYS: (1) Tin washboard set, blue, ca. 1935; (2) Tin cup and saucer; (3) Canasta Junior set, ca. 1950; all Mickey Mouse items — $25.00 (for 3 sets)

BOOKS: (1) *Mickey Mouse Runs His Own Newspaper,* Whitman Publishing Co., 1932; (2) *Mickey Mouse and the Dude Ranch,* Whitman Publishing Co., 1943 — $25.00 (for both)

ASHTRAY: Pie-shaped dish with six cylindrical compartments for cigarettes, model of Minnie sitting in dish — $60.00

POSTERS: Donald's Gold Mine, 1942; Old Army Game, 1943; and Vanishing Private, 1942; all Donald Duck — $45.00 (for 3)

POSTERS: Wet Paint, 1946; Chief Donald, 1941; and Fall Out, Fall In, 1943; all Donald Duck — $50.00

POSTERS: Spirit of '43, 1943; Lighthouse Keeping, 1946; Pelican and the Snipe, 1944; all Donald Duck — $65.00

BOOKS: (1) *Mickey Mouse and the Magic Lamp,* 1942, Whitman Publishing Co.: (2) *Mickey Mouse in the Treasure Hunt,* 1941, Whitman Publishing Co. — $25.00 (for both)

HINGEES (CARDBOARD CUT-OUTS): Cut-outs of Mickey and Minnie Mouse, 1944; Mickey Mouse in four cardboard cut-outs, ca. 1935; Mickey Mouse movie palette, ca. 1935 — $45.00

CELLULOID: Bambi and two bunnies at play, framed, 9" x 8", with the stamp original WDP — $400.00

CHARM BRACELET: Gold line chain with six 14k gold-enameled charms of characters from the movie *Pinocchio* — $65.00

PINS: Four in set—two in the shape of Mickey Mouse, one of Donald Duck, and one of Pluto — $30.00

JEWELRY: (1) Pocket watch, Longines Wittnauer, inscribed "Walt Disney" on reverse; (2) Mickey Mouse button; (3) Pluto ring; (4) Mickey Mouse carved wooden pin — $65.00

FORKS: Two silver child's forks with figure of Mickey stamped on handle — $15.00

BOOK: *Mickey Mouse and the Magic Carpet,* Whitman Publishing Co., 1935 — $30.00

BOOKS: (1) Pastoral, 1940; (2) Donald's Penguin, 1940; (3) The Gremlins, 1943; (4) Dumbo, 1941; (5) Br'er Rabbit Rides the Fox, 1946; (6) Bambi, 1948 — $30.00

PENCIL DRAWINGS: Two sketches of various Disney characters, 12" x 15" — $150.00

PENCIL DRAWINGS: Two sketches of various Disney characters, 12" x 17" — $120.00

BISQUE AND METAL FIGURINES: Bisque figuries are of Snow White and the Seven Dwarfs, Prince Charming and the Witch; Metal figurines are of Pinocchio and Geppetto — $35.00 (for set)

CELLULOID: Scene from *Snow White and the Seven Dwarfs* with an alert doe and buck in the foreground and foliage and birds in the background, framed, 8½" x 7½", signed by Walt Disney — $425.00

BOOKS: (1) *Mickey Sees the U.S.A.,* 1944; (2) *Little Pig's Picnic,* 1939; (3) *School Days in Disneyville,* 1939; (4) *Mickey and the Beanstalk,* 1947; (5) *Donald Duck's Adventure,* 1950 — $25.00 (for 5)

CELLULOIDS: Two from *Bongo Bear,* plus a framed still from *Fantasia* — $30.00

CELLULOID: Picturing Dopey and Sleepy sleeping on clouds with silver stars above, 10" x 6½", signed by Walt Disney — $575.00

SKETCHBOOKS: The sketchbooks of *Snow White and the Seven Dwarfs,* William Collins Sons, 1938 — $70.00 (for both)

BOOKS: (1) *The Art of Walt Disney,* Jarrold and Sons, Ltd., Norwich, 1945; (2) *He Drew as He Pleased,* Albert Hurter, Simon and Schuster, 1948 — $40.00

PAPER BASKS: Mickey, Minnie, Figaro, The Three Little Pigs, Snow White, Doc, Grumpy, Dopey, the Witch, and others are depicted, ca. 1935 — $55.00

PROMOTION VOLUMES: Contains celluloids, photographs, and color transparencies from *Mickey and the Beanstalk* and *Bongo,* 1947, and *Make Mine Music,* 1947 — $400.00

WRIST WATCH: Ingersoll, 1933, circular, Mickey Mouse indicates the time with yellow-gloved hands, flexible metal band decorated with two small figures of Mickey Mouse, includes original red box — $260.00

Description of Items	Auction Price
POSTERS: (1) Art of Skiing, 1941; (2) Art of Self-Defense, 1941; both Pluto	$35.00 (for both)
POSTERS: (1) Pluto at the Zoo, 1942; (2) How to Swim, 1942; (3) How to Fish, 1942; all Pluto	$40.00 (for 3)
POSTERS: (1) Pluto's Kid Brother, 1946; (2) How to Play Golf, 1944; (3) How to Play Football, 1944; all Pluto	$50.00 (for 3)
BISQUE FIGURINES: Mickey Mouse has a walking stick and gold hat, Minnie Mouse has an umbrella and a silver hat, ca. 1935	$35.00 (for both)
CERAMIC MUG: Decorated with Mickey Mouse in fireman's uniform, ca. 1935	$35.00
CAMERA: Black plastic, takes miniature pictures, Donald Duck, ca. 1950	$10.00
BISQUE FIGURINES: (1) Mickey Mouse riding on back of Pluto, holding on to Pluto's ears for balance; (2) Minnie Mouse, ca. 1935	$15.00
WRIST WATCH: Ingersoll, ca. 1935, Mickey Mouse indicates time with yellow-gloved hands, with original blue box	$120.00
TOOTHBRUSH HOLDER: Molded with picture of Mickey Mouse washing Pluto's face	$30.00
POCKET WATCH and WRIST WATCH: Both Ingersoll, 1933; wrist watch shows Mickey Mouse indicating time with yellow-gloved hands; pocket watch has orange and black-enameled fob	$200.00
WRIST WATCH: Donald Duck, Ingersoll, 1946, rectangular, light blue dial, original box included	$90.00
ALARM CLOCK: Mickey Mouse, Ingersoll, 1956, Mickey Mouse indicates time with red-gloved hands, with original box	$100.00
WRIST WATCH: Ingersoll, 1935, Mickey Mouse indicates time with yellow-gloved hands, the leather band is decorated with small figures of Mickey Mouse	$90.00
BISQUE FIGURINES: All in the shape of Donald Duck—one with quacking bill, one with upturned bill, and one riding a rocking horse, ca. 1935	$35.00 (for 3)
TOOTHBRUSH HOLDER: Front molded with picture of Mickey and Minnie Mouse standing side by side with hands on their hips, ca. 1935	$25.00
POSTERS: (1) Seal Island, 1949; (2) Water Birds, 1952	$20.00 (for both)
TOY: Musical band, four figures (two of Mickey and two of Minnie), each playing a different musical instrument, ca. 1935	$60.00
ART: Ink wash of Mickey Mouse by Claes Oldenburg, signed by artist and dated 1966	$2,000.00
ELECTRIC ALARM CLOCK: Movable figure of Mickey Mouse indicates time with yellow-gloved hands, green metal case with pictures of Mickey, Minnie, Pluto, and Clarabelle on band, Ingersoll, 1933	$300.00
TEA SET: Decorated with scenes from film of Peter Pan, 23 pieces, with original box, ca. 1950	$25.00
MAGAZINES: 13 copies of Mickey Mouse Merchandise and Promotions Magazine: 1935, 1936–37, 1938–39, 1940–41, 1947–48	$450.00
CELLULOID: Picture of Goofy holding a bedraggled Wilbur while scolding him, label on reverse side reads Courvoisier Galleries, 1939	$400.00
MAGAZINE: First issue of the Mickey Mouse Magazine, summer quarterly, 1935	$90.00
LAPEL BUTTON: 3½" round, features picture of Mickey Mouse and inscribed "Sincerely Yours—Mickey Mouse," ca. 1935	$70.00
BOOKS: (1) I Tre Porcellini [The Three Little Pigs], ca. 1935; (2) Topolino [Mickey Mouse], ca. 1935; both bound volumes in Italian	$60.00 (for both)
COMIC BOOKS: El Pato Donald, four bound volumes of the Spanish comic book; first semester, 1945; first and second semester, 1956; first semester, 1947	$35.00
LAPEL BUTTONS: (1) Mickey Mouse—2 buttons; (2) Donald Duck—7 buttons, "Wanna Fight" and 2 buttons, "Who's Afraid of the Big Bad Wolf?"; all ca. 1935	$110.00 (for 11)
MAGAZINES: Mickey Mouse Magazine, issues from Jan. 1933–Oct. 1935, with the exception of Oct. 1933, Jan. 1934, and Sept. 1935	$340.00
BOOK: Walt Disney's Version of Pinocchio, Random House, 1939. No. 93 of a limited edition of 100 books	$90.00
MAGAZINES: Mickey Mouse Magazine, issues from Jan. 1933 to Sept. 1933	$170.00
BOOK AND MOVIE PROGRAMS: (1) Fantasia, 1940, Walt Disney Productions; (2) two programs from movie Fantasia and one program from movie Song of the South	$40.00
MAGAZINES: Mickey Mouse Magazine (includes three copies of the Mar. 1937 issue, which is the special double cover with an invitation to the Mickey Mouse birthday party)	$55.00
BOOKS: (1) Pinocchio, Random House, 1939; (2) Pinocchio with Pictures to Color, 1939	$35.00
ALARM CLOCK: Ingersoll, face shows Mickey and Minnie Mouse embracing. A preproduction sample (never mass produced), designed by Alberto Horen	$200.00
WRIST WATCH: From the first series of Disneyland watches (only 500 produced), Mickey points to the time with white-gloved hands, ca. 1968	$40.00
MECHANICAL TOYS: In the shape of Pluto, yellow, inscribed "Watch Me Roll Over," three in set	$45.00 (for 3)
TEA SET: Decorated with Mickey and Minnie Mouse pictures, 13 pieces in set, with original box, ca. 1935	$100.00

BANK: In the shape of treasure chest, embossed with pictures of Mickey and Minnie Mouse, ca. 1935 — $40.00

CANISTER SET: Porcelain, a toy, 6 small and 3 large containers with lids to match, ca. 1935 — $70.00

WRIST WATCH: Round with Jose Carioca pictured on dial, ca. 1951 — $55.00

PINBACK BUTTON: Features Mickey Mouse in classic walking position, 3½″ in diameter, ca. 1935 — $40.00

MOVIE PROJECTOR: Decorated with Mickey Mouse decals, Keystone Manufacturers, also two manuals, film splicer, and two films, (1) *Krazy Kat* and (2) *Tom Mix Riding for Life,* in original box, ca. 1935 — $200.00

BAGATELLE GAME: Mickey Mouse, arch-shaped board pictures Mickey among numerals, ca. 1935 — $100.00

WRIST WACH: Ingersoll, Pluto featured on black circular dial, original box and manufacturer's instructions, ca. 1951 — $60.00

FIGURINE: Carved Castile soap figurine of Mickey Mouse, h. 4½″, ca. 1936 — $35.00

SONG SHEET: Theme Song, "Minnie's Yoo Hoo," from the first Mickey Mouse Club, inscribed "Copyright 1930 by Walter E. Disney" — $55.00

FIGURINES: Snow White and the Seven Dwarfs. Snow White is 4″ and Dwarfs are 3″, each inscribed with their names, ca. 1939 — $35.00

WRIST WATCH: Rectangular shape, shows Mickey Mouse indicating time with yellow-gloved hands, ca. 1948 — $40.00

GUM CARDS: Series R 161 (2 sets), 32 cards showing various Disney characters — $25.00 (2 sets)

CHRISTMAS CARDS: 23 cards in this set of Disney Christmas cards for the years 1933, 1935, 1936, 1937, 1938, 1939, 1940, World War II, 1944, 1945, 1947, 1954, 1955, 1956, 1959, 1960, 1962, 1964, 1967, 1968, 1969, 1970, and 1971 — $190.00

BANK: In the shape of a toy telephone with a cardboard figure of Mickey Mouse on the front, ca. 1935 — $50.00

PENCIL SKETCHES: Pegleg Pete used in the film *The Cactus Kid,* No. 16, No. 26, and No. 194, 1930 — $110.00

BOOK: *Lady and the Tramp,* by Joe G. Rinaldi, Simon and Schuster, 1953, autographed by Walt Disney — $40.00

Index